Mixed Media

Mixed Media

Feminist Presses and Publishing Politics

Simone Murray

Pluto  Press
LONDON • STERLING, VIRGINIA

First published 2004 by
Pluto Press
345 Archway Road, London N6 5AA
and 22883 Quicksilver Drive, Sterling, VA 20166–2012, USA

www.plutobooks.com

British Library Cataloguing in Publication Data
A catalogue record for this book is available from the British Library

ISBN   0 7453 2016 3 hardback
ISBN   0 7453 2015 5 paperback

Library of Congress Cataloging in Publication Data applied for

10   9   8   7   6   5   4   3   2   1

Designed and produced for Pluto Press by
Chase Publishing Services, Fortescue, Sidmouth, EX10 9QG, England
Typeset from disk by Stanford DTP Services, Northampton, England
Printed and bound in the European Union by
Antony Rowe Ltd, Chippenham and Eastbourne, England

for Helen

whose this both is,
and is not

Contents

List of Illustrations

Acknowledgements

Funding from the Commonwealth Scholarship and Fellowship Plan, the British Council and the Australian Research Council made possible the lengthy research and writing of this book.

Sections of this work appeared in earlier versions in *The European Journal of Women's Studies* 5.2 (Sage, 1998) and *Alternative Library Literature 1998–1999: A Biennial Anthology* (McFarland, 2000).

'The Communications Circuit' is redrawn from Figure 7.1 in 'What Is the History of Books?' [1982] from *The Kiss of Lamourette: Reflections in Cultural History* by Robert Darnton. London: Faber, 1990. p.112. Richard Collins cartoon first published in *Australian Financial Review*, 8 November 1995. Reproduced by permission of the artist. *Frost in May* cover reproduced by kind permission of Virago Press, a division of Time Warner Books UK. *Sexual Politics* cover reproduced by kind permission of Abacus, a division of Time Warner Books UK. *Promiscuities* by Naomi Wolf published by Chatto & Windus and Vintage. Used by permission of The Random House Group Limited.

Many women from the international feminist publishing movement generously shared their first-hand experiences in informative, engaging and occasionally raucous interviews: Sally Abbey, Philippa Brewster, Sue Butterworth, Carmen Callil, Stephanie Dowrick, Alison Hennegan, Hilary McPhee, Lilian Mohin, Ursula Owen, Alexandra Pringle, Dale Spender, Harriet Spicer, Elizabeth Webby.

John Sutherland and Kasia Boddy, both of the Department of English Language and Literature at University College London, read and commented upon this work in its earliest phases. Philip Errington shared an office the size of a prison cell, sanity-saving in-jokes and a stuffed fish for two years of this project's life.

Maureen Bell, Gail Chester and the Book History Postgraduate Student Network provided intellectual stimulation and moral support in the face of interdisciplinary indifference. Anne Galligan, Louise Poland and other members of the Publishing Research (Pu-R-L) listserve constituted a rare instance of publishing research concentration and community.

David Doughan and the staff of the Fawcett Library – now the Women's Library – in London carefully built and maintained an essential women's research centre despite flooded basements and years of under-resourcing, and generously shared their wealth of knowledge.

Anne Beech of Pluto Press UK recognised that the legacies of the feminist publishing movement deserved serious scholarly attention and championed this project accordingly. The extended Pluto Press team were admirably professional in seeing the book through to finished product, and are wholly exempt from the more scathing industry verdicts pronounced elsewhere in this volume.

Steven Pannell generously loaned computer equipment at a critical and impoverished point. Nick Caldwell and Maureen O'Grady assisted with illustration preparation in the pressure-cooked last months of the project.

Helen Gilbert, Graeme Turner and Frances Bonner, all of the University of Queensland, sponsored numerous make-work schemes when they were most sorely needed.

Sparring partner and valued friend Dan Neidle laid on free drinks and film tickets in the darkest, most isolative days of this project and refused to let my social atrophy be complete.

The postgraduate community of the University of Queensland's School of English, Media Studies & Art History offered collegiality, peer support and memorably good times in the writing-up phase of this project. Angi Buettner, Susan Luckman, Peta Mitchell and the School's academic and administrative staff were unfailingly generous with their ideas and friendship.

Although they were at interstate remove from the front line of writing, I thank all members of the Posse (both official and honorary) for occasional belief, healthy scepticism and forcefully re-engaging me with the world beyond the desktop.

My warmest thanks goes to Kieran Hagan for non-invasive support and get-away plans.

Still, Madam, the private printing press is an actual fact, and not beyond the reach of a moderate income. Typewriters and duplicators are actual facts and even cheaper. By using these cheap and so far unforbidden instruments you can at once rid yourself of the pressure of boards, policies and editors. They will speak your own mind, in your own words, at your own time, at your own length, at your own bidding. And that, we are agreed, is our definition of 'intellectual liberty'.

Virginia Woolf, *Three Guineas* (1938)

Introduction

I should begin by declaring, not an interest, but a lack of initial interest in another sense: a feminist publishing house is not a cause to which my heart responds. There are surely few occupations which can claim to need a sexist back-up less than novel writing? It is almost the only respected, paying art at which women have been busy nearly as long as men and with a comparable degree of success. Nor, contrary to a widespread modern myth about the Awful Lives of women in the past, did they once have to be George Eliots to get away with it ... In our own century the numbers of successful women writers (successful in the sense of being published, read, enjoyed, remembered, not necessarily well-paid of course) must be equal, or nearly so, to the numbers on the male side. Neither young nor old nor women nor men nor homosexuals should, if they are good at *writing*, need to occupy a professional reservation as if they were an endangered species.

Tindall, 'Sisterly Sensibilities, or, Heroines Revived' (1979: 144)

How green were our bookshelves, how black and white our lives, those long-gone days when sisterhood was global and every remotely right-on household sported the distinctive spines of Virago and The Women's Press. Once those bottle green and striped covers were a passport to the front lines. Now you might well find your favourite feminist author on the Penguin shelf, and grab your next blockbuster from the railway Virago stand.

In a word, feminist publishing has succeeded.

Briscoe, 'Feminist Presses: Who Needs Them?' (1990b: 43)

In the ideological and temporal distance that separates these two positions it is possible to trace the outlines of the most significant development in late twentieth-century book publishing: the emergence and infiltration into the cultural mainstream of feminist presses. Gillian Tindall's observations, extracted from a 1979 *New Society* review of Virago Press's fiction list, query the very *raison d'être* of a feminist publishing house, reading the past success of individual female novelists as evidence of a publishing industry gender-neutral in its operations and scrupulously apolitical in its self-conception.

Her breezily confident assertion that women novelists have been as well 'published, read, enjoyed [and] remembered' as their male counterparts has, since the time of Tindall's writing, been so thoroughly challenged by feminist analyses of canon-forming practices and the widespread erosion of the concept of critical neutrality that her observations now read as wishful thinking rather than as irrefutable analysis. Yet, to focus solely on Tindall's flimsy evidence of the careers of individual authors is perhaps to take aim at a soft target, leaving unanswered her larger, more unsettling, question: what is the political or literary justification for a feminist publishing house, and how may oppositional analyses derived from the second-wave women's movement be applied to an industry which in its structure and operating practices is intrinsically capitalist? The twin goals of political commitment and profit generation might be expected to pull any such feminist publishing operation in mutually incompatible directions.

The familiarity with which Joanna Briscoe in her article alludes to the distinctive green spines of Virago books and the black and white insignia stripes of The Women's Press's standard covers marks a cultural sea change during the intervening period over the idea of a publishing house geared towards writing by women. Over the course of the decade that separates these two quotations, feminist publishing successfully engineered the percolation of its politico-cultural programme into mainstream public consciousness. At the epicentre of this profound change in Western literary culture stand the numerous feminist and/or womanist publishing imprints which emerged in Britain between 1972 and 1999:[1] Virago Press, Onlywomen Press, Feminist Books, The Women's Press, Pandora Press, Sheba Feminist Publishers, Stramullion, Black Woman Talk, Honno, Aurora Leigh, Urban Fox Press, Silver Moon Books, Open Letters and Scarlet Press. While varying enormously in their political priorities, internal organisation, profitability and longevity, all of these imprints were united in their perception that the act of publishing is, because of its role in determining the parameters of public debate, an inherently political act and that women, recognising this fact, must intervene in the processes of literary production to ensure that women's voices are made audible.

The high profile of feminist houses in the periodical media and printed ephemera of the 1970s and 1980s women's movements might well have been predicted, but what distinguishes recent British feminist publishing from similar presses internationally is the extent of its penetration into the mainstream broadsheet press. The political and commercial metamorphoses of various British feminist presses have been widely (if not always rigorously or accurately) reported in the broadsheet media almost since Virago Press's inception at the height of women's liberation activism in 1972. High points in public awareness of feminist publishing include the success of Virago's Modern Classics reprint series throughout the 1980s, the twentieth anniversary celebrations of The Women's Press in 1998, and – most prominently – the sale of Virago to Little, Brown & Co. of the Time Warner media group in November 1995. The tone of this reporting, with its penchant for depicting ideological divergences between individual women as feminist 'feuds', its concentration on Virago and The Women's Press in preference to smaller – often more politically radical – imprints, and its perpetual doom-laden prophesying of feminist publishing's imminent demise, is revealing in its partisanship. Nevertheless, the fact remains that the general integration of feminist publishing into mainstream cultural life has been widespread and far-reaching. The names of individual feminist imprints have become cultural signifiers, alluded to without need for further explanation. They have become incorporated into the vocabulary of the culturally competent.

Events during the decade since Briscoe's article appeared mark the apotheosis of this trend towards mainstream cultural incorporation of feminist publishing: in December 1997 former Virago author Fay Weldon published her novel *Big Women* in hardback with the HarperCollins imprint Flamingo, and a four-part BBC screen adaptation was broadcast on Channel 4 in July 1998. By means of the curious Möbius loop effect of modern media, Virago Press, widely recognised as the model for Weldon's fictional publishing house, Medusa, had passed from being a purveyor of fiction to itself constituting a fictional protagonist (Lister, 1997; McCann, 1997; Sawyer, 1998). From the status of fringe cultural anomaly at the time of Tindall's article, feminist publishing had so migrated towards the mainstream of cultural recognition by the early 1990s that Briscoe hints at the pre-feminist publishing era as a type of distant dystopia, a strangely inconceivable and culturally anomalous period before 'the rebel-rousing [sic] days' when the 'floodgates for a mass of theory and fiction' were opened (1990b: 43). Arguably, Weldon's broad-brush satire on feminist politics and its curiously hostile portrait of women's collective endeavours can be read, paradoxically, as encoding an unintentionally progressive subtext: satire, in order to hit its mark, presupposes a high level of public familiarity with that which it targets.[2] Public lampooning ironically also testifies to public recognition.

In analysing the principles and practices of feminist publishing, this book is concerned chiefly with those presses, established and administered by women since the revival of public agitation for women's rights in the late 1960s, which took as their project the production and republication of women's writing. To stipulate such a definition is immediately to call into question its parameters: what of women's historical involvement in publishing? How do self-described feminist presses relate to the women's studies lists established by mainstream publishing houses? Does a women's press owned or funded by non-feminist sources cease to qualify as a feminist press per se? To institute any inflexible definition of what constitutes properly 'feminist' publishing practice is fundamentally to misconstrue the nature of that practice. Historical feminist publishing precedent, shifting ideological allegiances, blurred organisational boundaries, and problematic funding lie at the heart of the contemporary women's press experience, and so demand a workably fluid and protean conception of what constitutes feminist publishing. Through concentrating chiefly upon Virago Press, The Women's Press, Pandora Press, and radical/lesbian/women of colour-identified imprints such as Sheba Feminist Publishers, Onlywomen and Silver Moon Books, this volume provides case studies of varieties of feminist publishing practice, juxtaposed always with mainstream corporate feminist publishing, for which feminist houses represent both cultural precursors and commercial competition. The publishing industry landscape is too complexly intermeshed to support the idea that 'independent' feminist houses exist in isolation from their mainstream rivals: within the course of its trading history a press may change from being an independent to being a fully-owned corporate subsidiary, to a company sharing publicity and distribution networks, to a public company with majority directorial shareholding. Virago's history is in this instance ideally illustrative. No single unifying factor, aside perhaps from complexity itself, adequately encapsulates the feminist publishing experience.

The conveniently invoked shibboleth of 'independence' is an especially inadequate formula by which to judge what does and what does not constitute a properly 'feminist' organisation, because it assumes an organisational autonomy at odds with the financially interdependent reality of the publishing sector. Many of the most prominent feminist houses have at some point, or have since their inception, been partially or entirely owned by non-feminist media multinationals; most have at some time derived funding from mainstream banks or local government authorities; all have sold their publications to the general public and hence, presumably, also to male consumers. So inextricably interlinked are feminist presses with the realms of international media, corporate finance and mainstream book distribution that any such attempt to define feminist publishing activities by reference to a would-be separatist criterion of fully autonomous female endeavour must fail at the outset. Such an approach is not only rigidly exclusionary, but defines out of existence that which it would seek to analyse.

Determining the appropriate geographical framework for an analysis of feminist publishing is a similarly vexing process. For the feminist press movement exhibits a profound internationalism, both in terms of inspiration and in more concrete forms such as rights deals and co-publication agreements. At the same time, Anglophone publishing cultures by the later decades of the twentieth century had become nationally distinct, and any analysis of feminist publishing practice must accurately reflect these specifically national characteristics. Hence this discussion selects British feminist presses for detailed examination, analysing the specific issues and debates prominent in the British publishing jurisdiction. But it maintains this focus while introducing counterpoint examples from feminist presses in other Anglophone publishing territories, specifically the United States, Australia, Canada, the Republic of Ireland, India, South Africa and New Zealand, examples which reinforce or more often contrast with the British experience and thus indicate paths which British feminist presses did *not* take. The governing impulse is to allude to the breadth and variety of feminist publishing internationally, while providing a coherent analysis of a specific sector in all its national complexity. The British publishing experience outlined here should thus be understood only as analytical scaffolding, not as any variety of ideological blueprint. Further studies of specific national feminist publishing histories can only add to understanding of the women in print movement and its internationally pervasive cultural impact.

References to Commonwealth countries seem especially germane in this context, given that Britain's two largest feminist imprints were started by Antipodeans (Virago having been co-founded by Australian Carmen Callil, and The Women's Press by New Zealand-born Stephanie Dowrick). In addition, another expatriate, South African

Ros de Lanerolle, during her period at the helm of The Women's Press (1981–91) presided over an important reorientation of the press's identity towards writing from the developing world. The internationalism of feminist publishing notwithstanding, this discussion remains attuned to cultural debates that occurred *within* Australia, New Zealand, Ireland, Canada, India and South Africa contemporaneous with the rise of the feminist presses. These debates, especially as they reflect the vexing issues of post-colonial cultural politics, place Commonwealth women writers and publishers at the intersection of nationalist *and* feminist agendas, and to omit consideration of either context would be to misunderstand the well-springs of their writerly and publishing activity.

CONSPICUOUS BY ITS ABSENCE: THE MARGINALISATION OF FEMINIST PUBLISHING WITHIN ACADEMIC DISCOURSE

To move from the arena of public literary debate to the realm of academic discourse is to experience a jarring discontinuity, for the high public profile and imprint recognition enjoyed by feminist publishers in the print media at large is, in the more exclusive sphere of academic publications, seemingly entirely unfamiliar. A curiously anomalous situation reigns whereby a deep-seated shift in the dynamics of literary culture much remarked upon in the publishing world remains virtually undetectable through the written academic records – the monographs, anthologies, theses, journals and conference papers – by which the academic world monitors its changing interests. The absence of extended discussion about feminist publishing makes itself felt in a variety of ways. Frequently the subject is simply omitted entirely from discussions of women and literature, or, equally problematically, where publishing *is* referred to it is assumed to constitute a neutral link in the communications chain. The upshot of this widespread academic obliviousness to the dynamics of feminist publishing has been a curious analytical hiatus when considering the processes by which individual authorial impulse is transformed into publicly available text. The pre-publication phases in the communication network are analysed by a complex variety of methods, and, equally conscientiously, the multifarious interpretations of written texts by readers are exhaustively investigated. Yet the act of making a text public, which resides at the very centre of the literary communications circuit, remains obscured by a puzzling intellectual opacity. According to such a schema, the intricate political interconnections that web the production of literature appear magically to unravel at the exact point of publication – an ironic situation, given that political judgements and cultural value are, in decisions over publication, frequently at their most potent and explicit.

Over the course of the last decade the commonly encountered academic obliviousness to the politics of feminist publishing has begun to be replaced by a subtler form of academic dismissal: the glancing acknowledgement. Many critics, perceiving that their failure to address the politics of the publication process undermines their assertion that *all* forms of communication are inherently political, have nodded in the direction of the women's publishing boom of the last 25 years, but in terms generally so brief and glibly congratulatory that they fail to engage with the complex debates and dilemmas that infuse this sphere of feminist media intervention:

> The remarkably successful way in which [women's] silences have been filled in the last decade or two almost masks the magnitude of the achievement. Women's studies is now a force and a market: publishers such as Virago and the Women's Press [sic] are commercially successful and feminist criticism is an academic force carrying with it career possibilities. (Minogue, 1990: 4)

Glancing acknowledgements of this nature leave begging important conceptual debates in the area of women's studies, thereby doing a disservice both to the discipline and to feminist publishing practitioners.[3] It is exceptional that a field such as women's studies, which has paid rigorous attention to the means by which academic disciplines are constructed and imbued with intellectual authority, should have failed to address in-depth attention to the political and commercial realities underpinning its own development.

The academic phenomenon that Dale Spender and Cheris Kramarae term the 'explosion' of feminist knowledge over the last 30 years rests upon the substratum of the feminist presses, which both republished out-of-print texts with which feminism archaeologically unearthed its own history, and made available to women the works of contemporary feminist thinkers (Kramarae and Spender, 1992). Without prior evidence of such texts' profit-making capacity, mainstream publishers were unlikely to have sponsored their own feminist lists, thereby expanding access to the world of publication, which feminist writers now enjoy. Dale Spender, perhaps because of her own publishing experience with feminist imprint Pandora Press, is a rare exception among critics in drawing attention to feminism's own analytical blind spots:

> The feminist knowledge explosion has been inextricably linked with the emergence of women's publishing ventures, and what is surprising is that this fundamental feature of Women's Studies' growth and achievement has attracted so little research attention within Women's Studies – which has such a commitment to examining its own processes. (Kramarae and Spender, 1992: 17)

Feminism's casual obliviousness to the crucial role that women-run presses have played in ensuring the movement's success is open to challenge both on ideological and on practical political grounds. Firstly, it is intellectually inconsistent for any politico-cultural movement committed to investigating the partisanship of all rhetorical acts to overlook the policies and practices that facilitate its own pronouncements. Despite having brilliantly illuminated the gender prejudices and inequitable selection policies that inform the mainstream publishing industry, feminists have so far remained largely silent on the gatekeeping policies of their own presses. If the act of publishing is in all circumstances informed by ideological factors, have feminist publishers themselves not played a crucial role in setting the parameters of feminist debate, privileging certain strands of feminist thought over others? If, as the media industry maxim has it, the power of the press belongs to he who owns one, presumably – when circumstances permit – it belongs to *she* as well. On the basis of intellectual consistency alone, feminism is obliged to explore the political ramifications of its own control over the printed word.

In disregarding its own publishing history, feminism is, moreover, failing to inform its increasingly sophisticated media critiques with the benefits of practical experience. Taking as its initial rallying cry 'the personal is political' – a public nailing to the mast of its faith in the political validity of women's lived experience – academic feminism has, since the mid-1980s, engaged in increasingly rarefied philosophical debates as to its nature as a movement and its ideological priorities (Messer-Davidow, 2002). Such self-analysis has been intellectually profitable for feminism, and represents a habit of self-reflection indispensable for any evolving social movement. Nevertheless, it remains true that feminist theory must grow out of a dialectical relationship with feminist practice, and that by overlooking the publishing experience of its own presses feminism is ignoring a rich source of potential theorising on its own doorstep. Nor would the women who founded and who continue to run feminist imprints feel unduly burdened by any such academic attention. For as feminism in a sense retreated into the academy during the market-dominated and politically conservative period of the 1980s, many feminist publishers were left feeling abandoned by a movement that, on one hand, castigated them for cashing in on oppositional politics and, on the other, often relied upon their presses to further the academic careers of movement figures. As the most consistently successful of women's interventions into media production since the 1960s, feminist publishing has vast potential to reinvigorate women's studies' theorising around communication. The question that remains is why a sphere of media activity so successfully breached by feminism and about which so much first-hand knowledge exists should have been relegated to academic oblivion – fruitfully explored neither by the history of the book, nor by women's studies, nor by those powerfully ascendant interdisciplinary forces in the contemporary humanities: media and cultural studies.[4]

SEARCHING FOR WOMEN IN THE HISTORY OF THE BOOK

The academic sphere in which feminist publishing studies might be expected most easily to reside is the broadly interdisciplinary field of research clustered under the banner of the history of the book. This field of academic inquiry began with an impulse that harmonises well with the socio-political impetus of feminist publishing – scholars in France, Germany, Britain and the United States sought to reinvigorate traditional modes of bibliography by analysing book production against a variety of sociological, political, economic and philosophical frameworks. Furthermore, the chronology of this discipline's emergence would appear to coincide productively with the academic institutionalisation of women's studies: building upon path-breaking 1950s French studies in *histoire du livre* such as Lucien Febvre and Henri-Jean Martin's *L'Apparition du livre* (1958), book history gradually consolidated its position within academe during the 1970s, and evolved into a recognised field of research during the 1980s, receiving perhaps its most sought after imprimatur with the launch in the late 1980s and early 1990s of internationally linked History of the Book projects, tracing book development and literary culture in an array of countries (Sutherland, 1988; Darnton, 1990 [1982]; Jordan and Patten, 1995). Yet the enormous potential for cross-pollination between book history and feminist research has remained largely a lost opportunity, in part because of book historians' predilection for the seventeenth- to nineteenth-century period – centuries in which the embryonic nature of organised feminist politics necessarily resulted in fewer feminist publications (Myers and Harris, 1983, 1985; Chartier, 1989; Darnton, 1990 [1982]; Anderson and Rose, 1991). But this absence is due also to a latent conviction within book history that publishing history and women's studies represent mutually exclusive fields of enquiry. Book historian Nicolas Barker, writing in *The Book Collector*, is perhaps unintentionally revealing in his assumption that the two disciplines are set on diverging paths: 'Work is there, wherever you can find it; it will continue to exist when the searchlight of fashion has moved on from the history of the book to, say, women's studies' (1990: 24).[5]

One of the history of the book's most prominent practitioners, cultural historian Robert Darnton, characterises the inchoate diversity of the field as 'interdisciplinarity run riot' (1990 [1982]: 110), a situation in which novelty and openness to innovation might be expected to facilitate a cross-disciplinary project such as feminist publishing studies. Perversely, this appears to date not to have been the case. In so far as the field of publishing history can be said to have its nuclei, they operate without substantial reference to the findings and interests of feminist academics, resulting in a field at once fraught with the feared fragmentation of interdisciplinarity, yet at the same time unified in its resistance to broad-scale feminist intervention.[6] Enumerating briefly the main categories of research in book history, I propose to demonstrate feminism's failure to intervene decisively in the field before turning to one of book history's proposed ordering schemas, Darnton's 'communications circuit', to illustrate that even in its suggested avenues for further research, book history has thus far encoded implicit gender preferences.

The classic genre for tracing the impact of the book has been the national history: a chronicle of the development of printed texts in, for example, Britain (predominantly understood as England) from William Caxton to the paperback revolution, usually ceasing before the phase of large-scale rationalisation and conglomeration, which British publishing experienced during the 1980s. John Feather's *A History of British Publishing* (1988) is representative of its type, in particular in its total omission of gender as a differential in the publishing equation across 500 years. Despite its publication date of 1988, it reads more like a monograph from the 1960s: no female publishing employee other than Geraldine Jewsbury, a house reader for Bentley's in the mid-nineteenth century, warrants even passing mention; women appear either as monarchs, lending their names to convenient historical subdivisions, or as faceless low-level publishing operatives in mid-twentieth-century houses run on the '& Sons' model of patrilineal descent.

The progenitor of Feather's gender-oblivious approach is the long-lived 'classic' of British publishing history, Frank Mumby's *Publishing and Bookselling*. The fifth edition of the text, jointly attributed to Ian Norrie, magisterially pronounces upon the inferiority of female achievement with a certainty that belies its 1974 publication date:

> At the start of our period women played little part in the book world, except as authors. In that role they excelled, especially as novelists and poets, and still do, although their achievements in music and the plastic arts have never equalled men's. Similarly, women have been amongst the most gifted of booksellers in the twentieth century but have seldom, as yet, been permitted the same opportunities to rise to the top on the other side of the trade, except as editors of children's books. (Mumby and Norrie, 1974: 241)

Updating Mumby's text and correcting previous editions' 'many omissions' (1974: 9) in 1982, Ian Norrie somewhat belatedly noticed that 'the feminist movement' was now 'in full swing' (1974: 15), and added to the 'Independents, Old and New' chapter a handful of sentences on Virago's Modern Classics reprint list, noting the 'vivid mark' its director Carmen Callil had made upon contemporary publishing 'by exploiting the woman's [sic] movement' (1974: 158). In the brevity of Norrie's remarks, in his conception of feminist publishing as essentially parasitic in its relationship to the political wing of the women's movement, and in his focus on a single press rather than on the industry force that women's publishing by 1982 had come to represent, Norrie inadvertently demonstrates the chronic limitations for feminism of the survey-overview genre of publishing history.[7] A dynamic blend of feminist theory and publishing practicality, grounded in varied and detailed case studies, is required to do justice to the complexities of the modern feminist publishing experience. At its best, such an approach would aim not only to fill the gaps in traditional publishing and women's studies research, but – more profoundly – to prompt radical reconceptualisation of the nature and parameters of both disciplines.

That the history of the book is capable of such disciplinary reinvigoration under the influence of contiguous schools of thought is demonstrated by recent trends in analogous areas. The avowedly apolitical historical-survey approaches, which would seem to stymie efforts for a feminist appropriation of publishing history, could be expected to be equally non-conducive to class-based approaches. Yet the hybrid of popular literature and publishing history has been an academic growth area over the past two decades, sponsoring studies such as John Sutherland's exploration of the role of economic determinants in the production of literary culture, *Fiction and the Fiction Industry* (1978), Joseph McAleer's use of publishing house case histories to reconstruct the mass public's reading experience in the earlier twentieth century in *Popular Reading and Publishing in Britain 1914–1950* (1992), Ken Worpole's study of mass-market publishing, *Reading by Numbers: Contemporary Publishing & Popular Fiction* (1984), and Richard Todd's analysis of literary prizes' impact on the publishing industry and on bestseller lists, *Consuming Fictions: The Booker Prize and Fiction in Britain Today* (1996). The potential for reinvigoration and reconceptualisation of the field demonstrated by such titles is especially heartening given the resistance to feminist analyses demonstrated by other prominent genres of publishing history. The statistically based modes of enumerative and analytical bibliography would seemingly be as well suited to feminist-oriented enquiries as they are to traditional book history, yet the heavy reliance in British bibliography on the records of the Stationers' Company (a guild from which women were excluded) effectively militates against any such appropriation of the methodology for more politically engaged ends (Myers and Harris, 1985; Eliot, 1994). Other species of publishing history proffer blank walls and uncongenial environs for the feminist book historian: the intrinsically self-congratulatory nature of the publishing house history does not lend itself to analysis of the cultural judgements by which certain texts were rejected for publication. Similarly, technological and purely economic overviews of the printing and publishing trades appear to bear a residue of the ingrained hostility to female employment that characterised the printing unions from the nineteenth century until well into the 1970s: Marjorie Plant in her *The English Book Trade: An Economic History of the Making and Sale of Books* decorously confines herself to exploring 'the social and economic relationships which arose between masters and men' (1974: 7).

Faced with such disciplinary indifference to the history of women's interaction with the book trade, where is the feminist publishing historian to gain entry to this academic citadel, made all the more impenetrable by its constant self-description as tentative, permeable and open to innovation? The nucleus of studies around intellectual and cultural history represents the most profitable point of access for feminism into the history of the book. This view is founded partly on the receptivity to theoretical self-analysis that characterises the field, and in part on its firm contextualisation of book history within the overlapping spheres of economics, politics, philosophy, sociology and history. Moreover, in an academic sphere regarded with some justification as dusty and fogeyish, it is here that the most dynamic – not to mention readable – work is being produced. A field claiming to be besieged by a 'multiplicity of approaches' and lacking in 'binding theoretical coherence' can hardly complain that a further measure of interdisciplinarity threatens to wreak havoc (Jordan and Patten, 1995: 2; Sutherland, 1988: 576).

Rewiring Darnton's Communications Circuit

Cultural historian Robert Darnton in his essay 'What Is the History of Books?' (1990 [1982]) provides a diagrammatic schema for conceptualising book history, which has drawn significant attention in the field of publishing studies partly, one suspects, because the field is characterised by anxiety as to how its disparate elements might be made to coalesce into a semblance of disciplinary unity (Sutherland, 1988; Barker, 1990). Tracing the publication history of a book through a literary circuit, the stages of which include the author, publisher, printers, distributors, retailers and readers, Darnton situates the whole process within overarching economic, social, intellectual, political and legal landscapes (1990 [1982]: 112). It is Darnton's contention that in the tension between these broad contexts and the smaller-scale activity of print circulation the history of the book can be seen in the making:

Book history concerns each phase of this process and the process as a whole, in all its variations over space and time and in all its relations with other systems, economic, social, political, and cultural, in the surrounding environment. (1990 [1982]: 111)

Given that Darnton's diagrammatic overview represents the closest thing to a disciplinary blueprint that book history has yet produced, the feminist publishing critic cannot but read the model noting its absences as much as that which it incorporates. Darnton's book model is a mono-gendered construction, omitting entirely the involvement of women at any single point in the communication chain and, moreover, failing to discern that gender considerations play a determining role at *every* stage of his communications network, radically altering its nature for women. In encapsulating his goal as the quest to discover 'how exposure to the printed word affects the way men think' (1990 [1982]: 134), Darnton reveals not just an uncharacteristic (for a present-day US academic) rejection of gender-neutral language, but also an unspoken basic premise of his publishing history model. Book history is, in Darnton's model, fundamentally masculine in gender.

The particular text that Darnton tracks around his communications circuit is Voltaire's *Questions sur l'encyclopédie* (1770), a significant fact, for the model proposed bears the imprint of the European eighteenth-century French-language book trade. In order for it to engage meaningfully with the contemporary Anglophone publishing scene it would have to be radically amended by taking into account the role played by book reviewers, literary agents, rights departments, literary prize panels and the plethora of other contemporary literary stakeholders. Hence, despite Darnton's claims for the universality and transhistorical nature of his model – 'with minor adjustments, it should apply to all periods in the history of the printed book' (1990 [1982]: 111–13) – it is, crucially, a gender- and period-specific construction, imbued with the priorities of the twentieth-century academic historian as much as it is with the experiences of the eighteenth-century bookseller.

The field of book history is, however, not so littered with holistically structured intellectual schemas that historians of feminist publishing should be overly hasty in jettisoning Darnton's model. While remaining fully cognisant of its glaring omissions and eighteenth-century timeframe limitations, feminists would be wise to appropriate Darnton's model and radically reconceptualise it for their own purposes. Once adopted and adapted there is much to recommend it. Firstly, the fundamental principle encoded in the model, that of the interdependence and dialectical tension between the book industry and larger societal contexts, is vital to any politically oriented critical approach such as feminism. Indeed, in order to take into account the central role played by encompassing social revolt and

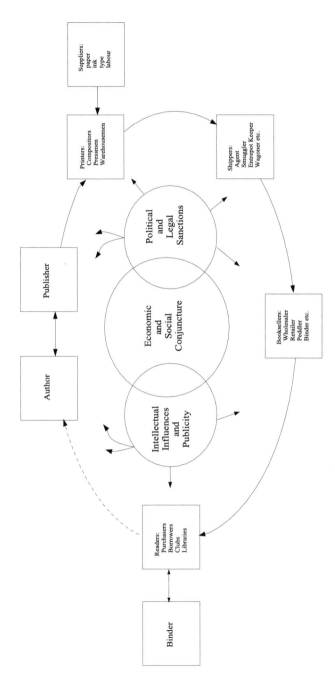

Figure 1 'The Communications Circuit' by Robert Darnton. Redrawn from Darnton's *The Kiss of Lamourette: Reflections in Cultural History*, London: Faber, 1990, p. 112. (Originally in 'What Is the History of Books?', 1982.)

15

political ferment in the revival of modern feminist publishing since the 1970s, Darnton's model could be usefully restructured so that the communications circuit is depicted as operating *within* the intellectual, economic and political spheres. Such a readjustment is mooted also in Nicolas Barker's 'Reflections on the History of the Book', though to support an historicist, not specifically feminist, position (1990: 22–3). The change here proposed would be beneficial in highlighting diagrammatically an oppositional press's position of unequal strength *vis-à-vis* the societal status quo. While it suggests the power discrepancy between independents and the mainstream (a fact invariably commented upon by feminist publishers in interviews), such a modified communications circuit acknowledges also the potential for individual agency within larger socio-economic systems. It is this bifocal element that is one of the most valuable insights of Darnton's model: an individual bookseller may be motivated to stock Voltaire's *Encyclopédie* because of a fashion in pre-revolutionary Europe for rationalist philosophy, yet his act may be prompted equally by the more immediate and personal spur of competition with a neighbouring bookseller (Darnton, 1990 [1982]: 114–19). Such a receptivity to the importance of individual action, within the possibilities presented by a sometimes hostile social milieu, is the kind of dynamic analytical approach that any study of feminist publishing must strive to emulate.

How else might Darnton's framework be appropriated to construct a feminist publishing history, which he appears to overlook? I propose several alterations to sketch in the outlines of a feminist 'communications circuit' (Darnton, 1990 [1982]: 112) appropriate for charting women's growing control over the printed word. Firstly, Darnton's model is posited upon the concept of *successful* communication; in his emphasis on how books move through the communications cycle he has little regard for what founders in the system, for what remains unwritten, for that which is rejected for publication, or for books refused retail space or denied distribution outlets. Hence, a feminist analysis of book industry operations would pay attention not only to Darnton's smoothly oiled cogs, but also to the hiatuses, disruptions and silences in the process. It would examine not simply a system for the communication of ideas, but also the same system's reverse manifestation as an instrument for *non*-communication and for the frustration of oppositional innovation. Locating the silences within a system in this manner generally involves evidentiary problems –

how to locate those books that do not exist? – but the ghosts of these silences and hiatuses haunt feminist publishing endeavours, and are frequently discernible by paying attention to the remedial measures in which feminist presses have engaged. For example, the UK broadsheet newspapers' unwillingness to review reprint paperbacks initially threatened Virago with commercial extinction; hence their small print runs of review hardbacks and their standardised Modern Classics cover design are doubly encoded with meaning – they amount to creative solutions to problems faced by industry outsiders.

Moreover, a recasting of Darnton's model for feminist usage would complicate its format and structure, rejecting Darnton's largely single-direction model for one better able to illustrate the subterfuge and tension characterising much feminist interaction with the publishing process. In particular, the unproblematic juxtaposition in Darnton's model of author and publisher belies the tensions inherent in the relationship, one strained especially among feminist presses by the risk of author poaching, and by the sometimes microcosmic community politics, which lead to the situation whereby a manuscript is submitted by an author known to the publishing collective.[8] Conversely, the model fails to accommodate individual feminist presses' efforts to reconceptualise positively the author–publisher relationship by infusing it with greater supportiveness, mutuality and consultation. The feminist publishing goal of reforming the conditions out of which literature is created cannot be done justice by Darnton's marginalising of the pre-publication phase, nor can the complexity of that relationship adequately be summarised by a deceptively simple diagrammatic arrow. The cumulative effect of these feminist restructurings of Darnton's model would be increased attention to hiatuses, communication impasses and feedback, to individual agency, alternative routes and circuitous channels: less quasi-scientific model than Snakes and Ladders board-game. For it is only through consulting the original documents, manifestos, articles and publications of the women's presses, enhanced by interviews with women centrally involved in the industry's development, that a critical medium can be struck between, on one hand, the acerbic, soap-opera-style representation of feminist publishing in Weldon's *Big Women* and, on the other, the somewhat bloodless geometry of Darnton's model.

SILENCES WITHIN SILENCES:
SEARCHING FOR PUBLISHING IN FEMINIST MEDIA STUDIES

If the communications circuits propounded within publishing studies can be adapted to feminist interests only by major rewiring, scholars with an interest in feminist publishing history could be forgiven for anticipating that women's studies – originally the academic limb of the 1970s women's movement – would offer a more congenial academic niche for their research. To an extent that is startling, this assumption readily proves to be false. Perhaps because women's studies developed contemporaneously with the burgeoning discipline of cultural studies during the 1970s and 1980s, feminist research in the area of media has demonstrated a marked preference for popular genres such as film, television, magazines and periodicals, pornography, romance literature and music videos (Baehr, 1980; Jackson, S. et al., 1993; Zoonen, 1994; Robinson and Richardson, 1997). In effect, this preference has meant that feminist publishing studies has fallen between academic stools: too literary in its associations to be annexed to feminist cultural studies; and too tainted with commercialism to fall within the purview of literary criticism (Chester, 1996: 146–7). The anomaly is that some of the foundational texts in feminist media studies were in fact published by the women's presses – especially by Pandora Press, which pioneered this market – thus these books in their very materiality bear witness to feminist intervention in media production (Betterton, 1987; Baehr and Dyer, 1987; Miller, 1990). Yet, perversely, in their content they frequently omit all mention of the topic. They are inherently paradoxical: indelibly marked with the stamp of the women's presses, but in their silence on the subject at the same time positively Trappist.

The fate of feminist publishing in being relegated to an academic no-man's land could arguably be attributed to shifts in the prevailing intellectual fashions of the past three decades. With a poor sense of academic timing, feminist publishing – according to such an interpretation – entered mainstream consciousness at precisely the point when critics were turning away from materialist analyses to pursue discourse-centred critical modes such as post-modernism, psychoanalytic theory and post-colonialism. Yet, such an explanation for the manifest absence of work on feminist publishing fails to convince on two grounds. Firstly, the boom in cultural studies during the 1980s and 1990s was never entirely dissociated from questions of economic substructure, demonstrable in analyses of favoured cultural studies media such as film (Bordwell, Staiger and Thompson, 1985; Dale, 1997), television (Ang, 1995; Gledhill, 1997; Geraghty and Lusted, 1998), and the pop music industry (Chapple and Garofalo, 1977; Negus, 1992). Moreover, the modes of textual analysis dominant in 1980s and 1990s academia need in no sense have precluded analyses of feminist publishing, as studies of post-colonial publishing industry politics in India and Africa amply testify (Altbach, 1975; Adaba, Ajia and Nwosu, 1988). Hence, with no inherent reason for cultural studies academia at large to have dismissed feminist publishing from critical regard, the troubling question emerges as to why – specifically – did the field of women's studies fail to register such an omission and to act to rectify it?

The implications of women's studies' pervasive silence on the issue are twofold. Firstly, it represents an internal contradiction in the theoretical construction of feminist media studies. Initially, research in this field took as its focus representations of women in popular media, many of which were interpreted as intellectually patronising and ideologically coercive stereotypes. Growing restive with this position by the late 1970s and early 1980s, feminist critics turned to more heartening evidence of women's proactive intervention in media production, analysing ways in which women's representations of women differed from those produced by less politically self-conscious mainstream media institutions. More recently, academic attention has focused on more theoretical conjectures such as the nature and significance of media mediation and the individual's agency to refashion cultural products (Bonner et al., 1992; Robinson and Richardson, 1997). The field's marked failure to engage centrally with the legacy of the women's presses represents a glaring omission in what has been, up until this point, an academic arena nothing if not theoretically self-conscious. Compounding the intellectual inconsistency of the field at the theoretical level is a commensurate practical loss in terms of evidence: whether through lower start-up costs or through less rigorously exclusionary distribution systems, feminist presses achieved the most high-profile and long-lived success of any feminist media enterprise. Within the UK, none of the feminist film-making collectives, film distribution organisations, feminist periodicals, academic women's studies journals, women's community newspapers, television production companies or independent radio programmes attained anything comparable to the financial success, public recognition and longevity of the feminist publishing houses – Virago Press and The Women's Press in particular. To overlook this rich store of experience and flourishing of feminist cultural confidence because of a preference for formats more demonstrably 'popular' than the book is to sacrifice a wealth of dynamic material on the basis of overly pedantic disciplinary boundaries.

Negligence, rather than any wilful intent to curb the ambit of academic research, probably accounts for the contradictory situation within feminist media studies. Yet the contemporary status quo is foreshadowed in a text that served as a foundation for much of the materialist feminist criticism which subsequently emerged in the field: novelist and short story writer Tillie Olsen's influential critical work, *Silences* (1980 [1978]). This volume, which concentrates critical attention on the circumstances – financial, domestic, cultural, familial and legislative – in which it is possible to produce literature, was timely for women's studies in linking women's publication history with the social and economic circumstances of women's lives. The text's opening section, a 1962 essay entitled 'Silences in Literature' (Olsen, 1980 [1978]: 5–21), was, as its title suggests, the intellectual seedbed of the volume as a whole, and in it Olsen movingly extrapolates from her own late-flowering literary career a broadly socialist-feminist theory for women's comparatively sparse literary output. Although Olsen adumbrates class, race and gender consid-erations that significantly constrain literary production, in addition to the further silencing tactics of self-censorship, artistic isolation and domestic and maternal burdens that prevent women from 'com[ing] to writing' (1980 [1978]: 39), her focus is predominantly on the pre-publication phases of writerly production. The process of publication is itself the unspoken silence at the heart of *Silences*. In only a bare handful of paragraphs (9, 41, 143, 170) in what is, as critics have often noted in exasperation, a scattered and somewhat repetitious text (Atwood, 1978: 27), does Olsen make even passing reference to 'publishers' censorship' (1980 [1978]: 9). Such criticisms are, moreover, usually centred upon publishers' genre preferences – 'there is no market for stories' (1980 [1978]: 143) – which force writers into using specific, perhaps uncongenial, forms, rather than on the publishing industry as an ideological filter with the commercial power to marginalise minority voices. Olsen's critique gives the impression that once a woman writer has leapt the hurdles represented by a lack of self-confidence, poverty, domestic responsibilities and an absence of writerly support, she has a clean, straight run until she must face the post-publication barriers of state censorship and the tricky water-jump of exclusion from academic syllabi. That access to publication, perhaps the most politically bemired and treacherous obstacle in this entire literary obstacle course, is glossed over with terse asides constitutes a fundamental misrepresentation of book industry realities.

Olsen's lack of emphasis on the ideological force of access to publication has been uncritically reinforced by much work in feminist media studies since the original US publication of *Silences* (1978). This gives rise to a curious contradiction, as to handle a copy of the book is to perceive a triple irony. The text is, in spite of its content, indelibly soaked with the spirit of the feminist presses: not only was the largest single section of the book, a reflection on the life and work of nineteenth-century American author Rebecca Harding Davis, written as an afterword to the first title in the Feminist Press Reprint series (Olsen, 1980 [1978]: 47), but Olsen by implication berates the mainstream publishing houses for allowing such a classic of American realist literature as Davis's *Life in the Iron Mills* (1861) to fall out of print and languish in obscurity.[9] Furthermore, in Britain, *Silences* proved a solid commercial success for Virago Press from the appearance of its edition in 1980, raising questions about the interrelationship not only of nineteenth-century and twentieth-century women's writing, but also of US and British feminist presses over the course of recent decades. It is the book's failure to acknowledge its embedding in the sphere of feminist publishing from its very inception that makes reading *Silences* such a frustrating experience: constantly avowing a broad-based analysis of communications systems and raising hopes for an inclusivist approach, it fails to direct the full force of its critical beam on the circumstances that make it, as a published book, possible.

Telling it Slant:[10] Reading Women's Studies for a Theory of Feminist Publishing

Silences, omissions and glancing asides do not, however, constitute the chill entirety of women's studies' commentary upon the phenomenon of feminist publishing. Recent work in the field has come to echo a refrain of consternation and surprise at an omission both glaring and theoretically unjustifiable. Florence Howe, founder of the oldest of the extant women's presses, The Feminist Press at The City University of New York, in 1995 regretted the absence of a full account of the last 25 years of feminist publishing, declaring that 'there has been no book on the subject' because 'no one has tried to write [the history] down' (Howe, 1995: 137, 130). It is a sentiment echoed in Mary Eagleton's insightful discussion of 'Women and

Literary Production' in the second edition of *Feminist Literary Theory: A Reader*, in which Eagleton makes audible a critical silence by asserting that 'the full story of the last twenty years of feminist publishing is still to be told ... one hopes, though, that someone, somewhere *is* writing a thesis on this aspect of feminist literary production since much knowledge and experience will otherwise be lost' (1996a 71).[11] Not to be outdone in terms of self-referentiality, Dale Spender and Cheris Kramarae in the introduction to their anthology of women's studies scholarship, *The Knowledge Explosion* (1992), delineate a necessary sphere of research even as they lament its absence from the pages of their own collection:

> That this considerable publishing achievement [by women] so enmeshed with the knowledge explosion and so open to challenge has been the focus of so little attention within Women's Studies is one omission; that it has not been pursued in more detail in these pages is another. (Kramarae and Spender, 1992: 19)

More recently, Stacey Young in *Changing the Wor(l)d: Discourse, Politics and the Feminist Movement* remarks that any attempt to understand the (US) women's movement requires analysis of the movement's symbiotic relationship with feminist presses, an analysis 'thus far marginal to (or absent from) studies of the movement' (1997: 26). Young declines, however, to develop fully a theoretical model by which this might be achieved (1997: 26, 59–60). By a curious turn of academic events, feminist publishing begins to take on the trappings of a phantom discipline – commented upon as much for its absence as for its contributions.

In commenting upon feminist publishing's Scarlet Pimpernel-like status in academia – 'they seek him here, they seek him there ...' – I do not wish to imply that this volume is created in a vacuum. Although no book-length critical study of feminist publishing from the 1970s until the present has yet appeared, research in analogous areas does exist and, if read with an eye for the politics of contemporary publishing, provides rich insights. Hence the title for this section, 'Telling it Slant', borrows from Emily Dickinson's famous line to suggest the tactics of cross-reading, argument by analogy, refraction and qualified acceptance by which the picture of feminist publishing might be constructed from close readings of the evidence women's studies has already compiled.

A group of works charting the interaction of women writers with cultures of print production, the majority of which were published in the late 1980s and 1990s, provides valuable methodological models. Gaye Tuchman and Nina E. Fortin's *Edging Women Out: Victorian Novelists, Publishers, and Social Change* (1989) usefully demonstrates the gendered nature of the publishing sphere, in itself rebutting Robert Darnton's implicit assumption in 'What Is the History of Books?' that the realm of public print is a sphere unmarked by gender codings. Exploring a similarly gendered pattern in relation to transatlantic nineteenth-century publishing, Susan Coultrap-McQuin in *Doing Literary Business: American Women Writers in the Nineteenth Century* (1990) provides a more optimistic reading of women's conditional acceptance in the public world of letters. Coultrap-McQuin emphasises women's strategic sleight-of-hand in adopting personae, which allowed them maximum flexibility to write about the world as they perceived it, an approach also furthered by Catherine Gallagher in her analysis of the ambivalent authorial practices of women writers from the seventeenth through to the early nineteenth centuries, *Nobody's Story: The Vanishing Acts of Women Writers in the Marketplace, 1670–1820* (1994). Yet the theoretical sophistication and archival thoroughness evident in such works cannot compensate for the fact that their attention is necessarily drawn to the subject of women *and* publishing, rather than that of women *in* publishing – making them studies different in kind from that attempted here. In considering women as active agents in the material production of literary culture, Paula McDowell's *The Women of Grub Street: Press, Politics, and Gender in the London Literary Marketplace 1678–1730* (1998) brings publishing history into belated dialogue with gender studies, though McDowell's chronological frame of reference makes drawing comparisons across the centuries a hazardous undertaking. Additional work on the fascinating nineteenth-century British house, the Victoria Press, an all-women printing and publishing operation of the 1860s and 1870s headed by pro-suffragist Emily Faithfull, focuses on women as outsiders in the London print trade, portraying their determined efforts to breach its exclusionary boundaries (Fredeman, 1974; De La Vars, 1991; Ratcliffe, 1993; Frawley, 1998). But once again sea changes in publishing techniques, formats and financing between the nineteenth century and the present mark out the Victoria Press as an interesting precursor to modern feminist publishing initiatives rather than as a direct progenitor.

for ch. 1

Analyses focusing upon the twentieth century proffer greater insights into the contemporary status quo, although frequently periodical publishing, rather than fiction publishing, constitutes these studies' primary frame of reference. Hence Dale Spender's exploration of ideological 'gatekeeping' by means of the refereeing policies of academic journals at once provides a key term for critiquing feminist publishing, while at the same time necessarily emphasising the distinctive character of academic journal publishing (1981). Similarly, Jayne E. Marek in her excellent *Women Editing Modernism: 'Little' Magazines and Literary History* (1995) demonstrates with well-selected evidence the inherently political nature of editorial control in early twentieth-century 'little' magazines, sponsoring a central tenet of this volume's theorising about the base-line power of wielding the editorial blue pencil. Yet periodical publishing, with its lower-scale investment, provision for advertising, and multiple authorship of a single edition, contrasts starkly with the financial realities of book-length fiction publishing, in which capital return is invariably slower and for which the construction of a marketable house identity is a primary necessity. Consistently, the medium in which analyses specifically focused upon book publishing have appeared has been feminist periodicals. Furthermore, the cogent articles that have appeared in the feminist press have frequently been penned by those with first-hand experience of feminist publishing practice. In this context, manifestos, commentaries, reports and position statements in publications such as *Spare Rib, Everywoman, Trouble & Strife, Quest, Sinister Wisdom, Women's Review of Books, off our backs, Refractory Girl, Feminist Bookstore News* and *Feminist Review* have provided the explicit theoretical orientation that pieces in broadsheet newspapers are inclined to suppress as overtly tendentious. It is precisely this falsely assumed mask of objectivity that the articles from feminist periodicals manage so compellingly to disrupt.

Finally, a bare handful of texts focusing in part upon feminist publishing's politics and practice have appeared, constituting the nucleus around which further analyses of the area must develop. Nicci Gerrard's *Into the Mainstream: How Feminism Has Changed Women's Writing* (1989) employs the author's experience as editor of Britain's *Women's Review* to survey changes in the field of women's writing throughout the 1970s and 1980s, benefiting from over 30 interviews with prominent writers in which they speak of their enhanced opportunities for publication in the wake of the feminist presses' success. Gerrard dedicates only one section of a single chapter to the topic of feminist publishing; however, the ambivalence recorded in her conclusions about the fate of the women's presses in the face of competition from vastly more powerful corporate multinationals has since proven unnervingly prescient. Individual chapters in other valuable texts provide instigatory analyses and important factual detail, but they have frequently been superseded by industry developments since their various dates of publication: *Rolling Our Own: Women as Printers, Publishers and Distributors* (1981) by Eileen Cadman, Gail Chester and Agnes Pivot records the origins and intents of British women's presses with avowed authorial support; Lynne Spender's *Intruders on the Rights of Men: Women's Unpublished Heritage* (1983) is touched by the creeping economic rationalism of the early 1980s, casting a gaze of ominous foreboding in the direction of the corporate publishing sector; and, more recently, Patricia Duncker's inclusion in *Sisters and Strangers: An Introduction to Contemporary Feminist Fiction* of a chapter dedicated to discussing 'the Politics of Publishing' underpins the readings advanced in her later chapters with a firmly materialist industry critique (1992: 39–54). Lastly, two guides to the women's press sector, Polly Joan and Andrea Chesman's *Guide to Women's Publishing* (1978) and Celeste West and Valerie Wheat's *The Passionate Perils of Publishing* (1978), convey the excitement of the early US women in print movement, but are now greatly out of date.[12] As contributions to an emergent debate around feminist publishing, these texts play a pivotal role, yet events since their various dates of composition bespeak an industry constantly in flux. It is this dynamic reality which gives the analysis that follows the status of a report from the field rather than that of a judgement professing magisterial finality. To declare the provisionality of one's findings is to acknowledge – and to embrace – the dynamic reality of feminist publishing as an ongoing commercial venture.

MIXED MEDIA:
EQUIVOCAL SUCCESSES AND SHIFTING PERSPECTIVES

Feminist publishing is beset by a dilemma that underpins the industry as a whole and each individual press at any point in time: the irresolvable tension implicit in the phrase 'political publishing'. How can a publishing house committed to securing cultural and political changes in favour of women hope to accommodate itself to a capitalist system that largely benefits from social stability and acquiescent female participation? Phrased differently, how can an oppositional politics hope to achieve commercial success within the ruthlessly competitive global publishing marketplace? Compounding the problem of a press's political identity are the risks attendant upon too great a commercial success: the decline of Virago's Modern Classics list was ironically hastened by its manifest popularity, a commercial strength that inspired mainstream rivalry and competition for rights to out-of-print women's titles. Feminist presses must walk an impossible line between political authenticity and commercial viability; between financially risky first-book authors and low-risk, profit-generating 'classics'; between ensuring sufficient turnover to remain solvent on the one hand, and, on the other, disguising any too flagrantly profitable operation for fear of imitation. Add to this already complex equation the uncongenial political and economic environment of the 1980s and 1990s for left-identified operations, and its microcosmic reflection within the publishing industry in a wave of press mergers, takeovers and bankruptcies, and the precariousness of feminist publishing becomes apparent. That an industry that began with such insignificant capital investment and low public profile achieved marked success within three decades is remarkable; that it did so against a grim background of recession and political retreat is nothing short of extraordinary.

The title of this volume, *Mixed Media*, captures something of this delicate balancing and profound ambivalence at the heart of feminist publishing. To propose any species of grand solution to the politics/profit conundrum would be hopelessly arrogant – involving, quite possibly, the total reconceptualisation of the current socioeconomic system – and it would, in any case, be mistaken to reason away the very source of tension that provides the key to understanding the feminist press industry. By concentrating on the variant strategies that feminist publishing houses have evolved, this volume proposes to grapple with the issues of political credibility versus company solvency from a variety of perspectives. Endorsement of any one approach is redundant in such a study, although, specifically in relation to radical collectivist feminist publishing, this volume does suggest that certain group policies aggravated rather than allayed circumstantial problems. More generally, this work's objective is to explore the variety of feminist print activity, and to demonstrate that, far from there existing an archetypal feminist press, the market in feminist books is now sufficiently large and diverse to support a multiplicity of approaches. The hostile rivalry between 'independent' presses and mainstream houses, which dominated discussion of feminist publishing (such as it then was) in movement periodicals of the 1970s, misses the fundamental point:[13] diversity and broad-based market penetration, rather than any abstract, unattainable notion of political 'purity', signal feminism's best hopes for survival in the publishing sphere.

The current paucity of book-length research on the subject of feminist publishing prompts this volume to militate simultaneously in three directions. Bibliographically, it locates sometimes obscure printed and archival material about feminist publishing and, where this material does not already exist, creates the same through interviews with feminist publishers. Secondly, it proposes a theoretical framework against which feminist publishing might be conceptualised, one coterminous both with publishing history and with women's studies, though resisting the gravitational pull of either field by refusing containment solely within one or the other. Thirdly, this work offers critical interpretations of how this primary (and rarer secondary) source material might be read against the proposed theoretical framework, allowing for a politically engaged evaluation of feminist publishing's achievements and difficulties to date. Scrupulous academic objectivity in the classical sense is a principle that this volume neither ascribes to nor attempts. Indeed, any such formulation would contradict at the outset the central perception with which feminist publishing originates: that production of the printed word and its interpretation constitute forms of *political* power. The upshot of such a position has been an attempt to replace the specious objectivity of pre-feminist criticism with a multifaceted analytical approach, which considers the construct 'feminist publishing' from a multiplicity of viewpoints – historically, politically, nationally and commercially. The hallmark of academic writing which rises to the threefold methodological challenge outlined here is a high degree of self-consciousness. Yet, given that in the pages that follow it is the lack of precisely this quality for which this volume takes publishing history, women's studies, and cultural and media studies to task, self-consciousness seems a necessary prerequisite of intellectual honesty.

1
'Books with Bite':
Virago Press and the Politics
of Feminist Conversion

By no stretch of usage can *Virago* be made not to signify a shrew, a scold, an ill-tempered woman, unless we go back to the etymology – a man-like maiden (cognate with *virile*) – and the antique meaning – amazon, female warrior – that is close to it. It is an unlovely and aggressive name, even for a militant feminist organisation, and it presides awkwardly over the reissue of a great *roman fleuve* which is too important to be associated with chauvinist sows.

> Anthony Burgess in a review of
> Dorothy Richardson's *Pilgrimage*, reissued by Virago
> in 1989 (quoted in Scanlon and Swindells, 1994: 42)

Twenty years since Marilyn French's *The Women's Room*, one of the most influential novels of that time, women's lives have changed. There is a new spirit in women's writing which Virago salutes with its new 'V' imprint. The launch titles are as diverse as women themselves, but the young authors share a liberating sense of irreverence and risk-taking. The 'V' aim is to avoid political correctness at all costs: these are books by women which speak to men as much as women.

> 'Wayward Girls & Wicked Women',
> Virago relaunch promotion (*Guardian*, 1997)

There is some considerable distance between being lambasted by a characteristically curmudgeonly Anthony Burgess for militant political chauvinism, and squeamish recoil from ideological commitment under the guise of avoiding 'political correctness'. That both of these quotations refer to the public face of Britain's Virago Press during the course of a single decade highlights the extent to which the women's publishing house has reinvented itself for a new generation of readers. Such a marked volte-face must derive either from a suspiciously late twentieth-century obsession with self-reinvention and novelty for its own sake or, more fundamentally, from a crisis of house identity suffered by Virago and its directors. Such a seizure of self-doubt can be pinpointed with unusual accuracy: the linchpin between the two faces of Virago outlined above is the sale of the press in November 1995 to Little, Brown & Co. UK, a subsidiary of the US-based multi-national Time Warner.[1] The sale, and the flurry of negative publicity that surrounded it, represented a critical phase not only for Virago, but for feminist publishing as a whole, as falling profits and uninspiring frontlists forced reconsideration of feminist publishing's agenda – a thorough-going industry soul-searching of the kind that Virago had not undertaken publicly in the course of its 23-year history. For this reason, the 1995 sale of Virago serves as a critical vantage point from which to survey the press's history and against which the company's post-1996 relaunch can be measured. Beneath the breathless rush of the new Virago's promotional copy, it is possible to discern a frantic search for the winning formula by which Virago formerly united its profits with its politics – and the belief that this elusive link is capable of being reconstituted in the consumer-dominated, politically skittish 1990s and beyond.

The sale of Virago Press to publisher Philippa Harrison's Little, Brown UK group for a rumoured £1.3 million on 2 November 1995 bears closer analysis because of the wider debates around feminist publishing which the incident sparked in the international media (Rawsthorn, 1995: 7; *Bookseller*, 1995b: 8). Essentially three strands are discernible in the journalistic coverage of the sale: the personality-dominated 'feuding feminists' angle (*Evening Standard*, 1995: 8; Shakespeare, 1995: 12; Porter, 1995: 1, 25; Rawsthorn, 1995: 7); the accusation of mismanagement and poor business practice (Pitman, 1995; Alberge, 1995: 3); and – most common among left-identified newspapers – the lament for a passing golden age of feminist and publishing history represented by Virago (Dalley, 1995: 21; Baxter, 1995: 9). The first of these approaches, that focusing on the personal animosity between Virago's founder, Carmen Callil, the firm's original director and former chairman [sic], and Ursula Owen, initially Virago's editorial director and later its joint managing director, follows the convenient journalistic practice of reducing complex issues to personal antagonisms. Epitomising this hostile coverage is Henry Porter's exposé of 'feminist publishers – their angry struggle' in his feature article for the *Daily Telegraph*, entitled 'The Feminist Fallout that Split Virago' (1995). Strategically juxtaposing photographs of Callil and Owen, Porter paints a scenario of maenadic fury, the obvious subtext of which urges that sisterhood is at best merely spectral – suitable for a rallying cry but a risible failure when put to the test.[2] In pursuing the feminist catfight line, the article ploughs an increasingly overworked media furrow. The early 1990s war-by-fax waged between tireless self-promoters Camille Paglia and Julie Burchill was belaboured in the mainstream press in precisely the same manner, as were the ideological differences between Australian author Helen Garner and younger feminists in the newspaper flurry over Garner's book about sexual harassment within universities, *The First Stone* (1995). According to such journalistic practice, the mergers and buy-outs of largely male-run multinational publishing companies are read as auguries of market trends; those of feminist publishing companies betoken nothing more significant than the hysteria of the wandering womb. As an unidentified 'ex-Virago' confided to Jan Dalley in her *Independent on Sunday* article: 'When men have boardroom battles, it's heroic

Figure 2   Virago's sale in late 1995 was widely interpreted in the international media as the end of an era. (Richard Collins cartoon first published in *Australian Financial Review*, 8 November 1995. Reproduced by permission of the artist.)

and Titanic and serious. When women do the same, it's a catfight' (1995: 21).

Of the many articles published about Virago in late 1995, those of most significance for the purposes of this discussion are the pieces appearing in the UK's centre-left broadsheets – the *Observer* and the *Independent on Sunday* in particular – for they invoke the issue of Virago's loss of independence to survey the general state of feminist publishing, and to reignite then latent debates about the political viability of such enterprises. During the high point of Virago's commercial success in the late 1970s and early 1980s, the substantial backlist sales generated by its fiction reprint series, the Virago Modern Classics, and its unmatched reader loyalty tended to obviate the need for any such debate. Virago was phenomenally successful, and commercial success was seen to constitute the litmus test of its publishing philosophy. The subsequent nadir of the company's fortunes in late 1995 is attributable to a variety of causes: a profit of barely £100,000 on sales of over £3,000,000 (a margin of under 5 per cent); the resignation of senior directors Carmen Callil, Harriet Spicer and Lennie Goodings within a period of eight months (*Evening Standard*, 1995: 8; *Bookseller*, 1995d: 6; Buckingham, 1995: 4); low staff morale; staleness induced by slow middle-level employee turnover; and ferocious competition from the feminist lists of mainstream houses for high-profile female authors and titles (Ezard, 1995: 3).

Yet, more pervasively, Virago's loss of direction is attributable to a crisis of confidence in the political and cultural role of a feminist publishing house, a deep-seated suspicion of its own irrelevance in an age that has broadly appropriated feminist positions as mainstream thinking, but which simultaneously eschews explicit gender politics as embarrassingly passé. Such defeat points, paradoxically, to the old-style Virago's victory: so successful was its publishing philosophy that its radical avant-gardism of the early 1970s appeared to the jaded mid-1990s as banally self-evident. Hence Virago's 1995 directors might have been forgiven for wondering whether they should preside over the company's demise or respond with a Mark Twain-like salvo to the effect that reports of its death had been greatly exaggerated.

Should Virago's sale to the world's largest media conglomerate be taken as evidence that feminism's battle for representation from the margins of political and cultural power has been won, and that its place in the cultural mainstream has been established? Alternatively, is the subsumption of Virago within the capacious corporate structure of Time Warner the final victory of market forces and economic rationalism over political commitment – the selling out of a feminist dream? It is in keeping with the complex ambiguities of feminist publishing that the fact of Virago's sale should be susceptible to both readings, but both represent an oversimplification of the issue. For Virago's 1995 crisis is attributable chiefly to a loss of confidence in what had, until that point, proved a delicate balancing act between the seemingly irreconcilable forces of politics and profit. By refusing to acknowledge that commercial success need necessarily vitiate political integrity, Virago attained a profile among the general reading public higher than that of any feminist press worldwide. The savvy and legerdemain by which such a delicate balance was achieved bears closer scrutiny, not only for the light that it casts on the fate of Virago Press in particular, but because it represents an optimal – though precarious – point on the continuum strung between feminist oppositionality and market centrality.

The characteristic that distinguishes Virago from many other feminist presses which sprang up under the invigorating influence of women's activism from the late 1960s is the duality of its self-conception: it perceived itself simultaneously both as a commercial publishing house *and* as an intrinsic part of the British women's liberation movement. With the mutation of international leftist politics towards the centre over the course of the 1980s and 1990s, it is difficult now to recapture the anomalousness of such a position in the socio-political climate of the early 1970s. With feminism regarding the progressive left as its natural political home, such a flagrant embrace of capitalist principles on the part of Virago engendered some suspicion, and attracted substantial criticism from the socialist wings of the women's movement (Owen, 1998b). Yet, the insistence that politics and profitability be brought into a working relationship is, in retrospect, a radical proposition.[3] Virago's *raison d'être* was to publish books informed by the feminist politics of the time and to make them profitable – in foundation member Harriet Spicer's terms 'to make profitable what you wanted to do' (Spicer, 1996).

The attempted unification of capitalist and feminist agendas placed Virago in a borderland position, between the feminist sisterhood (with its preference for experimental, collectively run co-operatives such as the British periodical *Spare Rib*) and the traditional power centres of mainstream London publishing (which regarded politically identified publishing – let alone *feminist* publishing – as a commercial non-starter and as a somewhat distasteful predilection). Nevertheless, Virago's protean house identity proved the key to its success. Because the press maintained a double outsider status in relation to both groups, it was able to weather the enormous changes in industry organisation and feminist thought that occurred during the 1970s and 1980s. Significantly, it was in the early 1990s – as feminism embraced the cultural possibilities of ambivalence and irony – that Virago appeared to harden in its political stance and to suffer recurrent financial losses. In the apt colloquialism of former Virago employee Sarah Baxter, 'Virago lost the plot' (1995: 9). The vagaries of fashion in feminist thought, not to mention the unpredictability of complex consumer economies, reward feminist presses that state their politics up front, but which are canny enough to factor in a buffer zone of ambivalence and allowances for revision. Provisional certainties, not lapidary pronouncements, have the best chance of securing market rewards.

The borderlands between divergent political systems and ideologies can, however, prove fraught and uncomfortable ground: original Virago member Ursula Owen speaks wryly of 'get[ting] flak from the left and right, but I'm fairly resigned to that' (Macaskill, 1990: 434). Alexandra Pringle, who joined as Virago's fourth member in 1978, casts the press's dual outsider status in a more playful light: 'Does it make you feel that you're under siege? Well, yes. But it's quite fun that, you feel you're out there battling ... up there on the barricades' (1996). This concept of strategic self-positioning in order to partake in both feminist activism and commercial publishing – but combined with a refusal to be defined or contained by either – is key to Virago's achievement and its current remarketing. Within this general framework of Virago as a political and publishing fringe-dweller – though a powerful one by reason of its fringe-dwelling status – this discussion analyses the company from its origins in 1972, including its post-sale relaunch in mid-1996 and taking into account subsequent seasons' developments. The first section presents a general overview of the company's history and its changing institutional niches, rebutting the misconception present in much writing about Virago's 1995 sale that Virago had, until that point, been a fully independent company (Ezard, 1995: 3; Henry, 1995: 13; *Bookseller*, 1995b: 8). Secondly, the discussion explores the facet of Virago's identity that is broadly feminist, focusing on Virago's complex relationship with the women's movement and with the academic wing of feminist politics – university-based women's studies programmes. The discussion then proceeds to site Virago within the context of the publishing industry, focusing on three key issues: the significance of independence for feminist presses; Virago's marketing of feminism for a mainstream readership; and Virago's role in the creation and appropriation of a market for feminist books. Lastly, Virago's current state of play is analysed, as is its most recent attempts to remarket itself as a trade publisher with special appeal to a younger, more politically jaundiced, readership. The structure of this chapter, analysing Virago firstly against the background of feminist politics and, in the second instance, against publishing industry dynamics, is the result of convenience rather than of any absolute theoretical distinction between the two spheres. Publishing and politics are, in the case of Virago, indisputably interlinked; the disentangling of Virago's relationship with first one and then the other area serves merely as an analytical device to cast light upon the unique position that Virago occupied at the cusp of the profit-driven publishing industry and the politically driven women's movement.

A KITCHEN TABLE IN CHELSEA:
SELF-MYTHOLOGISATION AND THE ORIGINS OF VIRAGO

The origins and publishing history of Virago Press have been so often recapitulated in the firm's promotional material that the division between past and present has all but dissolved – history is recycled as publicity in a manner that occasionally owes more to directorial agendas than to historical veracity. The self-mythologising strain in Virago is comparable in publishing history only with Allen Lane's famous championing of the early Penguin paperbacks: because both ventures were innovatory for their time, the fact of their existence – aside from any individual title they produced – has become in itself a badge of their founders' achievement. The origins of Virago lie in the oft-repeated detail that the press began at founder Carmen Callil's kitchen table in her home in Chelsea, and that it was fuelled by red wine and late nights spent arguing over the politics of the emerging women's liberation movement, all undertaken against a backdrop of economic buoyancy and political possibility (Lowry, 1977: 9; Macaskill, 1990: 432; Durrant, 1993: 93; Gerrard, 1993: 61). The company's initial self-description – 'the first mass-market publishers for 52% of the population – women. An exciting new imprint for both sexes in a changing world' (Virago publicity pamphlet, 1996: 1) – encapsulates both the optimism and the determinedly non-sectarian vision of the press for which its founders strove. The house's success over the following two decades and its immense brand-name recognition fostered celebrations not so much of the firm's individual achievements, but of the press's very existence: in 1993 *A Virago Keepsake to Celebrate Twenty Years of Publishing* neatly conflated in its title the individual press with the concept of feminist publishing. The self-celebratory tone of the book, distributed free to bookshops by Virago, earned the press censure from some sections of the women's movement who critiqued the discrepancy between Virago's profits in the 1980s and feminism's political retreat:

> In the Virago *Keepsake* a further shift has taken place; a move from the individual author to the Virago author, a celebration not of the women's movement, or of women's writing, but the survival of the press itself – a recognition of what it stands for, not so much in terms of political achievement, but brand loyalty and quality writing. (Scanlon and Swindells, 1994: 42)

The choice of year in which to celebrate Virago's twentieth anniversary was itself contentious. The exact date of the press's foundation – either 1972, when Callil registered the company, or 1973, when Virago's first title appeared and when Ursula Owen was granted shares in the company – tends to vary in Virago's publicity according to the political make-up of the board at the time of writing.[4] For a publishing house that conceptualises its very existence as a political achievement there is much feminist cachet to be had in presenting oneself as its sole founder.

The myth of Virago's genesis (an apt term, given the firm's wryly anti-Edenic bitten apple logo) often glosses over the exact financial conditions under which Virago's initial nine titles were produced. Between 1973 and 1976 Virago was an 'independently owned editorial imprint' of Quartet Books, publishing under its own name but with copyright and production of its titles controlled by Quartet (Virago publicity pamphlet, 1996: 1; Spicer, 1996; Owen, 1998b). Unsurprisingly, given that this same corporate niche was later to prove so uncongenial to feminist publishers The Women's Press,[5] Virago's former directors speak meaningfully of learning during those years about the importance of the power to publish. They evince a hard-won awareness that 'any requirement to refer to others on editorial decisions, however benevolent those others might be, is a constraint' (Owen, U., 1988: 89). Budgeting and editorial conflicts with Quartet led to a 1976 management buyout, funded by a £35,000 bank loan and personal pledges from Virago's directors. The period of independence that followed was one of steady expansion for the firm, with sales of the non-fiction Virago Reprint Library of early twentieth-century socialist and Fabian books such as Margaret Llewelyn Davies' *Life as We Have Known It* (1977 [1931]) and Maud Pember Reeves' *Round About a Pound a Week* (1979 [1913]) being compounded by the marketing triumph of the Virago Modern Classics. This later series, a fiction reprint list of 'lost' women writers whose out-of-print, copyright-free works were attractively repackaged for a new generation of feminist readers, achieved such success that its titles came to define the public image of the firm. Coinciding profitably with the rise of women's writing courses in academia, which were in turn fired by landmark texts such as Elaine Showalter's *A Literature of Their Own: British Women Novelists from Brontë to Lessing* (1978 [1977]), the Virago Modern Classics series blossomed, underpinning the firm's expansion into publishing fiction by living writers. The flagship series incontestably achieved its original aim of showing 'the imaginative range of women's writing and ... celebrat[ing] the scale of female achievement in fiction' (Owen, U., 1988: 93). The removal of the pejorative sting from the phrase 'woman writer' has proven to be the series' most influential legacy. Nevertheless, as Virago Modern Classics editor Ruth Petrie observed in 1993, at the time of its launch in 1978 (with the republication of Antonia White's *Frost in May* [1933]) it was non-fiction rather than fiction that the women's movement felt harboured the greater revolutionary potential:

> In those days [the mid-1970s] we all thought our politics were based in non-fiction writing, in issue-related titles. Fiction was what you gave yourself as a source of pleasure and distraction. It wasn't going to offer a commentary on life in quite the same way. (quoted in Norden, 1993: 15)

Virago experimented with a second period of corporate partnership with its sale in February 1982 to the Chatto, Bodley Head and Cape Group (CBC), which was to provide Virago with the high-outlay distribution and production services it required, but which would guarantee the press's editorial autonomy, thus differentiating the carefully negotiated arrangement from the invasive paternalism of the earlier Quartet alliance. Although Callil later justified the manoeuvre to a Women in Publishing forum as having 'written into it safeguards orchestrated by ourselves' (Callil, 1986: 851), Virago by 1986 had began to demur from an arrangement in which it was required to shoulder losses from other houses in the umbrella group, and under which it lacked access to 'information about what bits of [the] business were generating profit' (Jones, N., 1992: 21–2; McPhee, 2001: 208). With the (then) US-owned giant Random House poised to take over the CVBC Group, Virago instigated a successful management buyout in November 1987, netting substantial profits for the firm's directors but necessitating the closure of the flagship Virago Bookshop in London's Covent Garden as a condition of their financiers' backing.[6] Again, Virago's perceived prioritising of company profits over sisterly allegiance was criticised in the British feminist press, with *Everywoman* magazine tartly reporting that 'staff made redundant at the bookshop' would, according to Virago, 'unfortunately not' be employed elsewhere in the company (*Everywoman*, 1987: 11).

During the early to mid-1990s the series of recessions within the book publishing sector generally accentuated a loss of direction and quavering confidence within the firm. Repeatedly throughout the period Virago announced cutbacks in the frontlist, changes in editorial focus and retrenchment of staff – all undertaken without securing the desired result of long-term growth. Hence Virago's twentieth birthday celebrations and managing director Harriet Spicer's 1993 international promotional tour carry beneath their ebullience overtones of discernible unease; the *Virago Keepsake*'s strident best wishes for 'more than another twenty years of successful publishing' (1993: viii) betrays the suspicion that, though ideal, this outcome was not necessarily certain. Virago was attempting to ensure future sales by invoking the magic of a brand name that had in the past proven so bankable an asset; a standard promotional tactic, it was nevertheless a vulnerable one for a firm entering its third decade.

The period from 1993 to the company's sale in late 1995 was dominated by boardroom disputes, further staff and list cutbacks, and directorial resignations: a briefly returned Carmen Callil resigned as chairman in February 1995; managing director Harriet Spicer followed in July 1995; and publishing director Lennie Goodings compounded the trend by announcing her intention to quit in September 1995. This last departure was recorded in the *Bookseller* on 13 October, with a fellow Virago director attributing Goodings' departure to 'editorial differences, including the decision to publish books written by men' (*Bookseller*, 1995d: 6). With the sale of the company imminent, Goodings' recorded preference for independence may have also prompted her resignation, for two years earlier she had remarked that 'being independent has meant survival for us. We control our own costs and savings, we decide ourselves where we will compromise and where we won't. We choose the books we want to publish' (1993: 27). That new owner Philippa Harrison persuaded Goodings in November 1995 'to change her mind about leaving the company' and to take up the position of publisher for the now fully owned Little, Brown subsidiary would appear fundamentally to contradict Goodings's earlier avowals of press independence (*Bookseller*, 1995b: 8). Moreover, the commitment to women-only publishing attributed to Goodings was contradicted by the first list overseen by her as publisher to the Virago imprint, containing as it did *Sons & Mothers* (1996), an anthology co-edited by Matthew and Victoria Glendinning. Viewed in one light, these changes reflect the dynamic, strategic adaptability that has characterised Virago's history; viewed in another, they underline former director Alexandra Pringle's observation that 'Virago as we have known it is now completely over' (1996).

CONTINGENT SISTERHOOD:
VIRAGO AND THE POLITICS OF FEMINISM

An analysis of Virago's complex relationship with feminism results in a curious paradox: feminists tended to regard Virago as having more to do with publishing than with activist feminist politics while, simultaneously, publishers suspiciously regarded Virago as a feminist cabal, motivated first and foremost by a political agenda. That Virago could be branded both a bourgeois press producing glossy, middle-brow fiction for London's Hampstead and Islington middle-class left, and at the same time a house 'run on communard lines' (Tindall, 1979: 144) by 'militant feminist[s]' (Scanlon and Swindells, 1994: 42) hints at the complexity of left-wing and feminist politics in modern Britain. Yet it also indicates a complexity specific to Virago itself: a strategically multifaceted identity, which won the press attention and publicity for non-conformity in the journals of both the activist left and the right. Frequently it also earned Virago critical flak, from feminists no less than from conventional publishing circles, but this borderline position enabled Virago – metaphorically speaking – to snipe at both sides of the political battlefield, creating a controversial aura about itself, which proved a publicity gift. Virago's fraught and often controversial relations with one facet of the political spectrum – women's movement politics – constitute the focus of the discussion that follows. It considers first Virago's relations with the activist wing of the movement before turning, secondly, to examine its interaction with academic feminism.

Women's Business: The Selling of Capitalist Feminism

The tensions between political commitment and company profits, which in late 1995 triggered Virago's sale, were not, in the press's earliest years, perceived as insurmountable. Ringing throughout the press's foundation publicity and early position statements is, by contrast, a boundless optimism that a company providing books for which it knew there existed an eager, previously unexploited market, could not *but* achieve commercial growth. The contemporary women's movement and Virago Press could, these press releases imply, sponsor ever-increasing mutual expansion – a relationship of seamless symbiosis (Virago publicity pamphlet, 1977).

Accordingly, Virago was, from its inception, at pains to differentiate itself from the anti-capitalist underground publishing scene – Callil stating in a 1977 *Guardian* interview: 'I want to somehow get it across that we are not an alternative publisher and that quite ordinary women are feminists too' (Lowry, 1977: 9). The extent to which Virago's staff harnessed the corporate principle of profit generation to the political agenda of feminism is clear in Callil's positing of capitalist survival as in itself a political statement: Virago 'must survive. It is our duty not to go bust' (Toynbee, 1981: 8). Implicit here is a rejection of the victim syndrome among politically committed arts organisations, which US writer Robin Morgan has dubbed 'the crown of feminist thorns': the belief that noble failure in the interests of an oppositional women's cause is ethically superior to survival and success (1977: 13). Virago, while voicing a political critique, was in fact organised hierarchically, and run on anomalously Thatcherite principles of long hours, low pay and heavy workloads. Long-time Virago staff member and former director Harriet Spicer recalls that founder Callil's management style 'is not to work at all collectively' (1996). Callil, in one of many 'l'état, c'est moi'-style comments deployed in the media in a public relations onslaught spanning three decades, enthusiastically reinforces Spicer's assessment of a highly individual-orientated character: 'Collective! ... That was new to me, darling' (Porter, 1995: 25). Furthermore, Virago's corporate status dates from its inception, rather than being the formalisation of a previously unincorporated collective group. In 1972 Callil registered two companies: Carmen Callil Ltd, a book publicity enterprise, and

Virago Press, the publishing company, which was initially financed by the profits of the publicity operation (Durrant, 1993: 93). As has been noted earlier, the individual nature of this act has, as Virago rose to public prominence, been repeatedly underlined by Callil, as though to construct from the ferment of 1970s collectivity and sisterhood a prime mover in the feminist publishing firmament.

The second manner in which Virago firmly demarcated itself from the newsletter-and-mimeograph segment of ephemeral women's movement publications was in its self-declared intention to appeal to a mainstream readership – one that included men as well as women:

> The idea for a feminist house grew out of the feminist movement which was reborn in this country at the end of the '60s. Virago was set up to publish books which were part of that movement, but its marketing aim was quite specific: we wanted to reach a general audience of women and men who had not heard of, or who disliked, or even detested the idea of feminism. It was not enough for us to publish for ourselves. (Callil, 1986: 851)

This explicit appeal to a readership of males as well as females, one constantly reiterated in Virago's early promotions material, encapsulates its desire to appeal across a spectrum that included both active feminists and those (currently) outside the movement. Virago's founders felt that the potential expansion of feminism as a mainstream social philosophy was needlessly inhibited by the coterie content and hostile tone of many separatist women's movement publications, in which a position of ideological purity was adjudged more important than public accessibility. Virago, by contrast, evinced an astute tactical and commercial sophistication, marketing to both the mainstream and the margins by hinting at its variance from both. Potential readers from either conventional or politicised feminist backgrounds are offered a mixture of something old and something new; the product is familiar enough to both groups that their expectations will not be completely confounded, but either its content (in the case of non-feminists) or its format (in the case of self-identified feminists) should prove alluringly novel.

In order to appreciate the innovation of Virago's cross-spectrum marketing and Callil's controversial dictum that it was 'not enough for us to publish for ourselves', it is necessary to contextualise Virago within a women's movement with a (then) increasingly powerful separatist impulse. Second-wave feminists were acutely conscious of the fact that women's self-expression was highly constrained both in its formulation (by narrowly defined patterns of femininity acquired through conventional socialisation) and in its expression (by means of the denigration of women's speech, by their virtual exclusion from academic curricula, and by the small number of women's texts published as literary fiction).[7] Feminist interrogation of the silence surrounding women's experiences resulted in the prioritising of forums in which women could articulate their opinions unreservedly and without self-consciousness – an idea manifested in what became known as the consciousness-raising or 'rap' group.

In 1970s discussions of feminist publishing, the concept of the women-only forum is expanded into that of a 'women's independent communications network' (Arnold, 1976: 26) in which all stages in the writing, publishing, distribution, reviewing and sales chain are controlled entirely by women. This separatist impulse was – as Michelene Wandor's interviews with prominent second-wave feminists in *Once a Feminist: Stories of a Generation* (1990) attest – widely prevalent within the British women's movement, but its most sustained articulation is contained in US feminist publishing manifestos from the early to mid-1970s. June Arnold, co-founder of the US house Daughters, Inc., in a landmark 1976 article enumerates the principles that underpin separatist feminist media analysis: the political necessity of women controlling all aspects of the publication process; the belief that the mainstream media wilfully misrepresent or, worse, deliberately ignore feminist issues, and that politically committed feminists must therefore shun its products; and the conviction that not only are feminist presses subverting mainstream publishing houses, but that they 'are in fact the real presses, the press of the future' (Arnold, 1976: 20). Arnold alleges an absolute hostility on the part of mainstream 'Madison Avenue' publishing to the feminist project, dubbing the conventional press 'the finishing press because it is our movement they intend to finish' (1976: 19). The mainstream goal of annihilating feminist competition is, Arnold asserts, to be achieved through the combined tactics of publicly belittling feminist presses and selectively co-opting their market (1976: 19). While Arnold's analytical terminology relies heavily on a Marxist perspective of a 'revolutionary group ... taking over a government' (1976: 18), a model of questionable relevance to feminist politics, her analysis of the 'finishing press['s]' appropriation of feminist books – 'the least threatening, the most saleable, the most easily controlled or a few who cannot be ignored' (1976: 19) – is chillingly prescient.[8] In the contemporary publishing sphere, high-profile third-wave feminists such as Naomi Wolf, Susan Faludi, Natasha Walter and Katie Roiphe are all published under the imprints of multinational conglomerates, an ambiguous development explored in detail in the concluding chapter's discussion of the feminist bestseller.

Echoing the central tenets of Arnold's manifesto are notes for a talk prepared by US feminist media veteran Charlotte Bunch and published, in a material manifestation of her convictions, in the lesbian periodical *Heresies* (1977).[9] In Bunch's analysis, only absolute control can guarantee editorial autonomy and political integrity in a hostile marketplace:

> OUR PRIORITY must always be to keep our media alive, growing, and expanding: as a base of power made up of political and economic institutions of our own ... [and] as a means of controlling our words and how they are disseminated, even when we aren't popular. (Bunch, 1977: 25)

For both Bunch and Arnold, feminist politics and corporate practice are antithetical ideological entities. The former must always be predicated upon breaking the cultural stranglehold of the latter.

In outlining the growth of separatist feminist media theory during the 1970s, and Virago's self-distancing from many of its precepts, it is vital to take into account a distinctive third form of contemporary theorising: that emerging from women aligned with socialist-/Marxist-feminism. Unlike the liberal and radical wings of the women's movement, socialist-feminists in Britain did not establish their own publishing houses, instead more commonly working with men for existing left-identified imprints such as Lawrence & Wishart, Polity Press, Comedia and Minority Press Group. Nevertheless, socialist-feminists, especially those working around journals such as *Feminist Review*, articulated a firmly materialist critique, which, in its insistence on the means by which literature is produced, disseminated and consumed, influenced the establishment of presses such as Virago in fundamental ways (Barrett, 1980, 1988; Mulford, 1983; Kaplan, 1986). Socialist-feminist critics such as Michèle Barrett insisted that the standard New Critical practice of isolating a text from its circumstances of creation and publication could never adequately account for its nature, or even for the fact of its existence: 'To restrict our analysis solely to the text itself is to turn the *object* of analysis into its own means of explanation; by definition this cannot provide an adequate account' (1980: 100). This extra-textual mandate for criticism problematised and politicised previously sacrosanct domains of the literary text, allowing a press such as Virago to validate its publishing programme as an intervention into the spheres of book production, distribution and academic canon formation. Socialist-feminism's attention to those cultural industries responsible for producing the book contextualised Virago and made its project possible in ways that the company's founders have not always readily acknowledged: theoretically, it provided Virago with a political analysis and intellectual vocabulary to describe its project; while in practical terms it tied Virago into pre-existing networks of politicised women who supported the press's vision of gender-conscious publishing and lent their professional expertise to the fledgling enterprise.

The support of some socialist-influenced sections of the women's movement did not, however, provide the corporate-minded Virago with insulation from its feminist critics. With its determination to attract a mainstream, crossover readership, the press predictably fell foul of the shifting tides of 1970s feminism, and was accused by separatist sections of the women's movement of collaboration with the mainstream. A former Virago director recalls that the *Spare Rib* collective, a London-based group of 10 to 20 women producing the feminist periodical of the same name, 'disapproved of us'.[10] Yet, in a manner highly characteristic of early 1970s feminist circles, there was considerable overlap between the groups: two *Spare Rib* members, Rosie Boycott and Marsha Rowe, had been involved briefly with Virago in its earliest phase before moving to full-time participation with *Spare Rib*; and a Virago advisory group of around 30 academics, journalists, writers and publishers contained several feminists who identified with separatist and/or socialist causes. The mandate of the advisory group was to suggest to Virago potentially saleable new books or reprints, and in some cases to write introductions to the volumes to increase their appeal to the academic market. The highly individualistic managerial style of Callil – 'I was not collective-minded. I was a *leader*' – clashed directly with pressure for consensus decision-making from within the advisory group, resulting in a showdown, which former Virago members recall as a clash of personalities as much as of politics (Pringle, 1996; Owen, 1998b). The event has a symbolic resonance – highlighting Virago's compromised status from the point of view of influential strands of feminist thinking, yet also the firm's personal involvement with feminists sympathetic to such organisational politics. Ursula Owen, whose editorial experience and extensive involvement in London feminist and academic circles was crucial in developing Virago's list, remarks upon the 'huge moral support' provided by the network (1988: 90; Hattenstone, 2001). A former Virago director, by contrast, observes that 'it in a sense became too intrusive ... some people felt they had a bigger role in it and of course once the company was up and running the people who were running it wanted to run it. So it had a limited life.' The disbanding of the group in 1978 ended Virago's only loose organisational tie with the left of the feminist movement, the wing that was to be marginalised so decisively by the free-market Conservative politics of the subsequent decade.

Given the market-driven, private sector politics of the Thatcher period, Virago's adherence to modes of corporate organisation and its recognition of the vital importance of profit generation can be seen as prerequisites for its success and longevity. But accusations of Virago 'selling out' to the mainstream – of being a 'bad apple' in the feminist barrel – are not uncommon in writing on the British feminist publishing scene from the 1980s and 1990s (Scanlon and Swindells, 1994: 41). Amanda Sebestyen, a former member of the *Spare Rib* collective, in 1990 remarked upon the deradicalising of women's publishing with bitter-sweet acknowledgement of corporate feminism's dominance of women's politics (such as it was) during the 1980s:

> Now there's been such a proliferation of cultural feminism, not in the sense that we used to mean it as separatism, but there's so much women's publishing. I sometimes get asked to write things for them. We're a gang now, aren't we? You get asked, you're on people's visiting lists, it's nice they still remember you. This is all about the 1980s and about being on the make, which was very much despised and disliked by me and lots of my radical feminist mates, but people settle down. There's nothing wrong in wanting work that's interesting, or enough money, or a relationship: sometimes I do find it very twee, that's all. For one thing I think a lot of feminist writing has become dominated by the market. (Wandor, 1990: 143)

Virago's alliance of feminist politics and capitalist economics, encapsulated in Callil's vow that 'it is our duty not to go bust', outlived the collectivist feminist presses, many of which (for example, Feminist

Books, Black Woman Talk, Sheba and Stramullion) had folded by the end of the 1990s, largely through chronic lack of funding (Pitman, 1987). Perhaps the most telling comment on the state of play between collectivist and corporate feminist publishing by the early 1990s is also the most ironic: Sebestyen's critique of the 'twee[ness]' of mainstream women's publishing is contained in Michelene Wandor's *Once a Feminist* (1990) – a Virago title.

A critique from the left of the women's movement which did, however, register with Virago's editorial board was the accusation that the Virago Modern Classics list disproportionately favoured white writers of past generations over living black authors. The allegation of a specific omission on the part of Virago is tied to con- temporaneous debates within feminism as a whole over white feminists' tendency to homogenise the experience of all women to accord with their own. As African-American feminist and women's publishing practitioner Barbara Smith pithily surmises: 'Feminism that is not about freeing all women, which means working-class women, women of color, physically challenged women, et cetera, is not feminism but merely female self-aggrandizement' (Smith and Moraga, 1996: 26). Editorial director Ursula Owen, recasting the Virago house identity in line with the 1980s women's movement's changing priorities, acknowledges the silencing of which feminism – ostensibly a liberatory movement – has itself been guilty:

> In recent years we have published fiction by black British and American women, conscious of how, early on, we concentrated too heavily on the experience of white women, how black women have felt excluded from the account, and conscious too of the difficulties for a largely white women's press in getting such publishing right. (1988: 94)

The debate around racism within feminism, which rose to public prominence during the 1980s, operated in the publishing sphere in a still more complex manner: valid criticisms of Virago's tendency to cater for white, middle-class, heterosexual women also led directly to The Women's Press's contemporaneous 'Live authors. Live issues' publicity campaign.[11] Implicit criticism of Virago though it is, this differentiation of The Women's Press's target market from that of its rival in fact presupposes the continued existence of Virago as a point of reference – it implies that a gap is being filled, that a previously silenced voice is now being heard. This amounts, ironically, to a coded acknowledgement of Virago's achievement: subdivision of the feminist publishing market cannot but underline the success of the press which first established that market's existence.

'The Biggest Battle Still to Be Fought':[12] Virago, The Feminist Press and Academic Women's Studies

Despite controversy over the content of the fiction list, Alexandra Pringle is accurate in observing that 'the Classics made Virago respectable', providing the reader association, distinctive packaging and literary kudos for which the press had been striving (1996). The republication of the first of the Virago Modern Classics in 1978 – the highly successful *Frost in May* – signals not only a move into fiction in addition to feminist social history, but also the first tangible sign of Virago's interaction with the movement within academia for redis-covering women's fiction. In a *Times Literary Supplement* article about the Modern Classics, Callil outlines three key motivations behind the series: the first is a reaction against the conventional critical belittlement of fiction by women – 'to reveal, and indeed celebrate, the range of female achievement in fiction, and to bury, if possible for ever, the notion that women novelists are confined to this ghetto of the imagination' (1980: 1001). Secondly, Callil promotes the concept of a female canon, with writers of different generations and centuries 'writing back' to the works of earlier women writers, conscious of their position within and contribution to a female literary tradition: 'This is not to say that I do not see a female tradition in novel writing: I do – it is another aim of the Virago Modern Classics list to reveal this' (1980: 1001). Thirdly, Callil records the influence upon the firm's editorial selection of one of the epochal texts of feminist literary criticism, Elaine Showalter's *A Literature of Their Own: British Women Novelists from Brontë to Lessing* (1978). Showalter's text has since been critiqued, both for its recoil from explicitly theoretical critical approaches, and for its somewhat dogmatic classification of women's writing into discrete 'feminine', 'feminist' and 'female' periods (Moi, 1985: 55–6, 75–80). Yet its influence upon Virago in the late 1970s and 1980s is unquestionable: 'her judgements led directly to the reprinting by us of May Sinclair, Sarah Grand and Dorothy Richardson' (Callil, 1980: 1001). Additional beneficiaries of Showalter's research, via Virago reprints, were the literary reputations of Vera Brittain, Rebecca West, Katherine Mansfield, Winifred Holtby, Elizabeth Bowen and Rosamond Lehmann. Marking a rare point of confluence between academic research and the direction of the British publishing industry,

accounted for by the grassroots of WS – not discussed

A Literature of Their Own was, as current Virago publisher Lennie Goodings notes, 'the Bible of the now famous nineteenth and twentieth century [sic] fiction reprint series' (1993: 26).

Figure 3 The first Virago Modern Classics reprint title, Antonia White's *Frost in May* [1933] (seen here in its 1992 cover design) bears all the hallmarks of Virago's house style: dark green livery, restrained title-face, and a painting by a lesser-known artist. (Reproduced by kind permission of Virago Press, a division of Time Warner Books UK.)

Given the slightly earlier emergence of the women's movement in the United States, it is unsurprising that US feminist presses, catering to the country's vast tertiary education market, also perceived the financial and cultural potential of reissuing out-of-print women's fiction. The oldest and best-known of the extant US presses, The Feminist Press at The City University of New York, founded by academic and activist Florence Howe in November 1970, was the first to identify and supply this market with its 1972 republication of Rebecca Harding Davis' *Life in the Iron Mills* [1861]. This text, published with a lengthy afterword by socialist-feminist critic and author Tillie Olsen, comprised the first title in the highly successful Feminist Press Reprint series (Howe, 2000b: 9–10). The Feminist Press's reissue of this title coincides with the year of Virago's foundation, and certainly precedes the initiation of Virago's Modern Classics series in 1978, thus substantiating the assertion by Florence Howe that 'we were the first to begin to reprint the lost literature by and about women' (Tally, 1987: 287). Questions of transatlantic publishing influence are frequently fraught with contradictory claims to originality and innovation. Unsurprisingly, given the competitive nature of global trade publishing, none of Virago's directors will explicitly acknowledge a direct US precedent. Yet all the evidence indicates that Virago was certainly aware of The Feminist Press's prior reprint success: the initiation of The Feminist Press Reprint series some six years before the release of Virago's *Frost in May*; examples of cross-fertilisation between the lists of the two presses – particularly in relation to non-fiction and to Virago's subsequent republication of American writers Agnes Smedley, Zora Neale Hurston and Willa Cather – all Feminist Press Reprint authors; and, most conclusively, the meeting between Howe and Callil in the early 1970s, which Howe recalls in a 1995 article, her tone being very much that of setting the historical record straight:

> Virago's Carmen Callil, the British founder, visited The Feminist Press in the early 1970s. She was going to start a press that would restore British women writers. When asked how many books she planned to publish in the first year, she said, 'Twenty-eight.' When asked, 'Which twenty-eight?' she replied, 'The first twenty-eight I find.' (1995: 133)

This evidence is cited not to belittle Virago's achievement in successfully marketing its reprint series, but because, in Virago's overwhelming public identification with women's reprint fiction and in the haze of self-mythologisation to which the firm is prone, the role of precursors and rivals has been obscured. It is a reflection of the publishing industry's long-standing tendency to celebrate not the originator of an idea, but its most prominent practitioner.

The factor that most clearly differentiates The Feminist Press from Virago – and that by extension distinguishes American feminist publishing in general from British and Commonwealth women's presses – is the extent of its interaction with the academic community. Feminist publishing faces an ideological and financial conundrum when contemplating entry into the academic publishing sphere: on the one hand, all feminist presses share an awareness of women's traditional exclusion from the privileged arena of high culture, and a concomitant awareness that in order to write women into the cultural record, their achievements must be taught and critiqued by the academy – the self-appointed arbiter of cultural value. On the other – financial – hand however, academic publishing constitutes a discrete sector of the publishing industry, and the pre-established nature of its distribution channels and marketing practices presents a formidable barrier to new firms attempting to break into this lucrative market.[13] Feminist presses remain burdened by an awareness that the tertiary sector is a market which, though ideologically essential, is commercially difficult to access.

Perceiving the politically ossifying effect of the traditional US publishing–academy relationship, The Feminist Press initiated various policies to break the self-perpetuating cycle whereby feminist knowledges were denied academic endorsement. In 1981 they commissioned a study of the most frequently set university American literature anthologies and, appalled at the continuing under-representation of all but a handful of women writers, compiled a competing textbook, designed to provide both an alternative for staff already conscious of gender imbalance in existing texts and a corrective shock for those oblivious to the standard texts' shortcomings. In addition, The Feminist Press heavily marketed their American literature anthology by developing relationships with academic literary bodies and by embedding the press in the powerful US academic conference circuit (Lauter, 1984: 42). The fact that the press's director, Florence Howe, had in 1973 served as president of the powerful Modern Languages Association (MLA) gave the press an insider knowledge and academic embedding crucial to the success of such a risk-laden, high-outlay venture.

Virago, for its part, cannot be accused of failing to apprehend the importance of the academic market in Commonwealth countries, which constitute its primary market. In her speech to the 1985 Women in Publishing conference, Callil articulated the need for feminist presses to break into the academic market in terms reminiscent of the firm's founding political principles:

The biggest battle still to be fought by all feminist publishers is, I believe, the battle for the school and university curricula ... Until the body of women's writing is seen as central to the culture of our society, and therefore as something that must be taught in schools and universities, the work we do will continue to be an uphill struggle. (Callil, 1986: 852)

Several factors, some external to the company and others intrinsic to its decision-making processes, nevertheless problematised such a desire to capitalise culturally and financially upon the academic market. Principally, academic women's studies in Britain is less influential, less institutionally secure and less endowed than its American counterpart; it thus proves an uncongenial environment in which to launch a large-scale feminist marketing initiative. Britain lacked (and unquestionably still lacks) the powerful women's studies networks that provide a discernible market for feminist texts in the United States. Trev Broughton, analysing the British scene, sketches a community in which the casual one-on-one academic relationships that characterised the first UK Women's Liberation Conference at Ruskin College, Oxford in 1970 still predominate: 'university women's studies in Britain has been the result of a felicitous, but essentially sporadic and *ad hoc*, series of encounters between academic women from various disciplines and of various political outlooks' (1993: 73). It is a pattern mirrored in Virago's academic network, first with the loosely defined advisory group, and later with the one-on-one editor–academic relationships that survived its dissolution. Harriet Spicer remarks that Virago 'was not a religious attender of the academic conference circuit' (1996), and Alexandra Pringle recalls that direct promotion of the list to the academy was somewhat haphazard: 'we would occasionally produce a leaflet but that was about as far as it went' (1996).

In addition, Virago was at a disadvantage in its attempts to woo the academic market in that it lacked an embedded editorial relationship with campuses and was unable to provide the kind of capital-intensive marketing programmes necessary for launching a new textbook. Intervention in the lucrative – though competitive – university text market would have demanded a financial commitment that Virago, even in its years of greatest profitability, was unable to provide. Yet unwillingness, as well as inability, was a crucial factor in Virago's underdevelopment of this potential market. In conversations about Virago, staff both past and present consistently give the impression of academic feminism as something *other* than Virago's sphere – a tangentially related though clearly distinct phenomenon. The nature of Virago's interaction with British women's studies perhaps exemplifies many of the tensions implicit in forging a business from ideologically informed publishing: while Virago's directors comprehended the cultural and political desirability of intervening in academic publishing, financial constraints and an institutionally insecure and amorphous market prevented real cross-genre expansion. From an academic feminist point of view this could be construed as a shortcoming on the part of the firm, as an opportunity for influence lost through corporate lassitude. From a publisher's perspective, however, it instead represents good business practice: identify core markets, cater to their interests, and do not risk overexpansion by forays into ill-defined new fields. Virago, usually adept at exploiting its borderline position between conventional publishing and feminist ideology, here felt the chill of its exposed position. While independence lends a publishing house an enviable degree of editorial autonomy, the financial limitations endemic to small presses can result in lost opportunities to proselytise to a broader social spectrum.

'IT DEFINITELY NEEDED BLOWING APART SOME WAY OR OTHER':[14] VIRAGO AND BRITISH PUBLISHING CULTURE

Decisions over the feasibility of targeting academic markets involve feminist presses in questions of publishing priorities, public recognition and potential profits – all in themselves issues of substantial political and economic gravity. Yet it is the complex and multifaceted issue of press independence that strikes at the core of feminist press identity. From the re-emergence of feminist publishing in the early 1970s to the present time, it is the issue of independence that has dichotomised feminist presses, and that continues in its myriad mutations to dominate debate on the ideals and mechanics of women's political publishing.[15] While the feminist publishing sector as a whole reflects the unstable dialectic of commercial investment and social change, it is most often over the issue of press ownership that this latent tension becomes startlingly manifest. The reconciliation of oppositional politics and capitalist practice would appear to require supreme political optimism combined with the jaundiced wariness of the market veteran.

Virago's in-and-out relationships with corporate empires make it a prime example of both the benefits and the detriments of corporate involvement for a feminist firm: chafing against the constricting paternalism of Quartet Books, Virago briefly sampled the commercial risks of independence, later affiliated to the CBC Group, foresaw takeover of the group by Random House and re-established its independence while benefiting from a remaining 10 per cent Random House stake, before finally selling to Little, Brown UK as a fully owned imprint. The firm's ongoing dilemma typifies the classic feminist publishing conundrum: fired by a political desire for editorial and financial autonomy, most presses are nevertheless tempted by the possibilities for enhanced production, marketing and distribution available by compromising this cherished independence. Yet such a binary conceptualisation of the dilemma is not wholly accurate. Further complicating the debate is the idea of conglomerate membership as a means for furthering *oppositional* political ends, in that a house that markets to the mainstream through conglomerate-controlled distributors may be more successful in proselytising a feminist political message to a wider audience. Virago, in its borderline position, is no stranger to these ideologically-pure-and-no-bank-balance or sell-your-soul-to-capitalism debates. Former joint-managing director Ursula Owen rejects such a diametric conceptualisation of the debate, in its place positing a position in which subversion from within the system is not a left-wing cliché but a practical business possibility in a particular late twentieth-century economic climate:

> But since it is not possible to separate the economic and creative sides of a publishing house, no publishing house can be truly independent ... We want to reach an even wider audience, which we are convinced is there. Yet we want to stay radical in the widest sense of the word. Our early decision to reach the high street audience and people who do not regard themselves as feminists meant that in a sense we became part of the Establishment, but not of it. (1988: 98)

Feminist presses must locate for themselves a position on the continuum between an idealised independence, on one hand, and total integration into a conglomerate structure on the other. In its attempts over a 30-year period to reconcile the deeply held feminist conviction that control over speech is a form of political control with a market-driven desire for expansion, Virago has ranged across this continuum, negotiating distinct forms of cohabitation with each of its corporate partners. Its current position as a wholly owned imprint *here I'd rather have a chronological description of Virago's stages —*

of Time Warner Books appears to contradict its founders' earlier rhetoric about the necessity of financial and editorial autonomy – their avowals that the elusive 'power to publish' is the *sine qua non* of a feminist imprint. However, from the time of its inception Virago has insisted equally upon marketing for the mainstream, maintaining high production standards and adhering to professional business practice, all of which may be compromised by an insistence on full financial independence in the face of increasing competition. The various institutional arrangements that Virago has negotiated hence represent attempts to reconcile a feminist political agenda with a changing marketplace in which that political agenda does not enjoy majority support.

The question remains whether recent examples of renewed vitality within independent publishing make Virago's decision to sell a perspicacious reading of the business climate, or a miscalculation of the form of compromise that would best enable it to ride out current trends. The November 1995 sale in fact coincided with an increasing trend within publishing towards middle-sized, independent firms, the same market sector that was so decimated by the mid- to late 1980s impetus for concentration and mergers. Publishing within a conglomerate structure has proven a less than ideal practice, with multinationals frustrated at the publishing sector's seeming inability to generate profit margins above 10 per cent, and with authors affronted at being passed from editor to editor, without the opportunity to nurture a productive author–editor relationship (McPhee, 2001: 284–92; Schiffrin, 2001: 103–28; Epstein, 2002: 1–38). It is therefore ironic that, at precisely the moment at which literary energy within the London publishing scene appeared to be emanating from small- to medium-sized independents such as Bloomsbury, Granta, Fourth Estate and Serpent's Tail, Virago's sale to the multinational Time Warner was presented as a condition of its survival.[16]

It is worth speculating whether these signs of independent life on the fringes of conglomerate culture amount to a sea change within the industry. The developing observations of Charlotte Bunch – an organiser of the instigatory 1976 US Women in Print Conference in Nebraska – are salutary in this regard. A prominent advocate of lesbian-feminist publishing in 1970s articles such as 'Feminist Publishing: An Antiquated Form?' (1977), Bunch's political preference seems originally to have been for organisations run on collectivist and more experimental lines than Virago, emphasising the 'new ways of thinking and working' to which women-only media enterprises could give rise

(1977: 25). Yet, by the early 1980s, her conclusions about the feasibility of collectivist feminist enterprises in a politically conservative era favour compromise in the interests of survival. In a 1980 interview published in *Sinister Wisdom*, the fervent oppositionality of her earlier article is tempered by a recognition of the economic and societal constraints that feminist publishing must incorporate into its analysis, or else wither as a result of market naivety: 'I think that what I'm hearing is not so much that the vision failed, but that the realities got it' (Doughty, 1980: 75). While endorsing the goal of independence for feminist enterprises, and the original 'vision that we would be able to do it better if we controlled it ourselves' (1980: 75), she tempers this with the realisation that 'the vision does become slightly different in the 80s, and it has to be more of the vision of what it means to survive with economic realities' (1980: 76). Interestingly, the three means that Bunch proposes for feminist imprints to maintain their independence in stringent economic circumstances directly contradict Virago's founding principles and certainly its current practice. She asserts first, specifically in relation to periodical publishing, the importance of perceiving a press as valuable even if it does not meet 'the standards of the main culture's publishing world' (1980: 73) by bringing out its editions in accordance with yearly forecasts. Virago, by contrast, regarded the accuracy of its accounts and the regularity of its publishing schedules – in short its business professionalism – as a point of company honour (Owen, 1998a: 17). Tactically speaking, this was a necessary image-building policy for Virago in an industry already suspicious of the press's professionalism on the grounds of its political agenda. Secondly, Bunch proposes a lowering of production standards in order to cut operating costs, opting for one- or no-colour covers and utilising poorer quality paperstock, even though this undercuts the goal 'a lot of us had set out with: to create products that looked the way the society expected them to look' (Doughty, 1980: 74). Virago, with its conviction that feminist politics and B-format paperback aesthetics could be harmoniously reconciled, preferred to compromise on complete independence rather than to jeopardise its appeal to high-street booksellers or the loyalty of its established customers. Bunch's third suggestion proposes feminist subsidisation of women's presses to secure their financially viability (a highly contentious issue within feminism, which is explored further in Chapter 4): 'I think the real question that has never been answered is do feminists consider the existence of their own presses and publications important enough to subsidise them?' (Doughty, 1980:

74).[17] Virago in its earlier days was in fact indirectly subsidised by Callil's self-named book publicity company, and thereafter received indirect subsidy via the free labour and expertise of numerous committed feminists within the industry and academia. Yet the concept of Virago as a self-supporting business was central to Callil's brand of feminism; just as she could enlist capitalism for feminist politics by declaring 'it is our duty not to go bust', all of her manifold print interviews and my own conversations with her support the view that for Callil the successful management of a business is in itself a feminist statement, and that appeals for subsidy indicate a degree of professional (and hence political) incompetence.

Eve's Bite: Marketing Feminist Writing for a Mainstream Audience

Virago's belief in the mass appeal of eye-catching, well-designed titles is intrinsically linked to its feminist beliefs: the potential for feminist ideas – well-packaged and well-marketed – to take root in mainstream society was the wellspring of Virago's birth. It is this fact that distinguishes Virago's embrace of marketing from the attitude towards this quintessentially capitalist industry prevalent among low-budget, collectivist imprints. Radical feminism, believing that its ideals and principles stand in essential opposition to society's current patriarchal and capitalist principles, tends to eschew the dilution of its political stance through collaboration with mainstream marketing – however lucrative the potential sales impact might prove for individual presses. Virago, by contrast, in a stance consistent with its more conventional hierarchical and corporate structure, evidences a more ambivalent view of the mainstream. The company's marketing strategies suggest that it perceives the mainstream as, in essence, philosophically neutral ground; it acknowledges that feminist principles may not currently comprise the dominant paradigm, but believes that the mainstream market is eminently appropriable for a feminist agenda.

Within the context of third-wave feminism, typified as it is by a fascination with popular culture and an aversion to separatism (Wolf, 1993; Lumby, 1997; Walter, 1998), Virago's expansionist conception of the mainstream market reads as unremarkable. But read against the context of 1970s women's liberation politics pervasively informed by Marxist analyses of culture as complicit in producing economic inequality (Barrett, 1980: 97), it was a radical political tactic. Separatist lesbian feminism's allied suspicion of the marketable literary product as an envoy from 'the finishing press's' evil empire underpins June

Arnold's diatribe against publishers' 'advertising and promotion methods [which] manipulate women into buying something they don't want or need' (1976: 24). Rather than attempting to bypass such complex and well-established sales channels entirely (as Arnold and, to a lesser extent, Bunch advocate in their 1970s celebrations of a women's independent communications network), Virago opted to exploit these pre-existing channels for feminist ends – packaging and distributing its titles along mainstream lines. Initially Virago's sales were centred upon the network of feminist bookshops within London such as SisterWrite in Islington, north London and Silver Moon bookshop in the West End's Charing Cross Road. But display in mainstream outlets was from the company's inception a priority, and one which received symbolic fulfilment when market-dominating book and stationery retailer W.H. Smith – hardly a notorious distributor of subversive, left-wing tracts – devoted windows to feminist books (including numerous Virago titles) at the time of the first International Feminist Book Fair in June 1984 (*Bookseller*, 1984: 2420; Ardill, 1984: 21).

Ursula Owen confirms that cross-spectrum marketing was a central tenet of the firm's publishing policy from its inception: 'we knew there was an audience which would love the books we loved, but we were determined to get into the high street as well as the radical bookshops' (1988: 89). More specifically, Virago sought mainstream status within the shop layout of high-street booksellers by arguing vehemently against the display of its titles in a ghettoised 'feminist books' section. Its staff lobbied exhaustively for space on the general fiction shelves so that 'Virago books [would] be in every way integrated into people's lives and [would] reach the widest possible audience' (Pringle, 1996). Because Virago has consistently rejected diametrically opposed conceptions of 'radical' and 'mainstream', the company was able to argue that such book placement tactics did not represent a capitulation to mainstream values, but a strategic means by which to subvert them. Politically, the policy gave the company considerable marketing flexibility, enabling it to present its wares as simultaneously alternative/specialist *and* mainstream, or as Harriet Spicer artfully encapsulates the manoeuvre: 'to widen the definition of what is perceived to be mainstream' (quoted in Jones, N., 1992: 22).

Four elements underlie Virago's marketing success as one of the Anglophone publishing world's most highly branded fiction imprints: its name; its distinctive uniform cover design; use of the B-format trade paperback; and paperback original editions. The name 'Virago' was designed to be punchy, provocative and wryly self-ironic. It arose out of the atmosphere of the early 1970s women's movement, and was the name originally given to *Spare Rib*, until 'Spare Rib' was hit upon 'so Virago was booted off to be the name of the publishing company', according to Rosie Boycott, co-founder of *Spare Rib* and one of two women besides Callil involved briefly in Virago's formation (Bennett, 1993: 10). Tongue-in-cheek harridan associations were common among early women's movement publications – other titles include *Shrew*, *Harpies Bizarre*, *Refractory Girl* and *Trouble & Strife* – with the political objective being to destabilise mainstream stereotypes of feminists by so exactly adhering to them. This tactic of 'occupying' derogatory terms in order to defuse their negative connotations and infuse them with a new, positive zeal also informed Virago's choice of colophon: an apple with a bite taken out (Gerrard, 1993: 61). Like its biblical counterpart 'Spare Rib', the image was designed jokily to counteract that most pervasive of patriarchal myths, the temptation of Eve. In marketing terms its power lay in its cheeky appearance on the spines of Virago titles, alluding temptingly to the dangerously subversive knowledge to be sampled within the glossy green covers. Coupled with the name 'Virago', the apple logo mounts a challenge to browsing book buyers – part tease, part dare – a combination made newly dangerous for the 1990s grunge generation by a Virago catalogue featuring a bitten apple tattoo (*Guardian*, 1997: 3).

Yet if the imprint's name and logo were self-consciously feminist, its cover design was classically up-market literary. Standardised green covers were designed for maximum reader recognition, a deliberate borrowing from that other great post-war branding success – Allen Lane's colour-coded Penguin paperbacks: 'it was a conscious decision to acknowledge what Penguin had done with their colours and that we would make a colour' (Spicer, 1996). Where Virago departed from Lane's principles was in its pioneering use of the larger trade B-format paperback – now the staple of highbrow literary fiction imprints such as Picador and Vintage – and in its all-colour covers, frequently utilising works by nineteenth- and early twentieth-century women artists. Alexandra Pringle, who took over the editorship of the Modern Classics after the departure of Callil to Chatto and Windus in 1982, recalls heated production debates over the feminist ethics of using a female nude painted by a male artist (1996). The traditional exclusion of female artists from the art history canon made the selection of their works not only a political, but also a marketing, boon: Virago found that 'second-rate painters made better covers than first-rate painters ... because the image was unknown and therefore you didn't come to it with a preconception' (Pringle, 1996). Virago also capitalised on the burgeoning market for film tie-in editions, using stills from gender-themed films such as Sally Potter's *Orlando* (1992) and Mike Newell's *Enchanted April* (1992) on its covers, exploiting the recognition factor among film- and bookshop-going audiences. Underpinning each of these marketing and packaging decisions – imprint name, colophon, cover design and format – was a conscious decision to clothe generally oppositional texts in the guise of the mainstream, in order to reconceptualise and redefine the contours of the mainstream market. Virago, according to Alexandra Pringle, 'was quite different from a lot of other small presses in that it always wanted to succeed, always wanted to sell books, always wanted the books to look attractive and be marketed well' (1996).

While alluring presentation and clever marketing propelled Virago towards its goal of selling feminist books to the mainstream, the ossified practices of British broadsheet reviewers imperilled access to its newly discovered mainstream market. British newspapers traditionally accorded review space only to hardback originals, effectively triggering a publicity crisis by casting Virago's list of paperback originals and reissues into media obscurity. Virago devised various tactics to circumvent this archaic reviewing policy (already by the 1970s out of step with publishers' issuing practice and consumer preference) including issuing a tiny hardback run of new titles specifically to cater for reviewers, and posting large, brightly coloured slips around review copies stating 'this has never been a hardback'. But, as Virago's (then) publicity director Lennie Goodings admitted in 1990, 'we've rarely made it' (Macaskill, 1990: 434). The trade/reviewer stand-off was complicated, in Virago's case, by a political commitment to keep their books within the budget of the largest possible range of women, a policy decision that necessitated the mass-market paperback format. But because of its countervailing commitment to high production and design standards, Virago waged a constant battle to reconcile its competing aims of market appeal, availability and company profit: 'the books had to look good, they had to be as cheap as possible but we had to stay solvent' (Owen, U., 1988: 89). Virago's house policy of politically informed profit generation, and its resultant existence on the borderlands of both feminist politics and mainstream publishing, may have lent it agility in marketing terms, but it also created dilemmas of pricing and availability, which would not have resulted in such rigorous political soul-searching in a more conventional publishing operation.

Virago's expansion during the 1970s and 1980s testifies to the sales potential of oppositional texts if they are distinctively and attractively packaged. Other small-scale, politically informed publishing imprints that sprang up in Virago's wake were mindful of the selling-power of a distinctive cover design, imitating Virago's characteristic dark green spine with a black and white barbershop stripe (The Women's Press) or a cutting-edge saw-tooth design (Serpent's Tail). In another innovation, which publishing rivals were quick to imitate, Virago revitalised the idea that an imprint with a pungent brand-name identity could still command reader loyalty, a phenomenon that was regarded as having waned since the dropping of Penguin's uniform covers:

> Still today, in an era of publishing despondency, booksellers swear that the green Virago spine and distinctive apple logo continue to inspire an almost miraculous loyalty – among men as well as women – and that customers still come in simply to ask for the latest Virago please. (Pitman, 1995: 28)

This unique house identity was beneficial also in attracting writers to the Virago fold. Because the titles reflected off one another, the critical and feminist kudos of the house's leading authors such as Angela Carter and Margaret Atwood generated an aura of highbrow, left-of-centre credibility of which other titles could partake. It was on the basis of this cross-spectrum market appeal that Virago secured women writers who may otherwise have had qualms about signing to a feminist press for fear of missing a wider readership. Publication with Virago provided a package particularly attractive to right-on but critically ambitious female authors: the tang of oppositional credibility mixed with the reassuring knowledge that an attractive cover and elegant format ensured the work would still be stocked in the high street.

Wayward Girls & Wicked Women: The Radicalising of the Literary Mainstream

Virago's sale in 1995 harboured a symbolic resonance for both feminism and publishing, prompting soul-searching on a paradoxical situation that had been brewing in the industry since the mid-1980s: why, when more feminist books than ever before are available on bookshop shelves, are the majority of feminist presses either defunct or merely imprints of multinational conglomerates? If, moreover, the political conservatism that characterised Western democracies during the 1980s initiated a retreat by the left to cultural rather than directly political spheres, why has that consolidation of cultural power not worked to invigorate the independent, oppositional publishing sector? A situation rife with contradiction appears to have evolved whereby critiques of existing media power structures are published by corporations fundamentally implicated in those very structures (Klein, 2001). This situation marks either the apogee of pluralistic tolerance on the part of capacious media empires or, according to a more circumspect Marcusian analysis, a cunning neutralisation of such critiques' political bite (Marcuse, 1986).

Since the mid-1980s, a conceptual gap has appeared between the assumption of early women's liberation feminism – that ownership of a communication medium is an essential prerequisite for controlling the message disseminated by that medium – and the status quo within the publishing world. Two examples serve to illustrate how the existence of a burgeoning market for feminist books and an increase in the number of titles catering to that market was speciously interpreted as evidence of feminist publishing's health. Market growth was cited as a panacea for old-style feminists' unease at the poaching of the feminist market from feminist presses. Women in Publishing specifically asked Callil to address this ongoing threat in an address to its autumn 1985 seminar, proposing discussion of 'the future of feminist publishing houses attached to general houses: would their parent companies close them down if the market dropped away?' (Callil, 1986: 850). Surveying the history of Virago, its influence on the lists of mainstream houses and its prominence on the high street, Callil diagnoses that 'the outlook for women's publishing has never been brighter' (1986: 850), adroitly side-stepping Women in Publishing's implied point that a vibrant market for feminist books in no way presupposes the existence of independent feminist presses to supply that market. In a further example of 1980s preoccupation with markets eclipsing 1970s-style ideological debate over press ownership, Lennie Goodings's 1993 interview with the *Bookseller* celebrates a proliferation of new feminist publications, relegating to brackets (significantly) the names of the imprints under which they appeared:

> Feminism was shifting and finding new ground, and so was political publishing. It was with great delight that in the 1990s we witnessed the withering of post-feminism under the remarkably fine scrutiny

of Susan Faludi's *Backlash: The Undeclared War Against Women* (Chatto & Windus) ... At the same time as the pundits cried 'Feminism is dead', the bestseller lists answered 'Long live feminism!'. There, in 1992, alongside Peter Mayle and Michael Palin, were Germaine Greer's *The Change* and Marilyn French's *War Against Women* (both Hamish Hamilton), and new works by some of the grandes dames of feminism, Gloria Steinem (Bloomsbury) and Nancy Friday (Hutchinson) – preceded the year before by Naomi Wolf's *The Beauty Myth* (Chatto & Windus). (Goodings, 1993: 27)

Surface-level triumphalism on the part of feminism is here destabilised by commercial reality, uncomfortably suggesting a wholesale appropriation of feminist markets from under the blithely self-congratulatory gaze of the women's presses.

Such a negative reading is, however, contentious; debate over the shift towards mainstream publication of feminist works has generated variant readings of the status quo. The first of these interpretations, which might be labelled the 'feminism triumphant' reading, argues that the appearance of a mainstream colophon on the spine of a feminist text provides irrefutable evidence of feminism's successful self-establishment at the heart of contemporary culture. A second, more sceptical, view perceives, in the rush of publishers for feminist titles, a cynical commercial exploitation of currently fashionable subjects. Feminist communications theorists such as Dale Spender echo concerns of earlier decades in their awareness that, because mainstream houses have no ideological commitment to feminist politics, these 'women's studies' lists could be dropped as soon as the "fashion" has finished, the market has been saturated' (1981: 198). Industry evidence abounds to support this more cautious view: Naim Attallah's purging of 'unprofitable' third-world titles from The Women's Press list in March 1991; and Penguin editor Margaret Blumen's frank concession to publishing *realpolitik* in her assertion that 'publishing is not a charitable organisation. There's money to be made in feminist publishing' (Briscoe, 1992: 17).[18] The third, ambivalent, reading of the situation rejects both uncritical enthusiasm and knee-jerk suspicion in its view of the market, arguing instead for the position of cultural tactician. For in an age dominated by marketing principles, the injection of radicalism under a mainstream imprint may constitute the most effective means of subversion – one consistent with the oppositional politics of 1970s feminism, but enacted in a characteristically media-savvy twenty-first-century manner.

BITING BACK: VIRAGO'S 1996 RELAUNCH AND BEYOND –
'A PROUD PAST AND AN EXCITING FUTURE'[19]

The media relaunch of the new Virago in July 1996 was, like many self-proclaimed innovations, in actual fact an artfully repackaged version of a much older idea: that of selling women's fiction between glossy covers and with a hint of bad-girl allure. As might have been suspected given the copious use of the Virago apple icon and the prominent placement of the press's name in relaunch publicity, old was being remarketed as new – a further twist of corporate self-mythologising.[20] Timely innovation was, however, discernible in the new range of first-time author titles labelled as the 'Virago Vs', a list designed to capture a 20- to 30-something demographic which had grown disaffected with the standardised design and more explicitly political agenda of the former Virago list. Texts about the women's peace movement, gardening and food, which had come to feature in Virago's list by the mid-1990s, were here usurped by a sharper, bawdier, highly self-confident tone, with titles such as Jennifer Belle's *Going Down* (1997) and Lydia Millet's American pop-culture satire, *Omnivores* (1997). The arch irreverence of Helen Eisenbach's V title, *Lesbianism Made Easy* (1997), a spoof self-help book on sapphic chic, targets an audience that demands its lifestyle politics light and untrammelled by undue theorising or requirements of activism. Sally Abbey, senior editor for Virago at the time of the relaunch, encapsulates the dilemma of marketing to a generation that demands the personal freedoms won through feminist activism, but which shies at explicit political identification:

> We're aiming the Vs at that broader spectrum of women who were independent, politicised, who by all definitions would have been called feminist, and a lot who are feminists, who were put off by an old-fashioned look. (1998)

Virago's house policy is that its relaunch represents not a new development (although, as the V list indicates, there clearly *is* an attempt to attract new audiences) but a continuation of the old – 'as far as we were concerned we'd never been away' (Abbey, 1998). Hence, in the press's relaunch material it is the insignia of the old Virago that predominate: 'the word is VIRAGO' was the initial relaunch slogan (*Bookseller*, 1996: 1), coupled with an image of a seductively naked woman proffering an apple (*Guardian*, 1997: 1). In particular, house author Angela Carter is foregrounded, with the intention that Carter's critically acclaimed, sexually charged fables of gender subversion speak for the relaunched press as a whole. The identification of Carter with the firm extends to borrowing one of the late author's anthology titles – *Wayward Girls & Wicked Women* (1986) – for Virago's 16-page advertising insert in the *Guardian*: 'if any single author could be said to embody the spirit of Virago it would be the late Angela Carter, whose darkly humorous novels are filled with women and girls both wayward and wicked' (1997: 3). That this conscious re-presentation of the house's identity has proven lucrative is testified to by Abbey's statement that 1997 marked the highest trade turnover in the company's history (1998). The ballast of 1997's financial results was provided by Virago's paperback edition of Atwood's Booker Prize short-listed *Alias Grace* (1996), a top-selling Virago title only surpassed by Atwood's subsequent Booker winner, *The Blind Assassin* (2000), the bestseller profile of which prompted Virago to rejacket in paperback all of Atwood's backlist.[21]

Virago's traditional genius for packaging oppositional texts so as to attract not only a highly politicised feminist audience but, in addition, a mainstream audience of casual bookshop browsers, remains pertinent. The 1997 publication of former Women's Press author Andrea Dworkin's collected essays, *Life and Death*, offsets Dworkin's public identification with strongly 1970s-derived separatist politics with a covershot of artwork by Brit-Art cult artist Sarah Lucas. By scrupulously avoiding a cover graphic that might reinforce reader perceptions of the author as an anti-pornography campaigner with a readiness to indict men as the problem, Virago engineers a strategic introduction of radical feminist ideas into a demographic of readers seeking recreation, rather than political edification, from its reading. Moreover, the design decision is financially astute: doubling the potential audience for the book not only secures Dworkin's loyalty and theoretical kudos for the house, it moreover healthily inflates sales. It is a harmonisation of political credibility and commercial marketability as intrinsic to Virago as it is anathema to the public persona of Dworkin herself.

Integration into Time Warner has gained Virago access to titles published under other imprints controlled by the parent company, allowing for a title more strongly identifiable with a Virago readership to be fed into the imprint's list. Marilyn French's seismic 1970s novel about one woman's coming to consciousness, *The Women's Room* (1977), was in 1997 transferred from the Abacus imprint and, endowed with the literary-critical imprimatur of a Virago Modern Classic, vastly increased its sales, making the book an early success for the relaunched imprint.[22] Yet, this list-feeding fluidity could, if reversed, potentially dilute the integrity of the Virago house identity, allowing for Virago luminaries such as Margaret Atwood and Angela Carter to be stripped off the Virago list and marketed under the Orbit, Abacus or Little, Brown colophons – should 'anyone from the agent, the author, or the in-house editor think it would be better paperbacked or hardbacked on a different list' (Abbey, 1998). Moreover, Virago's editorial autonomy within Time Warner Books is widely asserted but, in the event, largely unenforceable. Philippa Harrison, former managing director and chief executive officer of Time Warner Books UK, was highly regarded within feminist publishing circles and, according to Abbey, 'very pro-Virago' (1998), yet the possibility remains – especially since Harrison's departure from the firm in October 2002 – that a title endorsed by the four-strong Virago editorial team could be vetoed at company board level.[23] The 1998 crisis at HarperCollins over former Hong Kong Governor Chris Patten's book, *East and West* (eventually published by Macmillan in 1998), highlights the reality that multinational corporations will not shy from wielding their commercial dominance to silence uncongenial political opinion (Neil, 1998: 12; Richardson, 1998: 11, 15; Klein, 2001: 191).

To peruse Virago's current catalogues is to marvel at the cultural centrality and market visibility of women's writing, and also to endorse the current management's perception that the visual and tactile allure of a well-designed, spot-laminated cover can facilitate the purchase of radically oppositional feminist writing. Unlike numerous other 1970s feminist presses, Virago discerned that inferior production values and utilitarian packaging actually militated against the proselytising of feminist ideas. That commerce and feminism are capable of being mutually enhancing, rather than mutually exclusive, is a belief that underlies Virago's 30-year history, and that casts the longevity of the firm, despite industry convulsions, as in itself a political achievement. Callil's vow that Virago was ideologically obliged 'not to go bust' has – perhaps especially in its latest incarnation – been stunningly upheld.

Yet the commercial necessity of minimising a book's political content in its cover design so as to avoid unduly alienating a skittish twenty-first-century readership must give any feminist critic of the publishing industry reason for pause. A readership that demands feminist-informed ideas, but only under the metaphorical brown paper wrapping of mainstream consumer culture, not only disassociates itself from its political history, but falls victim to the crass stereotypes of the women's movement long propounded in the mainstream media. Catering for this contemporary *Zeitgeist*, Virago promotes lifestyle politics without requiring political gestures beyond the act of consumption itself: 'By and large, I think people just respond to a cover, an idea...what they want is to be sold an idea – they're not buying into a club in the same way they probably once were' (Abbey, 1998). Viewed superficially, the depoliticisation implicit in this process appears unnervingly regressive. Yet, as Western political processes increasingly appropriate the techniques of consumer marketing, Virago Press may discover that the tense dialectic of politics and profit on which it has always based its publishing practice has become curiously redundant. For, in an age in which politics and marketing have become effectively indistinguishable, the embrace of consumerism in the name of the feminist cause may constitute a supremely expedient political tactic.

2
'Books of Integrity': Dilemmas of Race and Authenticity in Feminist Publishing

> We are idealists in our aims but realists in our publishing practice.
> We have to make difficult choices between 'good' politics and
> 'good' writing, between a too-expensive book and no book at all,
> between passion and survival.
>
> The Women's Press, 'Feminism and Publishing' (1979: 33)

In the early years of the 1970s, a newly revitalised feminist movement combined a focus on the position of women in society with the new left's conviction that the written word was subject to political control. One result of this fusion was a powerful critique of the contemporary publishing industry. Literary and commercial presses did not, feminists argued, occupy the role of benevolent men of letters, graciously eschewing base commercial motives in their crusade to disseminate culturally improving titles. Rather, such presses acted as gatekeepers for public discourse. By bestowing or withholding the crucial imprimatur of publication, presses furthered specifically *ideological* ends. Cultural practice in general, and publishing in particular, were reconceptualised by the women's movement as forms of covert political policing of a distinctly *un*free market of ideas. This recognition of the fact that the commercial book trade operated not according to the high-minded dictates of liberal tolerance but according to capitalistic, masculinist interests potentially in conflict with the second-wave feminist agenda was the primary understanding on which feminist publishing practice was based. Recognising that publishing was inherently ideological, the women's movement vowed to appropriate such practice for explicitly women-centred political ends. Radical political consciousness would, it was assumed, prevent feminist publishers from wielding the power to publish as a tool for silencing, as had mainstream presses before them. Political integrity – that notoriously slippery phenomenon – would act as a check on gatekeeper demagoguery.

Feminist publishing's belief in its ethical self-consciousness was, perhaps, what left the movement so vulnerable to attack in the late 1970s and 1980s from women of colour who felt alienated from the predominantly middle-class, first-world agenda of the feminist presses.[1] Searching in vain for prominent black authors on the lists of the women's presses, women of colour critiqued the self-selecting and elitist character of feminist concerns, arguing that only a women's movement representative of *all* women was worthy of the name (Smith, 1986 [1977], 1989; Gabriel and Scott, 1993; Smith and Moraga, 1996). The impact of debates around issues of race was not of course confined solely to the field of feminist publishing; it in fact radically reshaped the identity and profile of feminism as a social and cultural movement (Simons, 1979; Moraga and Anzaldúa, 1983 [1981]). Yet within feminist publishing, the debate initiated a return to critical speculation about the specific nature of feminist press practice of a kind not undertaken with such analytical vigour since the early 1970s: what structure characterised a truly 'feminist' press? What degree of multiracial representation on a house's list was appropriate? Could the cause of women of colour be strategically advanced through published writings, or was the presence of such women at editorial decision-making level an indispensable element of any multicultural politics? As attention turned to the varieties and priorities of feminist publishing practice, the mere existence of feminist presses was increasingly perceived to be, of itself, inadequate. Having achieved a degree of market leverage within the book industry, feminist publishing now came under attack from groups sufficiently close to its ideals to feel its impact, but sufficiently alienated from its campaigns to demand expansion of its agenda. As an internal critique, this rigorous reappraisal of the industry's aims was undoubtedly necessary and significantly overdue. Yet, like all internal debates, it ran the risk of creating divisive factions within the fragile feminist press community, which were vulnerable to exploitation by a largely hostile and avidly opportunist publishing mainstream.

In charting the development of this important internal debate over diversity within feminist publishing, this discussion identifies three phases, moving from an incipient awareness of feminist publishing's racial specificity, through challenges from alternative, women-of-colour-controlled presses, to agitation for representation of black women and women of colour at managerial level across the entire publishing industry. In tracing this pattern of development I am conscious of imposing a somewhat specious academic order on what was and is an infinitely interlinked and complex publishing sector. Further heightening the artificial orderliness of such an analysis are the wild discrepancies of scale that cluster about any such discussion of feminist publishing and its social context; for racial issues of far-reaching social significance were embodied in presses staffed by only a handful of women, although these presses in turn demonstrated a market for books by women of colour with broad-scale commercial and cultural ramifications. In this sense, feminist publishing acts as an intriguing microcosm of trends across Western feminism as a whole in the late 1970s and 1980s: it operates as a focal point where debates over access to cultural image-making achieve their most concrete manifestation.

The analysis of dilemmas of race in feminist publishing that follows focuses on those British women's presses most closely associated with multicultural writing – The Women's Press, Sheba Feminist Publishers, Black Woman Talk and Urban Fox Press – although the distinctive experience of several North American women's presses, in particular the ground-breaking Kitchen Table: Women of Color Press, is also invoked. Beginning with the issue of organisation and autonomy in feminist publishing, the discussion analyses how second-wave feminism – an intellectual and social movement in its origins critical of capitalist structures – moves into the publishing marketplace in order to proselytise its political message. Selecting for particular focus The Women's Press, Britain's second largest feminist house, and a press with a distinctive profile for promoting third-world and black women's writing, this discussion analyses how oppositional politics can achieve a precarious reconciliation with capitalist economics, and the multiple tensions that may arise as a result. Turning to publishing initiatives by women of colour, in particular the 1980s British presses Sheba and Black Woman Talk, the discussion considers challenges to the corporate nature of The Women's Press and collectivist presses' distinctive championing of writing by British black and South Asian women. Finally, the discussion focuses upon the vexed question of women of colour's access to editorial and policy-making positions within the publishing industry, calling into question the concept of 'authenticity' in debates over racial representations. These investigations prompt potentially unsettling questions about the directions in which feminist publishing is currently developing: specifically, can feminist publishing broker alternative and more favourable terms to ensure its future financial survival and continued cultural receptivity?

THE WOMEN'S PRESS:
LIVE AUTHORS. LIVE ISSUES. LIVELIER BOARDROOM

The Women's Press enjoys a high public profile and one of the most distinctive brand-name identities among English-language publishers. Its paperback titles sport a punning steam iron logo ('Press = iron – geddit?' as the *Sunday Times* once quipped), stripy spines (reminiscent of an iron cord), and original cover graphics (Macaskill, 1991: 84; Dowrick, 2003b). The press has come to be identified by the book-buying public, and especially by feminists, as indelibly associated with new varieties of feminist writing (Macaskill, 1991: 84; Birch, 1991: 39; Bonner et al., 1992: 100). In particular, the press has long traded in its advertising on its association with black and third-world women's writing and the committedly political, cutting-edge tone that this lends the firm: in the mid- to late 1980s it proclaimed itself the harbinger of 'Live Authors. Live Issues', in the late 1990s it promised 'Books of Integrity by Women Writers', and at the time of its twenty-fifth anniversary celebrations in 2003 it boasted 'Great Writing by Great Women' (*The Women's Press*, 1998: 1).[2] Given that two perceptions – that of a small independent press and that of a press committed to writing by women of colour – constitute the twin poles of the public perception of The Women's Press, it is salutary to outline a brief company history and to demonstrate that both assumptions are, in fact, highly selective representations of its corporate reality. Furthermore, this discussion takes The Women's Press's ambiguous status *vis-à-vis* issues of independence and of black women's writing as a starting point to spark broader discussion of the dilemmas surrounding feminist publishing as a whole. Firstly, can editorial autonomy ever be ensured without financial ownership or shareholding power on the part of committed editors? Secondly, what are the ideological ramifications of a press run predominantly by white women marketing itself as an outlet for the voices of women from a wide variety of racial groups?

The foundation of The Women's Press was prompted by the notable success of Virago, Britain's first feminist press, from its establishment in 1972. Relying on a list of forgotten women's classics that mainstream houses had allowed to drop out of print, Virago was able to capitalise on second-wave feminism's thirst for antecedents by producing feminist-informed texts in attractively packaged trade paperback format. The Women's Press followed in Virago's wake with initial steps towards its establishment being taken in 1977. It was set up both in emulation of Virago's proven success as a feminist publishing venture, and in challenge to Virago's monopoly on Britain's expanding feminist book-buying market. Like Virago, The Women's Press initially comprised a core of dedicated women, surrounded by 'a volunteer advisory group of feminists involved in publishing, scholarship and the media' (The Women's Press, 1979: 33). Yet from its inception, The Women's Press was keen to distinguish itself from its more established rival by casting its radical intent in the right-on language of late 1970s political psychology:

> We reflect the wish to externalise and thereby change and form women's reality, the reality of our perceptions, potentialities and selves. As feminist publishers we express the cultural element of a consciousness-raising dynamic, a questioning awareness of value and power which has its roots in each of our consciousnesses and its collectivity in the WLM [women's liberation movement]. (The Women's Press, 1979: 32)

The association between the two presses goes further than competition for the same market, and in fact runs also to structural issues of ownership and financing. Virago's first nine titles had been published with the necessary financial backing of Quartet Books, Virago only leaving the Quartet group in 1976 after sharp disagreements over the extent of its founder's editorial decision-making power. Early in 1977, Quartet was purchased by Palestinian-born businessman Naim Attallah's Namara group, a disparate collection of entrepreneurial, retail and publishing interests (Spicer, 1996; Owen, 1998b; Attallah, 2000: 64). Hence, when New Zealand-born editor Stephanie Dowrick contacted Attallah in mid-1977 with the idea of setting up a feminist press, Attallah was able to discern both an immediate market and an appropriate niche within his holdings for such an enterprise. Attallah and Dowrick entered into a business partnership with The Women's Press initially 'owned 51% by Quartet Books, Ltd.' while Dowrick controlled the remaining share, though the young company took pains always to emphasise that it 'work[ed] autonomously up to the stage of marketing' (Frank, 1982 :112; Dowrick, 2003b).[3]

The Women's Press presents a startlingly incongruous profile within the Namara group, sandwiched between Attallah's ownership of the right-wing *Literary Review*, and his managing directorships of Establishment hallmarks Asprey's and Mappin & Webb.[4] It is a politically precarious position for The Women's Press, and one that led to a degree of scorn from Virago quarters during periods when Virago was an independent operation. In large part this veiled disdain arose from Attallah's constant self-presentation in the media as an urbane connoisseur of women, suggesting a man with an archaic conception of gender relations. The dismissive tone of Virago's directors also betrays the moral superiority of a firm that had risked a management buyout rather than compromise its integrity by remaining within Quartet. For such reasons the directors of Virago generally considered The Women's Press a pale imitation of their own operation, a view that The Women's Press's second managing director, Ros de Lanerolle, perhaps unintentionally reinforced when she referred to her press as Attallah's ersatz Virago: 'I think he half regretted that he had let Virago go. And owning the Women's Press [sic] does have a certain cachet' (Macaskill, 1991: 85). Criticism was also forthcoming from outside feminist circles: baffled as to why Attallah guaranteed The Women's Press an overdraft to publish in the (then) virtually unheard of area of women's writing, business rivals slyly dubbed The Women's Press 'the Ayatollah's folly'.

The departure of Dowrick for Australia and the accession of Ros de Lanerolle to the managing directorship of The Women's Press in 1981 signalled a reorientation of the house's list towards de Lanerolle's own political interests (Dowrick, 2003a). As a South African political exile and seasoned anti-Apartheid activist, she expanded The Women's Press's investment in new Commonwealth and third-world women's writing and presided over the firm during the time of its greatest success in 1983 with the British publication of Alice Walker's bestseller *The Color Purple* [1982]. Yet the publishing recession of the late 1980s and early 1990s plunged The Women's Press into losses of between £105,000 and £300,000 (the exact figures are disputed by the firm's key players of the time) and precipitated a boardroom struggle for control of the press's direction (de Lanerolle, 1991: 4; cf. Jones, 1991b: 16). Attallah alleged that the losses were the result of overconcentration of The Women's Press list on risky third-world writers (Pallister, 1991: 38; Steel, 1998: 28); de Lanerolle countered with evidence that the operating deficit was, in fact, declining and that recessionary economics were the true cause of a drop in sales (1991: 4). It is a dispute that bears outlining as emblematic of the dilemmas which feminist publishing faces in its quest to remain simultaneously provocative and solvent.

In late 1990, in a move that provoked widespread opposition from de Lanerolle's supporters within the firm, Attallah appointed sales director Mary Hemming (a staff member more sympathetic to the owner's plans for the press) to the position of deputy managing director. The second stage in the increasingly acrimonious owner–director conflict was de Lanerolle's attempted buyout offer of £500,000 in February–March 1991 (Pallister, 1991: 38), the rejection of which resulted in Attallah maintaining control over the firm, its internal structure and publishing policy. De Lanerolle was subsequently offered the lesser position of chief editor at the press as a trade-off for relinquishing her role as managing director – a deal that she refused (Ahmad, 1991: 13). The results were catastrophic: de Lanerolle was forced by Attallah to resign and to accept a redundancy pay-out; Attallah appointed himself the firm's interim managing director; five of the small press's senior editorial, publicity and rights staff resigned in solidarity with de Lanerolle; and Stephanie Dowrick, the press's original managing director, was recalled to Britain to act as temporary head pending the appointment of Kathy Gale as joint managing director (Birch, 1991: 39; Hennegan, 1992: 6). Mary Hemming, having weathered hostilities that she has since summarised as 'a very awful time for the Press', was rewarded for her loyalty to Attallah with the post of joint managing director, working in partnership with Gale (Steel, 1998: 28).[5] As Rukhsana Ahmad observed at the time in *Spare Rib*, one of only a handful of publications to cover the events, the fracas 'might have earned the title of a boardroom coup if the cast had been all-male' (1991: 10).[6] What the affair highlights starkly for alternative publishing is the impotence of editors to set their own publishing agendas if they lack financial clout within a press's corporate structure, and the corresponding power of unsympathetic owners effectively to gag writing that they deem unprofitable, and hence to deny it public exposure.

This brief history of the firm is designed as a critical corrective to assumptions – based upon The Women's Press's commitment to edgy, oppositional women's writing – that the firm must be a feminist collective, or at least a small independent company struggling valiantly against publishing's notoriously low and slow profit returns. Though the press has indeed struggled, it is its existence as a wholly owned subsidiary of Attallah's Namara group that in fact goes to the heart of both its successes and its dilemmas. Attallah guarantees the press an overdraft (the extent of which is undisclosed though it is undoubtedly substantial), which grants The Women's Press the financial cushioning to publish and promote risky writing from marginal groups. But this same outside control of the purse-strings can obliterate a particular list direction if it is deemed to be unprofitable, thus seriously jeopardising The Women's Press's public profile among feminists aligned with minority women's causes. This corporate affiliation with Namara has existed since the press's inception; in a 1979 article in radical London-based periodical *News from Neasden*, an anonymous author (most probably Dowrick) writes of 'the support of our guarantor with whom we share formal "ownership" of the company' (The Women's Press, 1979: 33). Given how fraught an issue Attallah's power within the press was to become twelve years later, the fastidious picking out in typographical tweezers of the capitalist notion of 'ownership' appears both ironic and somewhat naive.

The second area in which closer analysis of The Women's Press's history refutes common public misconceptions relates to the press's association with writing by women of colour. Undoubtedly The Women's Press was a key player in promoting culturally diverse women's writing during the 1980s, with the success of Walker's *The Color Purple* (winner of the 1983 Pulitzer Prize for Fiction), Tsitsi Dangarembga's *Nervous Conditions* (winner of the Africa section of the 1989 Commonwealth Writers' Prize), and Pauline Melville's *Shapeshifter* (winner of the 1990 *Guardian* Fiction Prize). Beyond these individual titles, however, the press committed itself to dedicating a significant portion of its list – and a commensurate proportion of its advertising – to promoting writing by women from minority groups marginalised by early second-wave feminism: black women, women from ethnic minorities, working-class women, lesbians and disabled women. Ros de Lanerolle, in an article entitled 'Publishing Against the "Other Censorship"', expanded the original tenets of feminist publishing to their logical (and more representative) conclusion:

A fundamental principle of women's publishing has been the idea of space for those who have *not* had space in the mainstream. And if this applies to women in general, it applies particularly to some classes of women. Lesbians, for instance … [and] black women. (1990: 9)

Yet, in addition to ideological inclusiveness, this policy also made exemplary business sense, for agitation by women of colour for a representative voice within feminism opened up previously underexploited markets among book buyers from minority groups, while at the same time expanding book buying among white feminists who may already have been purchasers of The Women's Press titles, but who were keen to remain *au fait* with developments within feminist politics. In export terms, a list constructed along lines of racial and ethnic diversity also opened potentially lucrative channels for international sales and foreign rights trading. With authors from New Zealand, Australia, South Africa, Canada, India, the Caribbean and many Commonwealth African countries, de Lanerolle stated with justification that 'we now have one of the most international lists in publishing' (Neustatter, 1988: 20). It was a list that moreover fused symbiotically with the growth of post-colonial theory among humanities academics during the 1980s and 1990s (Cobham and Collins, 1987; Dangarembga, 1988; Nasta, 1991; Butalia and Menon, 1993).

De Lanerolle in a 1991 interview acknowledged that The Women's Press's high-profile 'Live Authors. Live Issues' campaign was adopted in part as 'a dig at Virago' and the slightly safe, middle-class tone of its Modern Classics series (Macaskill, 1991: 84). The implication, which The Women's Press was particularly keen in its marketing to emphasise, was that Virago had cornered the market on the late nineteenth- and early twentieth-century feminist canon, but that the new ground in radical and racially diverse feminist writing was being broken by The Women's Press. Yet this demarcation of Virago's and The Women's Press's publishing strengths into past and present spheres of influence oversimplifies and distorts in the way that all attempts to construct set house identities do. The reality of both houses' publishing interests reveals far greater diversity and multi-facetedness than the 'Live Authors. Live Issues' campaign suggests. Virago had much success in promoting contemporary authors such as Angela Carter, Pat Barker and Margaret Atwood, and achieved bestseller status and solid backlist sales with the five volumes of African-American author Maya Angelou's autobiography, beginning with the highly successful *I Know Why the Caged Bird Sings* (1969), for which Virago secured the British publication rights in 1984. This book, with its insistence on an African-American perspective, burgeoning civil rights struggles, and the circumstances of working-class women's lives, aligns perhaps more closely with The Women's Press's house identity than with Virago's. Yet, *Caged Bird*'s third reprinting within its first year of publication secured Virago's fortunes in the same manner in which *The Color Purple* had in the previous year secured the fortunes of The Women's Press (Angelou, 1984 [1969]:

iv). Angelou's autobiographical volumes became a financial rud.
of Virago's backlist for the whole of the following decade, with
numerous reissues, changes in cover design and television tie-ins.[7]

Further complicating the reality of the two houses's market identities
is The Women's Press's first list in February 1978 – featuring reprints
of forgotten women's classics including Elizabeth Barrett Browning's
Aurora Leigh & Other Poems, Jane Austen's juvenilia entitled *Love and
Freindship* [sic], and Kate Chopin's *The Awakening* (Dowrick, 2003b).
The list's nineteenth-century focus and its mirroring of the emergent
academic feminist canon is highly reminiscent of Virago. It highlights
the extent to which Virago and The Women's Press, as Britain's most
visible feminist publishing houses, constructed protean house
identities, which could be simplified into discrete niches for publicity
and marketing purposes but which, in reality, remained fluid and
multifaceted. In such a manner both houses could avoid being
identified too closely with yesterday's publishing trends and retained
sufficient manoeuvrability to be able to capitalise on a rival's
publishing successes by emulating its list strengths.

The Women's Press thus in many ways confounds the expectations
aroused by its own advertising. Although a significant percentage of
the book-buying public may well nominate it as the archetypal
feminist press, taking its cue from the press's high-profile twentieth
anniversary celebrations in 1998, the discrepancy between public
profile and company reality is marked. Far from independent, it is a
fully owned subsidiary of a corporate media group and has been since
its inception. The press has successfully marketed writing by women
of colour as central to its political identity, yet the ratio of black
authors to white authors on its list was – even under de Lanerolle's
radical influence – almost exactly the same as that at Virago: approximately 1:5 (Ahmad, 1991: 12). In 1998, the press still derived its
public identity from a minority of books on its list: in August 1998
the company sponsored a highly visible 'top 20 promotion' of books
by black and third-world authors, but this followed a previous publicity
campaign in March of the same year in which the press selected a
general 'top 20 titles' – only three of which were written by women
of colour (*The Women's Press*, 1998: 1). At stake is not an issue of racial
quotas, or of determining optimal representational formulae, but of
a press frontlisting occasional books by women of colour while its
list continues to be dominated by women from other social and
ethnic groups.

ese ambivalences and discrepancies in The Women's
ip to ideas of what constitutes feminist publishing,
n indisputably radical in other spheres, especially
to reconfigure author/editor/reader relationships.
merly, the press's aim at its outset was to achieve practical and attitudinal change in the way books were commissioned, edited and marketed, with on-going collaboration between author, editor and reader as the optimal goal. Reflecting on her four years at the helm of the press, founding managing director Stephanie Dowrick described the kind of institutional change in publishing practice that she pioneered: 'I wanted writers to feel there was a continuity of interest between them and the publisher and reader, and out of that support and energy would come a different kind of writing. I think sometimes it did' (Goodkin, 1992: 17). Borrowing from feminist models such as the collective (with its rejection of hierarchical organisation) and the consciousness-raising group (in which political discovery was designed to take place within an emotionally supportive environment) The Women's Press intervened in standard publishing practice, attempting to break down rigid demarcations between author, editor and reader.[8] On a day-to-day basis, such policies meant greater attention to unsolicited manuscripts, one of which – Jill Miller's *Happy as a Dead Cat* (1983) – achieved publication against the general odds of being rescued from the slush pile. In terms of editing, the feminist publishing ethos committed the press to allocate significantly greater resources than would most mainstream houses for the development of promising manuscripts, such as first-time author Ellen Kuzwayo's book *Call Me Woman* (1985). The book's structural editor, Marsaili Cameron, recalls nurturing the manuscript through multiple rewrites to ensure that the anti-Apartheid activist's vital message found its audience, resulting in an experience of editing that 'was a truly shared project' (1987: 125). The press also prioritised new writing, devoting greater than average list space to the financially high-risk area of first novels from literary unknowns: at one stage 60 to 70 per cent of The Women's Press titles were original publications, a fact proudly stated on the books' covers (see, for example, Nasta, 1991). The strain that this concentration on slow-return titles placed on The Women's Press's finances was alluded to by Attallah in 1991 as justification for his drastic reorganisation of the press and its list (Pallister, 1991: 38). Yet de Lanerolle's comments at the time reveal that it was not balance sheets alone which went to the heart of the conflict between owner and managing director. Rather, it was the kind of organisational

structure and its political positioning of the press *vis-à-vis* its readers, which ran counter to the conventional business expectations of Attallah. As de Lanerolle outlined in her July 1991 letter to *Spare Rib*: 'the major disagreements between Mr Attallah and the majority of the workers at The Women's Press were not simply about losses but about what we published and how we ran the company' (1991: 4). For, in de Lanerolle's analysis, taking publishing risks on first novels made a kind of political and financial sense, as it exposed the press to new purchasers of its books, purchasers who in turn may have themselves produced publishable manuscripts:

> We find ourselves part of a creative ferment when women are getting together in writers' workshops, reading to each other and criticising, running therapy centres and support groups – all generating vast quantities of information and campaign material that need to be shared with other women ... And the new readers these writers stimulate will be writing in their turn ... Our readers are our writers and our writers are our readers. (Macaskill, 1991: 84)

for Ch.5

Far more than conventional trade publishers, The Women's Press located itself within a broad-scale political and social landscape, cultivating contact with grassroots feminist organisations such as the London Rape Crisis Centre and the Work Hazards Group, partly in order to remain alert to new directions in feminist politics, and partly to know its main market. The press's self-conception was at times somewhat analogous to that of a community newspaper, pledged to alert its adherents to new trends and forthcoming events. Activities such as author readings, book launches and discussion groups were regarded both as ideological fillips and as sales events, a view entirely in accordance with feminist publishers' original conviction that the act of publishing is itself an ideological act. If so, why not harness profitability to a community consciousness-raising event and simultaneously enhance both awareness and the company bank balance?

OWNING YOUR OWN: DILEMMAS OF CORPORATE INVOLVEMENT

The incongruity of The Women's Press's ownership prompts two questions for a feminist analysis of publishing: firstly, do the ideology and political convictions of a publishing house's owner matter in feminist publishing and, if so, to what extent? Secondly, can editorial autonomy ever exist meaningfully without the guarantee of financial independence? The implications of the first of these questions are best analysed by investigating in further detail the specific personalities involved in The Women's Press so as to gain an understanding of how Attallah's media role has imposed a programme of self-distancing and damage limitation on the press.

Naim Attallah has consciously cultivated a media persona in his adopted country in which his outsider status as a foreign-born national can be neutralised through a complex combination of contrived exoticism and Anglophilia, making Attallah appear both entirely at home in the upper echelons of British society, yet at the same time not quite of it (see Badawi, 1987; Lawson, 1990; Dougary, 1992). The 'Sheikh of Soho' persona, coined originally by satirical magazine *Private Eye* – although it seems to have been willingly adopted and projected by Attallah (2000: 64) – encapsulates this ambiguous identity. By 'establishing Quartet as a finishing school for talented society gels', Attallah proved himself both an inside player in the British literary world, yet simultaneously a figure of detached otherness (Attallah, 2000: 64). A reputation encapsulated by one British journalist as that of a 'lascivious old chauvinist' (Dougary, 1992: 10) is compounded by a meticulously constructed urbanity in his published interviews, and a propensity for generalising sweepingly about the experience of the entire female sex – most notoriously in his 1987 tome *Women*, a collection of Attallah's selectively edited snippets from interviews with 319 successful and predominantly white women. To the imagined relief of The Women's Press, the book was published by Attallah's Quartet Books, although this did not stop the obvious and (to The Women's Press) disparaging connection being made: in feminist publishing circles it became known satirically as *Women: A User's Guide* (Lawson, 1990: 56).

Prior to 1991 there is scant evidence of Attallah having intervened directly in editorial decision-making at the press. Yet his remarks about the firm – its origins, its directors and its list priorities – over the course of its history consistently suggest a paternalism that does the press's publicity department no favours. Narrating the details of The Women's Press's foundation in 1977, Attallah chooses the imagery of romantic love and casts himself in the role of benevolent sugar-daddy: 'A year later this dynamic woman, Stephanie Dowrich [sic], came to me and said "Why don't you put your hand in my hand and let's form a company"' (Badawi, 1987: 10).[9] Similarly, Virago's 1976 buyout from Quartet, prompted by battles over the content of its early list, is described in terms of Virago's then managing director

Carmen Callil's alleged neuroticism: 'she was so at war with the boys that I had to let her go' (Badawi, 1987: 10). Given how conscious The Women's Press has shown itself to be of its public profile and the integrity of its image, such remarks by the press's owner threaten to tarnish its credibility, particularly among the more oppositional wings of feminism at which the press particularly targets its marketing campaigns. Styling their firm as the publisher of 'Books of Integrity by Women Writers', it is small wonder that The Women's Press's senior figures generally omit Attallah's name in interviews, waiting for the interviewer to first point out and query the seeming incongruity of the alliance (Steel, 1998: 28).

The contradictions inherent in The Women's Press's commercial foundation would appear to undercut attempts to market itself as a radical imprint, but they are in themselves insufficient to negate the firm's claims of commitment to women's writing. Feminist print enterprises started in the 1970s and early 1980s may more commonly have taken the form of collectives, but the particular circumstances of The Women's Press's situation – both radical in intent and financially cushioned – enable the press to publish a greater number and variety of women's books than most collectives are financially able to produce. The Women's Press's niche within the Namara group was crucial to its steady expansion after the release of its first list in 1978, for the overdraft that Attallah guaranteed the press protected the house against the cash-flow problems which beset small presses without a strong capital base. Freed from the requirement to turn a substantial profit in its first years of operation, the press was also untrammelled by interest payments on loans to banks, a financial exigency that, again, often sinks small publishing ventures. Former joint managing director Kathy Gale also recognised that private backers like Attallah, however they may interfere in list direction, are occasionally willing to extend credit in situations where banks cannot justify the continued financial risk. Of the 1991 dispute she remarks: 'If The Women's Press had been solely guaranteed by a bank, there's no question that it would have gone then' (Steel, 1998: 28).

The enormous sales and publicity success that Alice Walker's *The Color Purple* brought to the firm from 1983 onwards illustrate most critically the benefits of the company's sheltered niche within the Namara group. Upon securing the UK and Commonwealth rights to *The Color Purple*, The Women's Press published their edition to a smattering of reviews and slow sales, a situation that improved once the book was awarded a 1983 Pulitzer Prize for Fiction, and that was transformed into a sales deluge upon the release of Stephen Spielberg's 1985 film adaptation of the same name.[10] The impact of the bestseller on the firm was transformative – turnover increased within twelve months from £150,000 to £1,000,000; new titles rose dramatically from 17 to 60 a year (Macaskill, 1991: 82). Yet the enormous outlay of funds associated with a bestseller, and the need to subsidise frequent large print runs, mean that a bestseller can easily effect a small publishing house's demise. Ros de Lanerolle, reviewing the process that 'nearly killed us' (Macaskill, 1991: 82) asserted: 'in terms of sheer logistics, a best-seller is a mixed blessing for a small publisher, and we are conscious of having negotiated a number of rocks that might have wrecked us' (Gerrard, 1989: 23). While editorial and directorial acumen were important elements in the firm's weathering of its success, the financial buffer of Attallah's umbrella group was indispensable, initially in that it allowed The Women's Press to ride out short-term cash-flow problems, and in the longer term because the experience of publishing a bestseller such as *The Color Purple* greatly increased The Women's Press's public profile and imprint recognition. The fact that in 1998, 15 years after its original British publication, *The Color Purple* was still listed as The Women's Press's strongest selling title, heading its twentieth anniversary 'top 20' promotion (*The Women's Press*, 1998: 1), testifies to the text's crucial influence on the fortunes of its publisher – and by implication also highlights the financial substratum that enabled the press to survive and capitalise on its success.

Having benefited from the financial protection that a conglomerate structure can provide, The Women's Press in March 1991 experienced the flip-side of corporate ownership, namely loss of editorial independence and the power to publish. The incident illustrates in the sharpest possible terms the price that committed feminist publishers pay for the trade-off of corporate backing: job insecurity, reversals in list direction, and the tarnishing of a house's hard-won reputation for political commitment and integrity. The blow to The Women's Press's image as a champion of black women's writing was substantial, and is attributable to Attallah's comments in the press at the time: having trivialised the boardroom dispute as mere 'arguments amongst the women', he moved on to indicate that cash, not cattiness, lay at the true root of the power struggle (Pallister, 1991: 38). Attallah alluded specifically to an ostensibly misguided overconcentration on low-return black and third-world women's writing, stating that 'sales were suffering as a result' and that 'we have to get the balance right' (Pallister, 1991: 38). In a letter to the *Guardian* (29 March 1991) 23 of The Women's Press's authors – including Merle Collins, Michèle Roberts, Gillian Slovo and Sheila Jeffreys – publicly distanced themselves from Attallah's new management, and deplored the damage that his assessment of third-world women's writing as unprofitable had done to the press's reputation: 'Some of us, as it happens, are "Third World" women. In the light of Mr Attallah's remarks, it is only too evident that anything we might have to offer would be entirely irrelevant to his purposes' (Ahmad, 1991: 13).

Intriguingly, in an interview published only weeks prior to the March 1991 resignations, de Lanerolle outlined the various spheres of power within The Women's Press, firmly demarcating its owner's powers to intervene in editorial decision-making:

> His [Attallah's] part in the firm is to guarantee the overdraft. He expects it to be a viable financial venture, obviously. He owns all the shares but he doesn't interfere. Occasionally he may say that these kinds of books don't sell, but he wouldn't say 'Don't publish that book'. (Macaskill, 1991: 85)

What may appear in retrospect a disastrously ill-timed assertion of independence becomes more explicable when read not as a *description* of the status quo between Attallah and the press, but as a *prescription* by de Lanerolle of what degree of intervention by Attallah into the press's internal affairs was acceptable. Yet, if this was an attempt to circumscribe Attallah's role by creating a public expectation that he would not use his financial clout to coerce the press's management, it was a singularly unsuccessful one: the spate of firings and resignations followed within a month of de Lanerolle's interview appearing in print. Attallah, as the owner of the press, was the party in the dominant position during the ensuing dispute, and he was able to achieve his desired outcome: the dismissal of de Lanerolle; a revamping of the press's list priorities away from Commonwealth and third-world writing; and the appointment of a more commercially sympathetic management team. Former employees, authors and feminist sympathisers staged a war of attrition against Attallah, which included cancellation of his Frankfurt Book Fair travel bookings, defamatory leaflets, a stink bomb let off at Quartet's Frankfurt stand, and a boycott of selected Women's Press titles (Moncur, 1992: 23). But the petty scale of these retaliations further underlines the power discrepancy between the parties to the dispute. A letter from de

Lanerolle to *Spare Rib* at the time of the crisis recognises the comparative impotence of the feminists and their supporters, reworking the familiar (and here apposite) maxim that 'freedom of the press belongs to those who own one': 'The point is that Naim Attallah has the right to withdraw his support from the kind of publishing programme and the kind of women's enterprise that The Women's Press once represented, for *whatever* reason. He owns the press' (1991: 4).

Essentially, the affair highlights starkly for feminist publishing the enormous detriment in terms of loss of editorial power that involvement in corporate networks may bring. Certainly de Lanerolle concluded that independence was the *sine qua non* of a feminist print enterprise, and embodied this belief in Open Letters, the non-fiction house she co-founded and launched in 1992 – an enterprise still in its consolidation phase at the time of her death in 1993 (Hennegan, 1992: 7; Woddis, 1992: 26). De Lanerolle's bleak realisation that 'if someone owns 100% of the shares, the other directors have no power' suggests that feminist integrity and financial protection may – in the bruising competitiveness of the publishing marketplace – prove mutually exclusive options.

LOCAL COLOUR: REPRESENTING THE DIVERSITY OF BLACK BRITISH WOMEN'S WRITING

In the decade before the underlying tensions in The Women's Press's corporate structure erupted to public prominence, criticism of the press's outlook and style of working had already been articulated. The long-running debate around feminist publishing and its intersection with the politics of race led to the formation of British women's presses specialising in writing by women of colour – presses that were organised collectively and that were highly conscious of their political 'authenticity'. Two of the more prominent of these women's presses, Sheba Feminist Publishers (established in 1980) and Black Woman Talk (established in 1983) emerged at a time when writing by black women was beginning to be promoted by white feminist presses and, to a lesser extent, by the mainstream publishing industry.[11] But the *means*, rather than the simple *end*, of publication energised the collectives of Sheba and Black Woman Talk, both of which aimed to expand black women's involvement in all stages of literary production in order to militate against the publishing world's belittling view of minority women as 'exotic flavour of the year' (Black Woman Talk Collective, 1984b: 28).

The early manifestos of The Women's Press may have invoked the radical language of 'a conscious-raising dynamic ... which has ... its collectivity in the WLM', but by the early1980s its status as a corporate-owned and hierarchically organised business venture was apparent to radical black women involved in feminist circles. Partly in response to these supposed 'Establishment' elements of The Women's Press, and partly because they were unlikely to find a wealthy entrepre-neurial backer of their own, Sheba set up in 1980 as a women's collective, without the fiscal safety net of a guaranteed overdraft. As an anonymous member of the collective optimistically stated in *Rolling Our Own: Women as Printers, Publishers and Distributors*, 'we could either set ourselves a time limit and get money together and all that, or we could just literally plunge in' (Cadman, Chester and Pivot, 1981: 38). Similarly, Black Woman Talk was initiated in 1983 by a group of unemployed black women in London 'who felt strongly about creating the space and the means for our voices to be heard' (Black Woman Talk Collective, 1984b: 28). In the early years of the 1980s, with the (now disbanded) Greater London Council distributing public grants money for community-based alternative arts projects, black women's publishing groups were able to launch themselves with a speed and self-confidence that is hard to recreate in the vastly more constrained economic climate of the twenty-first century.

The fact that alternative feminist publishers sprang into existence so readily during the period is attributable, in part, to the generally buoyant economic climate of the early Thatcher era, but it is also due in large part to the period's continued boom in feminist book sales. The peculiar paradox of the 1980s is that, at the same time as the left and feminists steadily lost political and parliamentary ground, the influence of these groups in cultural and intellectual circles continued to rise. Without the background of this expansion in the feminist book market, the readership for works by black women would have been unable to sustain such a proliferation of radical women's presses. Expansion, and not saturation, of the existing market in black women's books therefore became the key priority for the newer presses. The likes of US authors Alice Walker, Toni Morrison and Maya Angelou had achieved bestseller sales for The Women's Press, Picador (an imprint of Pan Macmillan) and Virago respectively. But Black Woman Talk and Sheba insisted upon the need to make audible British black women's voices, so that the multifarious nature of black and South Asian women's experiences in Britain was not threatened by transcultural assimilation into the quite distinct perspective of African-American women. Hence Black Woman Talk, in an early position statement published in *Feminist Review*, regarded the success of Walker and other writers of colour with wary reservation, suspicious of the ease with which the challenge of their literary 'otherness' could be neutralised by publishing industry tokenism:

> More recently, it appears that there is a growing awareness amongst some of the established mainstream and feminist publishers of the need to make Black voices heard. Unfortunately, their enthusiasm to publish works by Black women, particularly from America, seems to stem from their recognition that such books have a lucrative market, rather than any genuine commitment to making publishing accessible to Black women writers in Britain. Afro-American women seem to be the vogue for feminist publishers such as the Women's Press [sic]. (Black Woman Talk Collective, 1984a: 100)

At the heart of such guarded assessments of the publishing industry's motivation lies a deep-seated opposition to literary ventriloquism on the part of white feminist publishers: a refusal to allow black women's writing to be fed through the cultural filter of white feminists' perceptions, and then to be marketed to largely white, middle-class audiences as diverting handbooks to black women's experience. Sheba, in particular, attempted to build into its organisational structures mechanisms for preventing such liberal appropriation of writing by women of colour, ensuring that both a white woman and a woman of colour worked on the editing of all Sheba manuscripts, and by using the expertise of black collective members in marketing titles to British ethnic communities. The media angle on black women writers as literary novelties was understood by such presses to constitute only a more oblique form of racism than outright literary exclusion. Cognisant of the reality that 'black women are often promoted by the mainstream media in ways that are racist', Sheba's *modus operandi* was designed as an ethical corrective: 'It's a small thing but its [sic] there as a kind of check' (Loach, 1986: 19).

From the vantage point of the early twenty-first century, the relative merits of radical black feminist publishers and The Women's Press may appear definitively settled: The Women's Press in 2003 celebrated its twenty-fifth anniversary; Black Woman Talk, Sheba, and the West Yorkshire-based press, Urban Fox, on the other hand, are now all defunct. If the primary responsibility of a political publisher is to remain trading, The Women's Press may be considered an overwhelmingly more successful feminist enterprise – the 1991 crisis notwithstanding. Yet both Sheba and Black Woman Talk were crucial in pushing the feminist agenda and breaking new literary ground during the politically difficult period of the 1980s (O'Sullivan, 2003: 29). For without these presses' insistence on British black women's experience and autonomous organising, the feminist publishing sector would be still more open to the charge of commercial co-optation of black writing without a proportionate ceding of institutional power. Having been marginalised first in the Black Power movement by the cult of black machismo, and later in the women's liberation movement, with its emphasis on white, middle-class careerism, black women by the early 1980s sensed that only autonomous organising would prevent the hijacking of their activist energy for others' political ends. That black feminists made their position broadly felt is evidenced by changes in the racial profile of The Women's Press's list by the mid- to late 1980s: stung perhaps by Black Woman Talk's singling out of the press for particular criticism in its 1984 manifesto, The Women's Press in 1987 produced Rhonda Cobham and Merle Collins' anthology *Watchers and Seekers: Creative Writing by Black Women in Britain*, as well as numerous novels by black British authors, including Joan Riley's classic of cross-racial dislocation, *The Unbelonging* (1985). In 1991 (immediately prior to the forced resignation of de Lanerolle) The Women's Press moreover produced Susheila Nasta's anthology *Motherlands: Black Women's Writing from Africa, the Caribbean and South Asia*, in the introduction to which the editor explicitly locates the text within a recent outpouring of multiracial British women's publishing. In so doing, Nasta manifests a consciousness of the text's political and publishing specificity, which would appear incongruous without the radicalising impetus of black women's imprints.

Yet, for all The Women's Press's success over the preceding 25 years in promoting the diverse voices of British women of colour, troubling ambiguities remain encoded in the company's organisational structure and outlook. There is a reluctance to draw the lessons of 1991 to their logical (albeit unsettling) conclusions. If, as Ros de Lanerolle was forced to acknowledge, freedom of the press belongs to those who own one, then only a stake in the financial ownership of a press can guarantee feminists' editorial autonomy and political integrity. Yet, on this count it follows by extension that only a press in which women of colour have commissioning power and managerial clout can avoid the taint of tokenism and the risk that black women's writing will again be silenced once the multicultural wave is deemed to have crested. In a final ironic twist, the market dominance of the twenty-first century has produced a bizarre state of play in the publishing industry: only those with firm economic power can now ensure the undiluted tenor of their oppositional politics. Early radical women's publishing theorists such as June Arnold have thus had their vision of an autonomous women's literary culture both stunningly fulfilled and – at the same time – utterly disproved.

BLACK INC.: BLACK WOMEN AND ACCESS
TO POWER IN THE PUBLISHING INDUSTRY

The crucial political importance of black women's autonomous organising within publishing was not confined to British operations such as Black Woman Talk, Sheba and Urban Fox Press, but manifested also across the Atlantic in numerous enterprises, notably in the form of New York-based Kitchen Table: Women of Color Press. In terms of organisation, scale and ideological perspective, Kitchen Table strikes interesting contrasts with The Women's Press. Editorial autonomy and the means to ensure it were grounding principles when US black feminist writers and critics Barbara Smith and Audre Lorde co-founded Kitchen Table Press in 1980 (Smith, B., 1998: xv). Smith's conception was of a feminist press in which the freedom to publish books that the editors considered important was backed up by financial independence: organisational autonomy would underpin and secure intellectual autonomy. Of prime importance was Smith's conviction that black women must ensure that their voices are heard in all stages of the production of their works, in order to avoid their oppositional message being compromised either by explicit editorial changes or by the more covert methods of silencing achievable by misrepresentation in marketing, poor distribution or low-quality production standards.[12] The concept of an 'authentic' publishing product, one determined at all stages by the groups about which it speaks, was Smith's fundamental conviction: paramount was 'our need to determine independently both the content and the conditions of our work and to control the words and images that were produced about us' (Smith, 1989: 11). Significantly, Smith identifies alternative and white-controlled feminist presses as just as likely sites for such literary disenfranchisement as mainstream houses:

> The founding ... [of Kitchen Table Press] was partially motivated by our need, as Third World women, to have complete control over both the content and the production of our words – control which is usually not available even when working with feminist and alternative publishers. (1984: 24)

In an important dialogue in May 1993, representatives of North America's various feminists-of-colour presses – Kitchen Table, Aunt Lute Books in San Francisco, and Women's Press of Toronto[13] – came together in an alternative session to the usual meeting of feminist and lesbian publishers at the industry trade fair, the American Booksellers Association (ABA). The edited account of their discussion, published in *Sojourner* magazine as 'Packing Boxes and Editing Manuscripts: Women of Color in Feminist Publishing' (1993), marks a watershed in the debate around racism in feminist publishing, as the representatives of the various presses express anger and disbelief at the increasing careerism and financial expediency they perceive among white-run North American feminist presses. Most revealing, in the context of the debate over tokenising black literature, are the observations of the group on the subject of internal press dynamics. The participants express a profound cynicism about the motivations of 'white women's presses', a political judgement catalysed by the alleged railroading of the joint-meeting by white feminists on the previous day. Lillien Waller of Kitchen Table Press encapsulates the group's conviction that any breaching of publishing industry power structures by black women is inadequate and subject to reversal unless it infiltrates managerial levels:

> The white women's presses – which is what they are even if they have one or two women of color working for them – are just that, ultimately: for white women. And if they happen to publish a few books by women of color, that's fairly incidental or they're riding the wave of some trend in colored people. (*Sojourner*, 1993: 11)

Waller's contention provokes urgent questions about the racial politics that underlie The Women's Press's foundation. It urges analysis not only of the content of The Women's Press list, but also of the politics implicit in the company's establishment and organisation. What contradictions can be read in the situation whereby a press run and dominated by white women specialises in publishing works by black and third-world women writers, to the extent of incorporating such writing into the press's core political identity?

Crucial to the emergence of a distinctive black feminist voice since the 1960s has been the concept of authenticity – the belief that representations of black women and their experiences should be self-determined, cast in their own language and should posit black women as their dominant point of view. Alexis DeVeaux conceives of this as:

> A struggle to express ourselves. To be heard. To be seen. In our own image. To construct the words. To name the deeds. Confront the risks. Write the history. Document it on radio, television and satellites. To analyse and live it. (quoted in Hernton, 1984: 144)

Arguably, this implies a contradiction implicit in the nature of The Women's Press's set-up. Feminist publishing enterprises took as their first premise the conviction that publishing was an industry dominated by white, middle-class males, and that the publishing decisions made by an industry so dominated would reflect the interests of the privileged group. By extension, presumably a feminist publishing industry in which white (and generally tertiary-educated, middle-class) women occupy decision-making levels will be to a greater or lesser degree removed from the central concerns of women of colour. Certain spheres of feminist publishing are at risk of promoting identity politics while remaining conveniently oblivious to the homogeneity of their own identity.

For feminist publishing the dilemma has two specific aspects. Firstly, can a feminist press staffed predominantly by white women accurately identify issues of vital concern to black women's lives, and market its books so as to reach this audience successfully? Secondly, given that feminist classics publishing has tended to be heavily reliant on academic works reclaiming a tradition of women's writing, and given that the industry's republication of these texts has helped to entrench a particular feminist canon, is there a risk of feminist publishing and women's studies colluding – perhaps unintentionally – to marginalise black women's writing? Responding to the strongly WASP tone of much early feminist literary history, Barbara Smith – in the foundation essay in this area, 'Toward a Black Feminist Criticism' – anatomises the silencing inflicted by a political movement that claimed to give voice to the culturally disenfranchised:

I think of the thousands and thousands of books which have beeı devoted by this time to the subject of Women's Writing and I am filled with rage at the fraction of these pages that mention black and other Third World women. I finally do not know how to begin, because in 1977 I want to be writing this for a black feminist publication. (1986 [1977]: 172)

In taking the initial steps to set up Kitchen Table in 1980, three years after the date of this instigatory essay, Smith went some way to alleviating the absence of avenues for black women's political and literary self-expression. Kitchen Table made a telling point about the feminist publishing industry's priorities when it obtained the rights to what is now a foundation text in black women's studies, Cherríe Moraga and Gloria Anzaldúa's anthology *This Bridge Called my Back: Writings by Radical Women of Color* (1983 [1981]). The title, which has since sold in excess of 100,000 copies for Kitchen Table and which won the 1986 Before Columbus Foundation American Book Award, was originally published by the Massachusetts-based Persephone Press, a 'white women's press' (Moraga and Anzaldúva, 1983: n.p.) which (the Kitchen Table edition of the book notes pointedly) allowed the book to drop out of print after a single print run (Nichols, 1995: 11). Having regained the rights, the editors chose to publish a second edition with Kitchen Table, and they underline in the preliminaries to this second edition that it has been 'conceived of and produced entirely by women of color' (Moraga and Anzaldúva, 1983: n.p.). The Kitchen Table edition became a startling bestseller for a small press, achieving ten reprintings and appearing on the curricula of women's studies courses internationally (Worrell, 2000: G1). The publishing history of this individual title prompts searching questions in the sphere of feminist publishing generally: can presses that identify publishing and politics as inextricably linked afford to remain oblivious to the political assumptions inherent in their granting of editorial control almost exclusively to white women? Furthermore, does such a press risk accusations of ventriloquism and political containment by publishing black women's writing according to white women's precepts and selling it to a predominantly white, middle-class readership?

In February 1995 Barbara Smith relinquished the position of publisher at Kitchen Table and in 1996 the press was adequately capitalised for the first time in its history, under the direction of a Transition Coalition Committee backed by The Union Institute in

).C. (Smith, 1998: xv, 205). However, the range of :s built into the transition agreement reveals that the ed at the impromptu feminists-of-colour ABA meeting ince attained currency within feminist circles. The Union Institute exerts 'no editorial control', *'no policy-making influence'*, '*no control* over day-to-day finances and operations', and it 'does not involve itself in the hiring of staff' (Grant, 1996: 1027), thus rebutting the overeasy and fallacious assumption of one onlooker that Smith had 'turn[ed] the press over to white women' (1996: 1032). Between 1995 and 1996 the transition team raised almost double Kitchen Table's former annual turnover by approaching grants bodies and private fund-raising ventures, and employed a salaried publisher to oversee press operations, raising hopes that Kitchen Table might have transcended the painful committed publishers' dilemma of choosing between political credibility and solvency. Had it attained such an elusive goal, it would effectively have evaded the two key problems that still pervade Britain's The Women's Press: women of colour would themselves have held editorial decision-making power, and they would not have been tied to the whim of unsympathetic financiers. Unfortunately, despite the funds injection co-ordinated by the Union Institute scheme, and even though salaried directorship of the press passed to a former board member, Kitchen Table closed in the summer of 1997 and 'has not reopened' (Smith, B., 1998: 209; Worrell, 2000: G1).

In The Women's Press's defence it should be stated that the company has, over the preceding decade, evinced an awareness that their staff make-up is white-dominated, and has attempted to ensure a more representative group of co-workers through placing recruitment advertisements automatically in the black *and* the mainstream press (Duncker, 1992: 49). But a marked under-representation of black women continues to characterise British literary publishing as a whole, and The Women's Press – despite its public image – is not immune to this imbalance. At the time of the 1991 crisis at The Women's Press, the firm did not have a single black woman editor, and Virago – with Melanie Silgardo – employed only one (Ahmad, 1991: 11). The threat, as black British critic and publisher Margaret Busby ascertains,[14] is that of a growing discrepancy between the market boom in black and third-world women's writing and a dearth of representatives from these groups in the publishing industry, let alone in positions of managerial and decision-making authority. Implicit *for ref @ CS eajsays 'your life'*

here is the suggestion that presses are cashing in on identity politics, without having to relinquish institutional power:

> Is it enough to respond to a demand for books reflecting the presence of 'ethnic minorities' while perpetuating a system which does not actively encourage their involvement at all levels? The reality is that the appearance and circulation of books supposedly produced with these communities in mind is usually dependent on what the dominant white (male) community, which controls schools, libraries, bookshops and publishing houses, will permit. (Busby, 1984: 12)

Writer and critic Barbara Burford, in an impassioned article for *Spare Rib*, reiterates Busby's analysis of resistant industry schema, but goes further than Busby in perceiving in commercial success itself potentially the greatest threat to the future evolution of black women's literature:

> As Blackwomen writing and being published in Britain today, we have to make sure that, this time, we do not remain a liberal fad, that we are not merchandised and commersialized [sic] into obsolescence. This time we must not allow ourselves to be turned on and off, and we must not disappear quietly, when it is decided that we as an 'issue' have suffered from over exposure. (1987: 39)

The question of whether it is predominantly white, liberal women who read black women's fiction is difficult to answer, primarily because statistics are rarely kept on the racial backgrounds of book purchasers, but also because a book's sales figures may not accurately reflect its readership. This discrepancy may carry particular weight with a market sector such as black women, whose generally lower socio-economic status may direct their reading habits towards borrowing from public libraries or acquaintances rather than book purchasing. Therefore a single copy of a Women's Press title placed in a municipal library could be read by hundreds of women within a few years of its publication. What can be assessed with greater accuracy are the race and gender backgrounds towards which The Women's Press markets its list, and the ways in which this contrasts with the house practice of Kitchen Table.

Dowrick founded The Women's Press with the conviction that feminist books should be packaged enticingly, a conviction that was underlined by the contemporary sales success of Virago's glossy Modern Classics series. In commentator Nicci Gerrard's words, both firms' marketing strategies represent an attempt to overcome 'feminism's discomfort with profit in connection with the arts, or with the lucrative business of packaging, marketing and selling creativity' (1989: 16). The political implications of cover design decisions are discussed by Smith in relation to Kitchen Table books when she asserts that the group would not package a black or third-world woman's book so as to suggest that it was the product of a more 'mainstream' author or in such a way that 'the only way to determine that it was written by a woman of color would be to turn it over and look at the author's picture on the back' (Smith, 1989: 12). The design policy stemmed from the press's insistence on authenticity and the political necessity of positing black women's experiences as central, though it sprang also from the press's identi-fication of its core market as people of colour – 'not solely women of color or lesbians of color, but the entire gamut of our communities' (Smith, 1989: 12). Kitchen Table viewed the white feminist readership as supplementary to this primary market: 'being explicit about our books' subject matter does not decrease this particular [white] audience, while it does ensure attention from our target audience of women of color' (1989: 12). In this race-specific conception of book design, links emerge with the contemporary British black-interest publisher X Press, the 'resolvedly commercial' house whose paperback covers invariably feature black protagonists as a device for attracting their target audience (*Bookseller*, 1996: 56). The sexual politics of these covers are, however, grist for a further design debate, echoing as they do the guns-and-women motifs of Blaxploitation films and the iconography of the cult of black machismo.[15]

I would suggest that Kitchen Table's prioritising of target markets through advertising arose from two causes. Firstly, it reflected the political conviction of the press's directors that racial oppression is the primary oppression encountered by women of colour, and that it is therefore politically essential to reach women of these groups via the context of their communities (Smith and Beverly, 1983 [1981]: 114–15). Secondly, it reflected the demographic strength and political profile that African-Americans have achieved in the United States. A similar programme of targeting books at black communities would not be financially viable for The Women's Press in Britain, as non-white communities in Britain tend to be more ethnically diverse and have still to achieve the level of political and institutional organising around issues of identity that African-Americans have striven to achieve. The Women's Press's conception of its primary market in terms of gender rather than racial identification stems also from its cross-racial list structure: given the high proportion of white authors published by the press, it would be unrepresentative and perhaps unprofitable to market its texts to attract a predominantly black or minority readership. White women do largely control marketing and design decision-making within the firm, yet there is no attempt to disguise the racial perspective of The Women's Press's books by black authors: indeed the covers of titles by high-profile black writers such as African-American Alice Walker positively proclaim – and celebrate – their author's racial identity.[16] The contrasting approaches to marketing displayed by the two presses arise, it appears, from the confluence of a number of factors: the individual racial identities of editors; their ideological perspectives on the nature of political oppression; and encompassing demographic and political contexts.

FEMINIST PUBLISHING – AT RISK OF BEING REMAINDERED?

How, then, should feminist communities and the wider literary world assess the current state-of-play in women of colour publishing? This discussion's motivation in counterpointing the nature of The Women's Press with its radical British rivals and with an American house publishing in broadly the same area is not to set up an ideological league table of feminist publishers, in which extra points are awarded for progressive organisational structures and deducted for non-feminist corporate owners. Rather, the foregoing examination of The Women's Press in the light of markedly different kinds of political print ventures aims to illustrate the varieties of response to the market for feminist publishing, and to investigate the ideological, financial and marketing implications of certain kinds of organisations. It is not so much a valorising of one system over all others, as an examination of the ways in which the market in feminist literature is capable of supporting a spectrum of feminist publishing endeavours. In particular, writing by women of colour – an area in which all of the presses considered in this chapter have focused their efforts – now faces the difficult transition from a distinct niche market into the general trade in upmarket literary fiction. While the public thirst for books by women of colour does not at present show signs of having been slaked, the key question for feminist publishers is how can they ensure that they, as opposed to multinational publishing conglomerates, continue to break the new ground in multicultural writing – *and* ensure sufficient profit from such publishing programmes to stay in business. Brand loyalty and reader recognition constitute key weapons in the trade arsenal of small alternative publishers, but in an increasingly corporatised and consolidated publishing environment it is uncertain whether 'books of integrity' will – in themselves – be sufficient to keep alternative feminist publishing alive.

Emerging at a particular moment in late 1970s feminist consciousness, The Women's Press made specific compromises to balance the demand for political integrity with the exigencies of commercial competition. The press saw as its highest priority the need to make feminist books available cheaply and plentifully to 'a double audience: feminists *and* the general reader in whichever area we are publishing' (Frank, 1982: 112). To this end, Dowrick and her successors at the helm of the firm sought to broaden the then-current definition of feminism to make it relevant to women from various racial and class backgrounds, seeking at the same time to construct a list that showcased living writers engaging with contemporary racial and cultural issues. Structurally, The Women's Press adopted a loosely hierarchised organisational model, rejecting the consensus decision-making of a collective, but attempting to retain an element of the creative support and collaboration that collectivism – at its best – can provide. Crucially, The Women's Press recognised that a feminist press can only act as a lever for social change if it continues in operation, and to this end Dowrick decided that firm financial backing, even if this necessitated outside ownership of the press, was a non-negotiable requirement. The decision resulted in a press better able to produce high-quality, widely distributed and well-marketed titles, and one able to survive the exigencies of rapid expansion and bestseller success, but one also in which final editorial control lay in the hands of an individual with debatable commitment to the ideology of the women's movement. Hence the 1991 resignations crisis at the press signals both an already remarkable longevity for a small press in a tumultuous industry, and the final clarification of where the power to publish actually lies in any fully owned publishing corporation.

For Kitchen Table, by contrast, the mere continued existence of a politically identified press was in itself inadequate, unless decision-making power lay in the hands of those whose cause was being promulgated. To that end, Kitchen Table was run democratically, prioritised employing women of colour and – despite criticism from some feminist quarters – published only writing by black and third-world women (Smith, B., 1989: 13; 1998: 200–1). Such a policy prioritised authenticity and editorial integrity over list expansion: though founded within a few years of each other, Kitchen Table published 15 books as compared with The Women's Press's current backlist of several hundred titles. Sheba and Black Woman Talk loosely identified with the version of identity politics publishing championed by Barbara Smith – Black Woman Talk going so far as to denominate Kitchen Table 'our sister press in America' (Black Woman Talk Collective, 1984a: 100). Yet without the driving-force of a writer-director of Smith's stature and perseverance, both presses folded under the weight of financial overextension and collective burn out.

The juxtaposition of these presses poses a fundamental question: has there now been sufficient public demand for texts by black women writers that a press run exclusively by black women such as Kitchen Table has become superfluous? Given the enormous sales and literary plaudits achieved by writers such as Walker, Morrison and Angelou – and the broader popularisation of black women's writing sponsored in particular by Oprah's Book Club – has the idea of a women-only house along the lines of The Women's Press now been politically superseded and rendered quaintly redundant? This discussion argues that conditions in the broader publishing industry make the continued existence of such presses an issue of political and cultural urgency. Although Virago and The Women's Press have succeeded in their aim of bringing writing by women – and in particular by women of colour – into the literary mainstream, there is a danger in assuming that cultural space, once won, is incapable of being reclaimed. Furthermore, to analyse a literary movement's success solely in terms of sales made and reputations established is to overlook the issue of political power as it is wielded within the publishing industry itself. The fact that women in general, and more especially women of colour, are still grossly under-represented in per capita terms at managerial level in the publishing industry highlights the difference between a publishing trend and achieved institutional change.

There is no reason why the mainstream trend for black women's writing, which first manifested in the mid-1980s, should not fall foul of publishing fashion, sinking as rapidly as it seemed to rise in the bookselling firmament. Given that the broader publishing industry publishes according to profit margins and not on grounds of ideological commitment, there can be no assurances that mainstream publishing channels will remain open to black women's writing, especially to those texts of an experimental cast and those informed by strongly oppositional politics. Hence the issue of editorial control as wielded by women cannot be dismissed. The most pressing issue for extant feminist houses such as The Women's Press is how to maintain revenue flow *and* political bite while competing against vastly more powerful mainstream firms for the market in writing by women of colour, which they – in a sense – are responsible for having first identified. It is a juggling act made more difficult still by feminist firms' need to adapt and grow this writing and its markets so that the voices of women of colour remain generally audible once the fickle attention of the mainstream publishing industry has shifted elsewhere.

3

Opening Pandora's Box: The Rise of Academic Feminist Publishing

> Our task, as I understand it, is to see that women's everyday life concerns are not lost in the jargon of the academic world. For us, the editors, the action-plan must entail making connections between knowledge and action.
>
> Tahera Aftab, 'Lobbying for Transnational Feminism'
> (2002: 153)

Viewed from the perspective of the early twenty-first century, the alignment between academia and feminism appears comparatively unproblematic. Largely neutralised as an activist political movement through a combination of fragmentation within and co-optation from without, feminism would seem to have found a congenial bolthole in the academy – a site of residual prestige where its cultural politics and research methodologies have found widespread acceptance, and where many of its founding figures have been able to carve out professional niches as the tide of activism, which first brought them to prominence, continues its long retreat. One upshot of this institutional embedding has been a countervailing 'disciplining' of feminism itself, as the formerly activist movement steadily accrued the institutional apparatus of syllabi, canons and 'founding mothers' (Scanlon and Swindells, 1994; Howe, 2000a; Messer-Davidow, 2002). Yet if any sector of Western professional life encourages women unblushingly to declare themselves feminists without fear of institutional rebuke, it is surely the academy.

Given this contemporary alignment, it can be hard to recapture the deep-seated ambivalence with which early second-wave feminism regarded academia, and the implications of this strained relationship for academic feminist publishing, both at the time and since. Second-wave feminism's belief in collectivism, direct political action and the importance of locating an 'authentic' female voice put it at odds with the select number of women who had, in the face of significant institutional prejudice and collegial hostility, secured footholds within academic power structures. On one hand, the second-wave movement recognised the political utility of academic women – whether as authors of publishable manuscripts or as informed advisors on editorial advisory committees, their weight added institutional credibility and intellectual ballast to an often fractious and still embryonic movement. Moreover, academic women were in a position to seed feminist ideas within educational curricula, thus influencing both younger generations of potential movement recruits, as well as older women returning to tertiary education after marriage and child-rearing – an often disaffected group whose coming to political consciousness provided much of the second wave's activist energy.

Yet, at the same time, second-wave feminism was somewhat suspicious of the careerist individualism necessary for carving a career in hostile educational structures, and viewed with opprobrium many earlier female academics' Beauvoirean tactic of writing about women from a quasi-masculinist speaking position – if writing about women at all. Female academics appeared simply less in need of feminist intervention than the majority of women, who were, by contrast, viewed as too often without access to tertiary education, confined to ill-paid semi-skilled employment, and denied the economic freedom to leave abusive domestic environments. To the extent that any group of pre-second-wave women enjoyed easy access to publication, academic women appeared to occupy a position of comparative privilege. As Ellen Mizzell recalls, 'middle-class women with cushy jobs in universities didn't need any help in making their voices heard; the problem was to shut them up' (1992b: 36). Though themselves mostly university educated, the activist publishers of the second wave were given to dismissive generalisations to the effect that 'any woman writer who could write a best selling saga, a romantic love story, a good thriller, or a good academic book, could see herself in print'. 'Literary and radical' writers, without the regular salary, institutional advantages and proximity to commissioning editors commonly characterising academic life, were 'harder to reach', and hence constituted feminist publishers' primary constituency (Nicholson, 1982: 77).

While accurately registering these ambivalences within second-wave feminism, it is important not to draw too absolute a distinction. The second-wave feminist publishing movement was always too fragile and financially precarious to rule out categorically any potentially sympathetic group of women; market ferocity had the practical effect of tempering ideological rigour. Hence second-wave publishers such as Virago and The Feminist Press did cultivate networks of academic women, particularly to serve on advisory panels assessing

manuscripts and potential reprints, or as writers of new intro-
tions to women's classics reissues. But academic women featured l.
prominently as authors of library monographs or tertiary textbooks
on the list of either house. Definitional ambiguity further defeats
any overeasy categorisation of feminist publishers into 'academic'
and 'non-academic' groupings. For no feminist publisher ever self-
described as solely an 'academic feminist publisher', in part because
the audience for academic works was never large nor reliable enough
to support such finely targeted niche marketing, and in part because
the exclusivist connotations of the 'academic' tag sat uneasily with
the second wave's belief in connecting with women's lived experience
and grassroots activism (Frank, 1982: 91). For the women's presses
discussed in previous chapters, the academic feminist audience
represented a publishing bonus – an important reservoir of
sympathetic reviewers, potential adopters of fiction reprints and
original novels as set texts, and intellectual cultivators of a future
feminist-informed readership – but a market always more ancillary
than primary in character.

This chapter shifts analytical focus to examine a less commonly
acknowledged force within the feminist press movement. Discerning
a gap in the publishing landscape for feminist-informed non-fiction,
which would appeal to the growing number of women's studies
courses offered at tertiary level, a group of presses sprang up internationally, of which The Feminist Press (US), Pandora Press (UK),
Scarlet Press (UK), Open Letters (UK) and Spinifex Press (Australia)
are among the better known. Rather than analysing these presses in
isolation from the feminist publishing movement as a whole (in
itself an artificial distinction), this chapter seeks to contextualise
their publishing mode within various book industry networks –
figured here as a series of concentric circles. Firstly, selecting Pandora
as an emblematic operation, the chapter charts the fate of this
particular non-fiction feminist publisher, embedding Pandora's
narrative within the experience of earlier feminist presses, which
Pandora had, to some extent, been established in order to emulate.
Secondly, the discussion moves outwards from the feminist press
sector to examine the uptake of feminism by mainstream academic
publishers, acknowledging once again the impossibility of drawing
neat distinctions between 'independent' and 'mainstream' presses,
not least because Pandora itself blurs this distinction. The discussion
explores in detail the professional advantages and political drawbacks
of multinational involvement in feminist knowledge creation,

demonising and the glibly celebratory verdicts
ɔur such examinations. In the third section, the
ɲacro level of analysis to consider women's studies
ɪnism broadly as disciplines constituted by, and
ɪed with, publishing history. Alert to the scope of
ɪeɪɪɪɪɪɪst-ɪntormed publishing within the multinational, university press and independent sectors of the book trade – in addition to self-described feminist publishers – the analysis considers how the discipline of women's studies has been conditioned by publisher preferences in terms of the content, format and modes of disseminating its research findings. In the heat of the arduous task of smuggling feminist ideas past the academic gatekeepers into the marketplace of ideas, feminism has paid markedly little attention to how that marketplace in turn variously modulated, encouraged and inhibited feminist expression. Between the original scholarly publishing of second-wave feminism and today's glossy gender studies catalogues from multinational academic publishers such as Sage and Routledge lies a subterranean yet richly revealing history of modern feminism. It is moreover a history that requires unearthing if feminism as a discipline is to be alive to the material underpinnings of its own intellectual development and professional practice.

PANDORA PRESS: 'WE WERE ONLY DISAPPOINTED THAT WE HAD BEEN BOUGHT, AND WERE THEN TO BE SOLD'[1]

Britain's Pandora Press occupies a liminal position in the history of feminist publishing. Its foundation was made possible by the prior existence of Virago Press and The Women's Press, as these houses' championing of the still novel concept of feminist publishing and their experimentation with reprint fiction demonstrated the existence of a market that received publishing wisdom had up until that point denied. Pandora, officially established within the (then) privately owned academic trade publisher Routledge & Kegan Paul (RKP) in 1981, has particular historical significance in that it marks the point at which mainstream British publishing first acknowledged the potential profitability of feminist titles and began a concerted campaign upon what had previously been a specialist and somewhat fringe market. Pandora emerged out of RKP's first tentative forays into women's studies publishing in the late 1970s with a feminist studies list overseen by former RKP publicity and editorial assistant, Philippa Brewster (1999; 2003). With the success of Dale Spender's

Man Made Language (1980), a socio-linguistic analysis of gender power as manifested within everyday speech, it was apparent to RKP's directors that a market existed for feminist-focused academic texts, and that the titles would gain greater market visibility if published under a separate imprint. Resistance to pushing such titles on the part of RKP's conservative sale representatives indirectly assisted Brewster and Spender in lobbying to establish a specifically feminist imprint – to be allocated its own sales force – as they were able to argue that unsympathetic sales staff were effectively inhibiting RKP's return on its publishing investment. According to Spender, this tactic in the event proved 'a stroke of genius on our part because it allowed Routledge to dissociate itself ... from those mad women and their women studies' (2003).[2] Pandora's origins within a long-established, scholarly, non-fiction house such as Routledge distinguish the press from the first and most academically orientated of US women's presses, The Feminist Press. For Pandora, as an imprint of a commercial publisher, relied entirely upon sales to fund its operations, especially in a publishing environment increasingly under pressure from economic rationalism and industry consolidation. Florence Howe's Feminist Press had, on the other hand, early established its identity as a not-for-profit operation, and thus qualified for tax-free status and grant endowments – quasi-public sector benefits which provided some cushioning from marketplace fluctuations (Collins, 1975: 102; Frank, 1982: 90).

Brewster rightly discerned that Virago and The Women's Press lacked the necessary seed capital and professional networks to capture the burgeoning market for academic women's studies in more than a haphazard and serendipitous way. Hence Pandora's profile was carefully crafted as a generalist, feminist, non-fiction house positioning itself between the tertiary education market and that mythical beast of British trade publishing – the intelligent lay reader. In selecting the name 'Pandora', the press was in accord with a then prevalent fashion for reprogramming female figures from classical mythology with feminist associations – a predilection obliquely satirised by Fay Weldon in dubbing her fictionalised, ersatz Virago publisher 'Medusa'. Pandora was, moreover, a figure particularly resonant with connotations of forbidden and dangerous knowledge ready to be unleashed upon an unsuspecting world, though – as (then) Fawcett librarian David Doughan suggested to the imprint's founders – in opening her casket, Pandora had also released hope into the world (Brewster, 2003; Spender, 2003). It proved a highly marketable image, which the press's proposed alternative name – Pleiades Press – could not hope to equal. Pandora won out as she was 'a little more gutsy, daring to open the box in the first place', as former Pandora employee Harriet Griffey recalled some years later. Besides, Griffey adds with a decidedly non-mythological pragmatism, Pandora 'worked better as a logo' (1998b: 8).

Constituting Pandora under the aegis of prominent trade publisher RKP undoubtedly offered the advantages of investment capital, extensive warehousing and distribution infrastructure, along with an established publishing profile in Anglophone universities worldwide. But the obverse of this arrangement was that Pandora was at no point an independent enterprise along the lines of mid-period Virago, or even a company with the (periodically) hands-off management of Namara in relation to The Women's Press. Working for a wholly owned list, Pandora's staff were employees of RKP and thus subject to the firm's managerial decisions on the commercial viability of a specialist feminist list. Throughout the second half of the 1980s this structural vulnerability in Pandora's operations manifested itself in almost biannual ownership changes as Pandora was sold off, acquired and stripped off for resale in the tumultuous climate generated by global stockmarkets' new-found interest in book publishing. RKP, including Pandora, was bought by Associated Book Publishers (ABP) for £4.5m in March 1985 in an attempt to create viable economies of scale in the industry (*Bookseller*, 1985b: 1255). In June 1987 Pandora was once again absorbed as ABP was in turn taken over by Canadian-based multinational International Thomson Publishing (ITP) at a cost of £210m, with ITP stripping off the ABP general list and restructuring the company as a legal, professional and scholarly publisher (*Bookseller*, 1987: 2301). Pandora's management faced a further wave of rationalisation in February 1988 when ITP, disappointed with Pandora's profit contribution and its fit within the firm, sold the list on to Unwin Hyman, a house hungry for a feminist list to match the women's studies imprints by that time becoming de rigueur among British publishers (*Bookseller*, 1988: 242; Menkes, 1988: 16; Willis, 1988: n.p.). Brewster notes that Pandora could have bought itself out at the time of the Unwin Hyman sale, but consciously chose to retain the resource backing of a major publisher (2003). Nevertheless, in a move symbolic for the fate of academic feminist publishing as a whole, in little over two years Pandora was again sold on to Rupert Murdoch's recently merged book publishing group, HarperCollins, a subsidiary of the global News

Corporation media conglomerate and a market pioneer in recalibrating book publishing for maximum profit generation. Second-wave feminists, aghast that the radical vision of women-controlled publishing had dwindled to a mere 'milk cow for Mr. Murdoch's other concerns', widely lamented the sale as a 'disaster' and 'the worst of bad news' (Hennegan, 1992: 6; Sullivan, 1998: 17; Spender, 2003).

Given the yawning ideological chasm between Pandora's editorial politics and the managerial ethos of News Corporation – a company with 'no commitment to the product, only to the performance' – it is unsurprising that Pandora's seven-year stint within HarperCollins was characterised by a climate of pervasive distrust and by fractious working relations (Spender, 2003). In commercial as much as political terms, Pandora's fit within the publishing conglomerate appears ill-considered. Pandora had emerged from the stable of RKP and was thus no commercially inexperienced part-time feminist collective. But the single-minded intensity with which HarperCollins pursued profit above all other considerations could not but represent an uncomfortable alignment for any press espousing an oppositional politics, albeit by this time increasingly an oppositional *cultural* politics. Brewster recalls former HarperCollins CEO Eddie Bell – long a Murdoch favourite for his track record in weaning publishing from its gentlemen's profession affectations to confront modern commercial realities – informing her that Pandora was '"going to lay golden eggs for us"' (Hennegan, 1992: 5). Part of Pandora's envisaged utility to HarperCollins appears to have been as a holding imprint into which the company could feed 'feminist titles' culled from other lists acquired in its formative buying spree, and there were long-running attempts to merge the imprint with HarperCollins' mind/body/spirit list (*Bookseller*, 1990a: 74; Brewster, 2003). The strategy helps to explain the curious melange of avowedly 'feminist' and more ambiguously couched 'women's' titles bearing the Pandora imprint produced during the period. The liberal feminist associations of titles such as Scarlett McGuire's *Best Companies for Women: Britain's Top Employers* (1992) sit uncomfortably with previous Pandora publications that broadcast their affiliation with radical and socialist limbs of the women's movement, such as Hilda Scott's *Working Your Way to the Bottom: The Feminization of Poverty* (1984), the Cambridge Women's Peace Collective's *My Country is the Whole World* (1984) and Gabrielle Palmer's *The Politics of Breastfeeding* (1988). Pandora's list during the period manifests in microcosm the gradual slippage from activist feminism to female-focused cultural politics, which characterised

Western feminism as a whole during the course of the 1980s and 1990s. Responding to the same socio-political developments, Virago opted to invoke the insurgent cachet of house authors Angela Carter and Margaret Atwood to rebrand itself for the ethical consumerist agenda of the 1990s. Pandora on the other hand – saddled with the Murdoch drive towards consumer-driven, lowest-common-denominator populism – faced an uphill struggle to assure audiences of its radical credentials.

By the time the effects of the early 1990s recession were being registered in the book industry, News Corporation faced a pressing need to reduce its immense corporate debt. This resulted in the sale of numerous media assets, among them the increasingly disenchanted Pandora, which was publicly declared for sale in March 1991 (Birch, 1991: 39; Jones, 1991b: 16). Scenting an opportunity to recast the press according to her own vision of an independent 'strong feminist publisher', Brewster negotiated strenuously during the following six months to raise sufficient capital from both movement and industry figures to mount a management buyout (*Bookseller*, 1991a: 852; *Bookseller*, 1991b: 829; Hennegan, 1992: 5). Bell publicly lent support to the idea, insisting in the trade press that Pandora's sale was prompted solely by its generalist list 'finding itself in competition with our other imprints' (*Bookseller*, 1991b: 829). Brewster had alerted HarperCollins to such a risk of intra-firm competition at the time of the original purchase, but the fact ostensibly only came to the notice of senior management in the straightened environment of a publishing recession (Jones, 1991b: 16; Brewster, 2003). Despite 'enormous goodwill' from industry colleagues and sympathetic feminists, Brewster's buyout bid eventually failed, due not to insufficient purchasing capital but rather to a lack of funds to subsidise daily operating costs (*Bookseller*, 1991b: 829). Upon announcement of the buyout plan's demise, Brewster and commissioning editor Candida Lacey were made redundant by HarperCollins, although they were subsequently invited to join (then) Random Century imprint Jonathan Cape, along with a handful of loyal authors (*Bookseller*, 1991b: 829; Woddis, 1992: 26). Lacking a competitive bidder, Pandora remained within HarperCollins until its January 1998 sale to north London independent Rivers Oram Press, but it presented a politically anaemic profile largely bled of oppositional bite (Griffey, 1998a: 5). HarperCollins' new Pandora director Eileen Campbell stated in 1992 that Pandora would continue 'publishing books by women for a wide range of women in the 1990s, which enables [sic] them to be better informed and make appropriate choices' (Hennegan, 1992: 5). The telling shift from publishing radicalising treatises to publishing consumables for the professional women of market-rationalised Tory Britain undoubtedly echoes the general tenor of the times. It highlights with particular starkness the contradictions between leftist politics and market consumerism, which had from the beginning been implicit in the feminist publishing project.

Pandora Lists

The most high profile of authorial defectors from Pandora in the wake of its sale to HarperCollins was celebrated novelist Jeanette Winterson. Allowing that 'in an increasingly corporate world it's getting harder and harder to make an ethical decision, either about the brand of baked beans you buy or the House with which you publish', Winterson nevertheless felt unable to remain in the Murdoch stable, and instead contracted with Jonathan Cape for UK and Commonwealth hardback rights, and with Random House's Vintage imprint for paperback rights (Winterson, 1991 [1985]: xv). There is irony in the fact that such discussion of Pandora as does occur in the contemporary press commonly frames the publisher as the discoverer of Winterson, now among the top echelon of critically and commercially successful literary authors (Gerrard, 1994: 7; Field, 1995: 38–9). Pandora's primary focus on non-fiction and academic markets more commonly functioned to relegate contemporary women's fiction to a secondary place on its lists. This is evinced by the fact that RKP's editorial board initially declined to issue Winterson's groundbreaking first novel *Oranges Are Not the Only Fruit* in hardback, limiting the firm's financial commitment to a paperback edition released with little fanfare in March 1985 (Winterson, 1991 [1985]: xii).[3] Its subsequent word-of-mouth success culminated in *Oranges* being awarded the Whitbread First Novel Award in 1985, and being adapted as an acclaimed BBC TV mini series in 1990, thus launching Winterson's writing career and amply justifying her dedication of *Oranges* to Brewster, 'who was the beginning' (1991: v).

More representative of Pandora's publishing activity were generalist non-fiction titles, which might be expected to cross over from scholarly or undergraduate audiences to a general readership seeking information about a specific issue, but likely to be alienated by footnote-laden academic monographs. In part, this focus on readable feminist scholarship signified a tacit acknowledgement by Pandora that Virago had come to dominate the market for early twentieth-century women's reprint fiction and politics, and that The Women's Press had become synonymous in the public mind with multiethnic and developing-world women's writing (Brewster, 2003). Pandora was best able to play to its institutional and editorial strengths by embarking on larger non-fiction projects, involving lengthy publishing lead-times, an often delayed return on investment, and the cachet for authors of publishing with a long-established educational publishing house – all of which RKP was able to offer the fledgling imprint.

At the time of its first branded list in 1983, Pandora's market profile was still being fine-tuned. What strikes a contemporary reader perusing Pandora's first titles is how evidently the firm was still testing the waters of the feminist publishing marketplace: its Elizabeth Gaskell *Four Short Stories* (1983) strongly echoes Virago's reprints, or perhaps The Women's Press's early reissues of Elizabeth Barrett Browning and Kate Chopin, themselves imitations of Virago titles; Michelene Wandor's anthology *On Gender and Writing* (1983) and Dale Spender's *There's Always Been a Women's Movement This Century* (1983a) are perceptibly designed to appeal to students of the growing number of university women's studies courses in literature and history; while Deirdre Beddoe's *Discovering Women's History: A Practical Manual* (1983), the first title in the Pandora Handbooks series, more obviously hedges its bets between professional historians and the broader market for amateur genealogy and local history tinged with feminist inflection. Where Pandora perceptibly hit its stride was with the Mothers of the Novel series of eighteenth- and early nineteenth-century women's fiction reprints published from 1986 onwards, which took their selection cues from Dale Spender's Pandora-published critical monograph *Mothers of the Novel* (1986), and their market appeal from introductions penned by recognised contemporary writers such as Jeanette Winterson, Margaret Drabble and Fay Weldon.[4] Pandora was imitating the reissuing of out-of-copyright women's classics pioneered in Britain by Virago, which in turn had imitated the publishing strategy of The Feminist Press, but covering an earlier historical period than either press had yet trialled. Attempts by Pandora to create still further canons of women's writing followed, specifically the Australian Women Writers: The Literary Heritage series, also overseen by Spender, which reissued of out-of-print nineteenth-century novels by Australian women writers in a project timed to coincide with Australia's 1988 bicentennial celebrations. Counterbalancing such reprint fiction offerings were Britain's earliest list in feminist cultural and media studies (an area that was to witness substantial growth during the 1980s and early 1990s, especially for the newly abbreviated Routledge), a sustained commitment to publishing around lesbian issues (competing with local radical and lesbian presses Sheba Feminist Publishers and Onlywomen Press for the newly detected lesbian-feminist market), and a popular crime fiction list (publishing original works alongside titles acquired under rights deals from US lesbian pulp publisher, Naiad Press).

Yet, while publishing themes emerge from across the Pandora list, the early sense of hedged bets remains palpable. In part this reflects Brewster's industry experience at balancing titles on a multifaceted list, using the more saleable books to cross-subsidise less immediately commercial projects. But the sense of tentativeness surely also derives from the climate in which Pandora reluctantly found itself operating: buffeted from corporation to conglomerate against a background of publishing recession and record redundancies, Pandora had in addition to confront the feminist book market's splintering into myriad sub-specialities by the mid-1980s (*Bookseller*, 1991a: 851–3). Attempting to assemble a constituency of readers from among this ever-changing politico-cultural kaleidoscope, Pandora was both victim of and catalyst for the feminist publishing sector's increasing fragmentation. *stage*

ACADEMIC FEMINIST PUBLISHING WITHIN CONGLOMERATES: 'ANY SELF-RESPECTING PUBLISHING HOUSE NOW HAS A WOMEN'S LIST'[5]

The body of academic work specifically concerning itself with feminist publishing is to date negligible. Yet within this delimited field, and within the wider discourse of broadsheet literary pages and book industry periodicals, it has become almost truistic to observe that an explosion of publishing around feminism and women's studies has occurred since the early 1980s (Jopson, 1986: 34; Jay, 1993: 70; Hancock, 1994: 20; Brown, 1998: 9; Sullivan, 1998: 17; Sen and Bhowmik, 2002: 187). A quick glance at the Spring and Autumn Books catalogues issued biannually by book trade periodicals such as *Publishers Weekly* (US), the *Bookseller* (UK) or *Australian Bookseller and Publisher* over the course of the last two decades reinforces the suspicion that academic publishing may well be perpetually in crisis, but that every crisis has its silver lining. That a literary-political ecosystem of readers, bookshops, literary magazines, scholarly journals and academic conferences exists to supply and support such publishing endeavours is overwhelmingly attributable to the activism and entrepreneurial energies of the second-wave women's movement. But feminist presses' frequent commercial naivety in the context of increasingly market-driven economies, coupled with a never fully resolved and rarely articulated disquiet over the marketing of feminism (analysed at length in the following chapter) ensured that the market unearthed by feminist publishers was open to colonisation by mainstream presses. Such trade publishers were only too eager to follow up indications of demand with corporate-produced supply. Yet the mainstreaming of the feminist market is not merely the doom-and-gloom scenario of cynical co-optation and commercial exploitation too often oversimplified in the movement's own press (Ravenscroft, 1989: 6–7; Douglas, 2000: 1). Mainstream imitation and modulation of feminist publishing indirectly saluted the achievements of the originating movement, and through professional publishing practices was able to bypass many of the organisational failings that had earlier inhibited popularisation of movement thought (Jones, J., 1992: 178; Naher, 1994). Politically worthy brand loyalty could not expect to outflank alluring production values and efficient distribution for ever; Ellen Mizzell observed in 1992, as the boom years of independent feminist publishing showed incontrovertible signs of waning, that 'no one buys a book any more simply because it has a green cover or a dinky little iron on the spine' (1992b: 36). Even loyal industry proponents were forced to concede by the early 1990s that 'feminist publishing isn't what it used to be' (1992b: 36).

Within the specialised sphere of academic publishing, the impact of feminist ideas on traditional disciplines tended to register in three distinct phases, though their exact sequence was often obscured by overlap and time lags. Firstly, a spate of books mounted a feminist critique of a discipline's reigning canons and sacred truths, upbraiding established disciplines for their gender blindness and obliviousness to the sexist assumptions underpinning their methodologies. Thereafter followed a second publishing wave centred upon reclaiming a given discipline's 'lost' female pioneers, precisely mirroring the shift in literary studies from critiques of patriarchal literature such as Simone de Beauvoir's *The Second Sex* (1953) and Kate Millett's *Sexual Politics* (1972) to feminist publishers' reprint libraries of women's classics. Finally, and particularly by the late 1980s once feminist ideas had thoroughly percolated through scholarly agendas, there emerged a movement of specifically theoretical disciplinary self-reflection. This third wave of academic works tended to reject earlier 'women and' models of canonical reform as flawed by their essentially complementary ethos, and strove instead to reconfigure disciplines root and branch by insisting upon female experience as a central analytical, methodological and theoretical concern.

During this process of exciting intellectual ferment, influential academic feminist work increasingly issued from multinational humanities-focused publishers such as Routledge, Sage, Blackwell and the larger university presses, which successfully grafted the oppositional chic of newly post-modern-inflected cultural politics with glossy cover designs, quality paper and eye-catching point-of-sale paraphernalia well beyond the budgets of most feminist publishers. Such new-found diversity and prominence of feminist-informed publishing was not, however, without its associated costs. The following discussion broadens its focus to consider mainstream academic publishing's reconstitution of feminism as a saleable commodity, analysing the phenomenon in light of both cultural and political concerns. It explores in particular the ramifications of this industry shift in terms of editorial independence, press 'authenticity' and publishing practice – existing conundrums within the feminist publishing sector rendered newly problematic by feminism's subsumption within mainstream publishing.

Mainstreaming Feminist Scholarship

In many ways, the existence of mainstream publishers' catalogues in women's studies or (increasingly) gender studies boasting hundreds of backlist and new season titles would appear the spectacular culmination of second-wave feminism's campaign for curricular reform. Women's studies' founding tenet that the concerns of women should be central to the academic study of humanity would appear irrefutably fulfilled by evidence such as Routledge's recent catalogue offering hundreds of titles in the field, all available internationally, and many in revised and updated editions. Yet assessing the achievement of the feminist publishing project has always hinged upon the exact criteria used to evaluate such success: is it best evidenced by the number and health of feminist houses; the quantity and prominence of feminist-authored titles across the publishing spectrum; or by the penetration of feminist ideas into mainstream culture? The question is a subset of an encompassing debate between separatist and mainstream elements within second-wave feminism as a whole, which conditions not only the publishing nodes of Darnton's communications circuit (or a feminist-inflected recon-struction thereof), but the entire literary community from the point of production through distribution to readerly consumption. Aspects of this pervasive debate are shot through any appraisal of gender and materialist literary production: witness Virago's previously noted inability in its early phases to secure paperback reviews in British broadsheets; in pleas for feminist book buyers not to purchase their titles at discount from Internet retailer Amazon.com but to remain loyal to feminist bookstores (Douglas, 2000: 1); in independent women's publishers' request for academics to set feminist-produced texts on reading lists and thus demonstrate their support with more than empty rhetoric (Hawthorne, 2001: 11). These shifting sands of the separatist/mainstream argument, and its many permutations and internal subtleties, are explored in detail in this volume's subsequent chapters, which investigate radical and mainstream feminist book-making respectively, testing each side's claim to the feminist high ground.

Determining the exact criteria by which to measure feminist publishing's achievement is complicated still further by a stream of thought within the movement that paradoxically equates success with self-extinction. The Feminist Press, proudly billing itself as 'the oldest women's press in the [US] nation', nevertheless has always conceived of its work as essentially corrective, filling the gaps left by mainstream publishers until they spied the obvious error of their ways. As Florence Howe has frequently reiterated, 'I thought of this press [in 1970] as something that would last a year or two, and all the publishers in the world would realise they were ignoring women and there'd be no need for us' (Howe quoted in *Chronicle of Higher Education*, 1999: A26). In essence, this is a feminist publishing credo structured around self-engineered redundancy: success is measured by publisher imitation; market penetration by commercial eclipse. Admittedly there is an element of disingenuousness to press founder Florence Howe's oft-repeated sentiments along these lines: to restate the envisaged superfluity of one's press when celebrating a tenth, or even thirtieth, anniversary is surely to speak with one's tongue just a little in cheek.[6] But the remarks are representative in highlighting a dilemma confronted by all oppositional cultural movements that achieve mainstream visibility: does success reside in the political 'purity' and independence of a cultural producer; in the broad-scale public impact of its ideas or in a liminal position at the margins of the cultural mainstream, where pushing the artistic envelope constitutes a way to balance – if not reconcile – political and practical commitments?

Production and Distribution Contexts

A key advantage of feminist scholarship's move into mainstream academic publishing since the early 1980s has been the sheltering infrastructure provided by mainstream publishers in an era of rapid industry consolidation and escalating costs. While rates of participation in Western higher education soared as the post-World War Two baby boom demographic moved into the university sector during the 1960s and 1970s, the individual spending power of students gradually declined in real terms over subsequent decades as government grants were frozen, and library spending across Western economies suffered stringent cuts in line with the newly embraced user-pays orthodoxies of economic rationalism (Croom, 1993: 135–8). In a countervailing trend, 'complete package' undergraduate textbooks increased both in scope and price, often spawning costly additional teaching and learning tools such as workbooks, colour transparencies, cassettes, CDs and websites. One result of this particular constellation of trends was that the financial outlay for publishers' commissioning and development of undergraduate textbooks grew exponentially during the 1980s and 1990s. If institutional adoptions could be secured, especially in the vast US undergraduate college market, publishers could be guaranteed attractive and reliable annual revenues (Mallis, 1982: 39). But the steadily entrenched pattern of high initial outlay and delayed return focused intense pressure on curriculum-setting academics as publishers' point of entry to the college market – a costly courtship based on assiduously cultivated publisher–academic relations, co-ordinated networks of university sales representatives and glossy inspection materials (Croom, 1993: 139). All of these developments absorbed publishers' working capital at a rate that cash-strapped feminist presses could ill afford to replicate (Griffin and Wilson, 1982: 80). The sense of being in competition with a vastly more powerful and better resourced academic publishing sector underpins feminist publishers' insistence that committed academics contemplate the broader ideological implications of their textbook choices. Susan Hawthorne of Melbourne's Spinifex Press states:

> Having our books set on courses in schools and universities can make a major difference. If course instructors have to decide between a Spinifex book and a book published by a large university or multinational company, we hope they'll choose the Spinifex book, as it will make a difference to us. (2001: 11)

Co·publishing

Other feminist publishers have sought to breach the seemingly impregnable ramparts of the multinational publisher–university coalition by entering into co-publishing and licensing agreements with mainstream publishers. The Feminist Press piggybacked on US college market leader McGraw-Hill's infrastructural advantages during the late 1970s to gain entrée for its twelve-volume Women's Lives, Women's Work series into mainstream US secondary schools (Dunning, 1980: 69; Howe, 2000b: 15). The press similarly sought to benefit from the specialist market knowledge of Indiana University Press in co-publishing Mary R. Mahl and Helene Koon's limited-run academic monograph *The Female Spectator: English Women Writers Before 1800* (1977) (Frank, 1982: 92). The strategy, for all its pragmatic cost-sharing, nevertheless risks mirroring in microcosm multinational co-optation of feminist endeavour, with the colophon of the feminist publisher merely politically rubberstamping the profit-making of a larger – and still politically uncommitted – commercial entity.

Imprint Identity

The phenomenon of imprint identity in book publishing operates as a kind of literary co-operative: each title on the list benefits from the brand associations of the umbrella imprint, but each title must equally contribute to sustaining the imprint's brand integrity if all titles are to gain by association. The concept of transferable brand prestige was artfully manipulated by feminist houses such as Virago to imbue relatively unknown writers with the critical acclaim and political credibility of an Atwood, Carter or Barker through list proximity. In a countervailing manifestation of list identity, however, feminist academics may derive increased professional prestige, and thus promotional prospects and job security, through bypassing the oppositional cachet of feminist houses to publish instead with an established educational publisher. In so far as such a manoeuvre contributes to the visibility and academic respectability of women's studies, it could be construed as a strategic gesture, one cognisant of the politics of academic publishing and willing to play them in the interests of the discipline as a whole. However, given the tensions between liberal-feminist careerism and collective-minded activism present at the origins of second-wave feminism, such a manoeuvre more commonly ignites ideological differences long simmering beneath the surface of feminist publishing. By extension it moreover invokes the scaffolding of separatist-mainstream contestation that encompasses the field.

A site at which these individualist versus collectivist tensions ha particularly manifested themselves in recent years is the intersection of publishing politics with debates around international development. As Western feminisms sought, during the late 1980s and early 1990s, to buttress their claims to serious academic consideration by investing heavily in post-modern and post-structuralist 'high' theory, developing-world feminist publishers lamented what they perceived as a self-interested cult of feminist theory superstars maintained at the cost of addressing real world concerns of the majority of women, especially around struggles for reproductive rights, health, education and freedom from violence and sexual exploitation (Aftab, 2002: 155). Urvashi Butalia, founder of India's Kali for Women press and a key proponent of developing-world women's publishing, implies that feminist academics thirsting for mainstream Western publishing imprimatur risk forgetting the founding principle of the feminist press movement – that publishing is an inherently political act:

> No sooner had feminist publishers created a market, ... the large, mainstream houses – ever ready to seize on a new opportunity – moved in. With them came all the things women writers, hitherto cast into the shade, had been looking for: stability, acceptability, a mythical objectivity, a presence alongside other, more 'respected' writers, financial security, a wider reach, and so on. (2000: 1710)

Similar accusations of author poaching by mainstream houses have long constituted a bone of contention in the publishing industry as a whole, and in feminist publishing circles in particular (Clardy, 1986: 7–8). Yet they achieved prominence against the background of an international marketplace intent upon maintaining developing nations as captive book markets through buttressing territorial copyright agreements, but less interested in two-way exchange with the specific intellectual concerns of 'periphery' academics (Menon, 2001: 177; Sen and Bhowmik, 2002: 186). The distinction between theoretical engagement on one hand, and demonstrably improved standards of living on the other, has often been unduly dichotomised in resultant debates among feminists. But, at the same time, developing-world critics are undoubtedly correct in discerning a multinational publisher preference for internationally saleable macro-level theorising over nation-specific – and often also language-specific – micro-level empirical analysis (Sen and Bhowmik, 2002: 188). An uneasy suspicion has arisen among developing-world scholars that,

ic theory might scrupulously posit all feminisms as
:ional publishers clearly regard some as more equal

ᴅ~~ᴊᴀᴅ~~ ... AGES OF MULTINATIONAL ACADEMIC FEMINIST
PUBLISHING: 'THE COMMODIFICATION OF TRANSGRESSION'[7]

The fate of Pandora Press during much of the 1990s as it was steadily
ingested into the Murdoch maw is emblematic for feminist
publishing's troubled experience with the multinational publishing
sector. Independent feminist publishers have long emphasised the
inevitable contradictions implicit in working for political change
from within multinational corporations; while good books
undoubtedly do emerge from such collaborations, the commitment
of the owning firm is always primarily commercial rather than political
in motivation. Should the feminist imprint fail to generate sufficient
profit for the owning corporation, it will be unceremoniously sold
on. Rumours in the book trade press at the height of the feminist
publishing boom to the effect that HarperCollins was 'looking for a
women's imprint' hint at the commercial opportunism driving such
corporate acquisitions (*Bookseller*, 1990b: 5). Once the 'hot topic' of
feminist publishing was deemed by industry analysts to have cooled,
managerial executives found feminist titles no longer added
oppositional lustre to the HarperCollins list, but rather generated
inexpedient internal competition (Ehrlich, 1973: 268).

As a result of second-wave feminism's origins in the neo-Marxist-
influenced student and anti-war politics of the late 1960s and early
1970s, vigorous critique of mainstream publisher profiteering from
the newly lucrative 'woman book industry' developed early in
movement writings (Ehrlich, 1973: 268; Arnold, 1976: 18–26; Griffin
and Wilson, 1982: 83–4). Ironically, it was less broad-scale public
rejection of independent feminist publishing than its enthusiastic
embrace that stumped the movement's intelligentsia. For second-
wave feminism lacked a sufficiently nuanced critique of capitalism's
interface with leftist cultural politics to explain mainstream
enthusiasm for feminist books in a climate of general economic
conservatism, other than to disparage such developments as the
'exploitation' or 'selling out' of movement ideals. It is this debate
over the cultural and commercial 'selling' of feminism – alluded to
earlier in relation to Virago's 1997 relaunch – which has yet to be
adequately theorised by scholars of feminist publishing and the

women in print movement. It is a question which goes to the heart of capitalism's astonishing ability to appropriate and commodify seemingly oppositional ideas in order to package and sell them back to the same subcultural groups from which they originally emerged. US literary commentator Ted Solotaroff, addressing the related issue of the multicultural arts industry, adroitly encapsulates this oxymoronic twist to contemporary cultural politics:

> One of the ironic paradoxes of capitalist triumphalism is that it fosters as a market what it seeks to curb or neutralize as politics. The most glaring example is rap music, but one sees multiculturalism driving educational and academic publishing and increasing[ly] literary publishing, as well as the theater. (1995: 149)

The resultant dilemma for the left, and for feminist publishing in particular, is how to rationalise a persistent consumer thirst for ideas increasingly marginalised in mainstream political life. The problematic result of feminist publishing's attempt to operate within such contradiction is that a movement at root suspicious of market capitalism has come to rely on sales figures as a barometer of its cultural health and social relevance. Second-wave feminism had, in foundational texts such as Friedan's *The Feminine Mystique* (1963) and Greer's *The Female Eunuch* (1970), been searingly critical of the commodification of women, especially of the substitution of housewifely consumerism for genuine female agency, which it saw as perpetuating the Western world's restrictive cult of femininity. But this same movement largely failed to anticipate how successfully the women's movement could commodify its ideas or – as has become increasingly apparent in the academic publishing sector – how lucratively those ideas could be commodified by others on its behalf.

An important qualification to register is that such debates over the appropriate relationship of the women's movement to capitalism divided not only feminist publishers from mainstream presses, but divided feminist houses themselves. Carmen Callil of Virago Press, for example, has consistently emphasised a view of commercial success as itself a feminist principle, and presses established in the wake of the collapse and failure of the first wave of radical presses, such as Spinifex Press (established in 1991), have reiterated their publishing professionalism as the key to their expansion and ability to continue producing politically engaged books (Brown, 1998: 11; Hawthorne, 2001: 10). Thus, trenchant anti-capitalism was never as all-pervasive a principle of second-wave politics as a retrospective reading of documents from the era might initially suggest; accusations of bourgeois liberal individualism were lobbed at women within feminist publishing houses as freely as they were targeted at female academics seeking to publish with mainstream conglomerates.

One effect of uncertainty over how to measure feminist publishing's achievement – whether according to movement or marketplace criteria – placed feminist editors under particular pressure around the problematic issue of list dilution. For multinational houses eager to jump on the bandwagon of feminist publishing, a feminist imprint frequently served as a convenient means to collate women-focused titles from multiple house lists and to brand them with a specious political unity. Just as feminist imprints acquired by multinational houses may have bestselling titles transferred out of their lists without editorial or authorial consent, multinational houses frequently transferred 'women's' titles *into* feminist imprints, with little regard for the academic niceties of a given text's gender politics. Such manoeuvres could be engineered without necessarily securing the acquiescence of a feminist imprint's publishing director. Consolidation of the book industry during the second half of the 1980s resulted in an increasing number of acquisition and commissioning decisions being taken by publishing boards, in which editorial staff might be outvoted by sales, marketing and production directors. Moreover, the increasing trend towards constituting each imprint (or even each title) as its own cost centre, in an attempt to entrench greater fiscal responsibility at editorial level, meant that feminist commissioning editors were not always at liberty to reject commercially reliable books because of qualms over their political value (Schiffrin, 2001: 91). In this light, it is easier to explain the appearance on Pandora's post-1990 list of titles such as Angela Phillips' *The Trouble with Boys* (1993), which seem to speak more to fears of youth delinquency stirred by the conservative fear-mongering of Murdoch-owned tabloids than to Pandora's original feminist publishing ethos. By contrast, publisher Liz Fidlon's foregrounding of gender politics at the time of Rivers Oram's purchase of Pandora from HarperCollins implies a return to political basics after a period of damaging flirtation with commercial expediency:

> The fit of the authors and subjects made Pandora a natural acquisition for us. It publishes non-fiction works by women that are accessible, original and at the cutting edge, and we plan to

strengthen and extend its list. Books like Gabrielle Palmer's *The Politics of Breastfeeding*, for example, remain important and need to stay in print. (quoted in Griffey, 1998a: 5)

Its title redolent of an earlier, avowedly radical phase of political activism, *The Politics of Breastfeeding* here signifies a return to the original independent ethos of feminist publishing, a movement buffeted and bruised from its fraught attempts to reconcile political commitment with multinational profit motive.

Standardisation of Book Publishing Processes

Debates over feminist publishing's subsumption within the mainstream book industry tend to focus upon comparative analyses of book content, attempting to calibrate changes in list foci and direction with changes in ownership. While such analysis remains relevant, it has the unintended effect of overshadowing changes to the publishing process itself, a context as charged with political implications and theoretical contest as is publishing's more easily documented textual output.

Market leading academic publishers manage to produce the vast number of backlist and frontlist titles proffered in their catalogues by standardising the publishing process so that it operates with maximum commercial efficiency. To this end, publishers' websites advise would-be authors to submit book proposals in standardised format and, upon arrival at the firm, commissioned manuscripts enter into an intricately co-ordinated process of commissioning editor review, line-editing, pre-publicity copy-writing, production scheduling, advance marketing preparation, briefing of jacket designers, notification of sales representatives, printing, binding, warehousing and shipment. Because of the overwhelming industry targeting of academics as arbiters of required course reading, the whole process must be synchronised with the (usually northern hemisphere) academic year, and post-publication feedback from academics is keenly solicited via requests for promotional blurbs, reports on inspection copies, and through the publishers' 'calling' system of academic sales reps. In terms of rationalising a notoriously unpredictable business, academic publishers have some advantages over houses with an exclusively trade focus. Textbooks that have achieved broad-scale adoptions in secondary and tertiary markets yield relatively reliable annual sales, and can be predictably shepherded through subsequent updates and editions to preserve academic publishers' market share from the predatory encroachments of second-hand book traders (Croom, 1993: 140).

In protest at the multinational publishers' assembly-line model of book production, second-wave feminists advocated a publishing process in which authors were asked not to feed their manuscripts into a corporate machine, with the finished book spat out the other end, but were instead centrally involved in a collaborative, consultative process. In this commitment to re-envisaging book production processes, feminist publishers were strongly influenced by 1960s experiments in co-operative and communal organising, which posited reform of means as much as of ends as a central political principle; as publisher and book history researcher Louise Poland observes, 'arguably, a refusal to separate the process from the output is central to feminist publishing' (2001: 133). A particular hallmark of second-wave feminist publishing was an espoused commitment to non- (or, at a minimum, less-) hierarchical modes of organising, collaboration on all stages of book production, skills sharing among staff and authors, training of both press workers and local communities, and an encompassing environment of vigorous debate and self-criticism about all aspects of press activity (*Co-operator*, 1985: 9–10; Jones, J., 1992: 175–6). Interestingly, allegiance to such ideas emerges almost as often from non-collective presses as from the collectives that tended to constitute the second-wave's preferred organisational model (see Chapter 4). Ailbhe Smyth of Ireland's Attic Press, a non-collectivist feminist publisher, which since 1997 has operated as an imprint of Cork University Press, distinguished Attic's *modus operandi* from multi-nationals on the basis of the 'personal relationship between the press and authors. We're not a musical chairs situation, with editors coming and going' (Barbato, 1990: 34; cf. Battles, 1998). The Women's Press (UK), which, as events of 1991 amply demonstrated, was in no sense co-operatively owned nor a collective, nevertheless repeatedly broadcast its commitment to dismantling the editor–author hierarchies of traditional 'gentlemen's' publishing:

> We want to involve our authors as much as possible in the actual process of the production of their work, breaking down the usual power relationships of the publishing world. We try to combine a constantly evaluated political perspective with extremely high 'professional' standards. We do feel a commitment to our authors as writers with long careers; i.e. we are not interested in a single book as a single 'product'. (Dowrick quoted in Frank, 1982: 112)

The cost of positioning a feminist press as a c(
publishing operation, writers' community and w(
centre was that others were liable to take the pr
(Nicholson, 1982: 78). The unceasing daily deman..
editing, marketing, publicising, distributing and accounting for a
small press threatened exhaustion and burnout in most individuals
(Bereano, 2001: 20). In combination with the requirement to engage
in parallel processes of ongoing political critique and constant
ideological self-scrutiny, such agendas resulted in large numbers of
feminist enterprises folding under the daily grind of living out
collectivist ideals.[8] This already difficult situation was further
compounded by feminist presses' shouldering of a double-load in
the context of economic recession and cuts to public funding (Lynch,
1998: 41–3). Joyce Nicholson, a member of publishing, distribution
and bookclub operation Sisters Publishing, active in Melbourne during
the early 1980s, outlines how the impossible burden of adhering to
a properly 'feminist' publishing process could result in a group of
talented and politically conscientious women straining relationships
both with outside business contacts *and* with the local women's
movement. Instead of granting unsolicited manuscripts the standard
industry response – a cursory reading of the first few pages followed
by a pro forma rejection letter – Sisters 'agonised over both the
manuscripts and the way we rejected them. We wanted to encourage
women to write. We felt we must say something constructive in our
rejections, and must not undermine the author's confidence'
(Nicholson, 1982: 78). The group's worthy feminist organising
principles had the debilitating effect of creating inordinate workloads,
staff exhaustion, a backlog of manuscripts and authors saddled with
long delays in receiving replies – 'thus compounding the crime of
our rejection' (Nicholson, 1982: 78; McPhee, 2001: 160–1).

Given the high costs and delays that collectivism imposes on
introducing feminist ideas to the marketplace, academic feminist
authors would appear justified in submitting their manuscripts to
multinational scholarly publishers. Such presses offer not only better
prospects of career advancement in the longer term, but the short-
term guarantee that the author's book will be adequately promoted
and will, still more crucially, in fact appear promptly in bookshops.
Nevertheless, multinational publisher processes exert their own toll
on feminist scholarship in the form of preferred subjects and formats
for research, an institutional pressure that has passed largely
unexamined in feminist scholarship to date. Multinational publishers

of ideas and debate to modern academe. In this sense, publishers of all hues influence the construction of academic disciplines both directly, through commissioning and acquisition decisions determining what is able to be read, cited, set on courses and stocked in bookshops and, indirectly, as publication track-records become ever more crucial in determining academic promotions and tenure. Feminist critics have long recognised the specifically political nature of the power to publish. From outside established academic power structures feminists have critiqued the pseudo-objectivity of scholarly institutions, which colluded to marginalise and silence feminist research (Spender, 1981). Having gained increasing admission (albeit in some cases grudgingly accorded) to those power structures, feminists retained the intellectual insight of the formerly excluded and remained admirably cognisant of the power they themselves wielded to mould the contours of academic scholarship. From the earliest stages of the second-wave publishing movement, practitioners such as Florence Howe recognised the intangible ideological effects of embodying ideas in material form: with the publication in 1972 of the first volume in The Feminist Press Reprint series, Rebecca Harding Davis's *Life in the Iron Mills* [1861], the press became 'aware that [the book's] publication was to change the ultimate purpose and achievement of The Feminist Press, for we were publishing symbiotically with the development of women's studies' (Howe, 2000b: 10). This is not to argue that feminist presses are entirely devoid of political myopia regarding the political implications of their own practice, as the vigorous internal debate over race and racism in feminist publishing demonstrates (see Chapter 2). But feminist press activity appears strikingly politically self-conscious when juxtaposed with the blissfully unproblematised self-conception of multinational publishers, who proudly proclaim their commitment to 'publishing the very best in Women's & Gender Studies'.[9] Multinational publishers have, through two decades of merger and acquisition, in addition come to control the bulk of academic journals, as well as an expanding array of Internet-based subject 'arenas', through which scholars and prospective students can glean information on suitable courses, relevant educational institutions, forthcoming conferences and – unsurprisingly – the firm's appropriately targeted textbooks and monographs.[10] Conflation of multinational publisher self-interest with disciplinary definition on such a scale makes the relative paucity of debate on the gender politics of academic publishing all the more striking. Or perhaps not. It is a brave – or professionally foolhardy –

author who would propose to a multinational publisher a study of the deleterious effects of corporate publishing's near-monopoly on scholarly research. To the extent that multinational firms have evinced commercial interest in publishing studies, they have by and large confined their investment to practical book industry manuals and to studies of the cultural politics of the book which remain safely historical in their ambit.[11]

What's in a Name? Women's Studies/Gender Studies/ Feminism/Sexuality

The uptake of feminism across the scholarly publishing sector seeded feminist ideas and analyses within an array of traditional disciplines. The traces of this complex process of institutional exchange and intellectual influence can be registered not only in publishers' catalogues but also in feminism's changing nomenclature to describe its academic project. The second-wave movement took time to agree upon an umbrella term for its mission to introduce women's perspectives into scholarly curricula, trialling 'woman studies', 'female studies' and 'feminist studies' before achieving consensus in favour of the more immediately familiar 'women's studies' tag (Stimpson, 1975; Howe, 2000a; Messer-Davidow, 2002). There is thus no intrinsic merit or political inevitability to the term 'women's studies'. Its gradual eclipse by the now preferred publisher categories 'women's and gender studies', or simply 'gender studies', has the benefit of expanding the field's analytical scope to encompass the socio-cultural construction of multiple 'other' sexualities: lesbianism, male homosexuality, queer identities, transgenderism – and the no less socially constructed and politically maintained normativity of male heterosexuality.[12]

Yet feminist scholars of publishing are right to give pause in considering whether this 'rac[e] to acquire titles that will sell in the store and be adopted in the classroom' has sacrificed a focus on women as specifically *political* subjects (Jay, 1993: 70). The implicit risk is of women being pushed to the margins of the discipline as simply one of a number of manifestations of social difference, in spite of the fact that women's studies' founding *raison d'être* was to secure a niche of scholarly activity in which women would not, for once, be sidelined. In a plenary address to the 1997 National Women's Studies Association conference, Florence Howe critiqued the trajectory of women's studies away from engagement with an activist political base, towards a sphere of careerist intellectual specialisation, diagnosing 'Women's Studies giving way to Gender Studies as a change without constructivist power' (Douglas, 1997: 16). That such verdicts echo the early second-wave's suspicion of male-identified female academics, and that this unease is now articulated in the US national conference for women's studies – as Howe remarks, originally 'the academic arm of the Women's Liberation Movement' – bears witness to feminism's transformation *by* academe as much as to feminism's transformation *of* its institutional contexts (Douglas, 1997: 16).

The latent drift towards abstracting and 'depoliticising' feminist research has been compounded within the related site of academic publishing by publishers' preference for projects in which gender forms part of the analytical vocabulary, but which would not be understood as 'feminist' in even the broadest activist sense of the term. Gender, like indices and appendices, threatens to become a standard – and largely apolitical – part of the scholarly publishing apparatus. Joan Catapano and Marlie Wasserman, commissioning editors at Indiana University Press and Rutgers University Press (Wasserman is also a director), note with the jadedness of the seasoned slush-pile reader: 'it is the unusual manuscript submitted for publication consideration that does not purport to be informed by gender analysis' (1998: 22). Smaller scholarly publishers, especially in the United States where the market for men's studies is vibrant and spans political affiliations from the cultural studies-inflected left to the Republican party-aligned new right, may be tempted to publish commercially promising though intellectually dubious studies of masculinities, which avail themselves of the term 'gender studies' but which may be actively hostile to feminist agendas (Robinson and Richardson, 1994: 88–91). Second-wave feminists, steeled by their experiences of mainstream press politics, have been vigilant in scrutinising such editorial practices for divorce of 'feminist' publishing from feminist process. Alison Ravenscroft, a member of Melbourne's all-women Sybylla Co-operative Press, disparages the women's studies list of Australian mid-sized independent Allen & Unwin as the creation of 'male publishing executive' John Iremonger (Ravenscroft, 1989: 6). In building the list, Iremonger sought out early-career academics in newly interdisciplinary fields such as women's studies and cultural studies to pen titles capable of consolidating and popularising these invigorating new approaches, in the process constructing a list that earned Allen & Unwin the reputation of 'Australia's leading academic feminist publisher' (Hancock, 1994: 20; Webby, 1998: 478). Yet, despite the presence on the list of authors such as esteemed Australian-born feminist philosopher Elizabeth Grosz, significant strands within second-wave feminism were vociferously critical of the compromises implicit in working with a mainstream corporation to proselytise progressive politics – in the (perhaps retrospectively ironic) words of Philippa Brewster, 'to *use* the establishment and *retain* the politics' (quoted in Jones, J., 1992: 176).

Models for Conceptualising (Academic) (Feminist) Publishing

The accusation that a women's studies list – albeit one regarded by senior feminist academics as the best locally originated list in the country – is tainted by male management once again evinces the mainstream/separatism divide that suffuses extant commentary about feminist publishing. In its relentless binarism, it is a model that has too often served to straightjacket commentary into arid debates over political 'credibility' versus market 'responsiveness' – relative terms employed with loaded self-interest that works to stymie rather than provoke debate.

Perusing the body of research on feminist publishing, it is striking how inadequate this static binary model has proven to the task of describing the multiple paradoxes within which academic feminist publishing now operates: gender is a key topic of analysis in most humanities and social science disciplines, though not in anything resembling an activist political mode; feminism remains prominent within mainstream and independent academic publishing, while women's studies departments atrophy; the political left is marginalised in Western democracies, but left-inspired cultural agendas are successfully commodified by multinational corporations, which in turn benefit directly from the deregulatory economic policies of those same economic rationalist governments. Feminist publishing is seemingly both everywhere and nowhere, depending upon the criteria one selects to register its presence.

Given the dissemination of feminist ideas – if not organising principles – across the whole of the book publishing spectrum, it is more responsive to contemporary realities to jettison binary categorisations in favour of a continuum model capable of conveying the variety of the sector: from independent feminist presses at one extreme, through feminist/women's studies lists within independent houses and university presses; further along might be found feminist lists within mainstream houses; still further towards the other extreme exists 'gender studies' publishing across the academic sector; and, at the far extreme, mainstream trade publishing of 'women's books', which may, to a greater or lesser extent, incorporate feminist

approaches. Feminism thus emerges not as an optic
study of academic publishing (as a putative sub
'feminist academic publishing') but as a variable ir
publishing process and across all types of publishing acu... ,
extension, and extensive reformulation, of Darnton's communications circuit model. That research alive to the diverse interplay between
feminism and the book industry exists to date in a tiny minority of
studies ironically marks a failure by feminism to fulfil its own three-
part schema for disciplinary reform. The initial phase of 'feminist
critique' has been amply fulfilled through studies of the mainstream
publishing industry's pre-existing gatekeeper hostility towards
innovative, women-focused research (Spender, 1981; Kramarae and
Spender, 1992; Chester, 1996). The secondary phase of feminist
recovery has been substantially undertaken in published accounts of
feminist press histories, studies utilising archival deposits of feminist
publishers, and in myriad front-line reports from practitioners
detailing the realities of quotidian feminist press operations
(Nicholson, 1982; Howsam, 1996; Brown, 1997; Lynch, 1998; Murray,
2000b; Bereano, 2001; Poland, 2001). Yet curiously, the third phase
of specifically theoretical disciplinary self-reflection pursued in other
fields of feminist scholarship appears, in the field of feminist
publishing, to have stalled or become mired in rearguard debates
rhetorically counterpoising independent and mainstream houses.

Such developments harbour an unfortunate irony, for feminism's
great virtues as a scholarly tool have been its readiness to investigate
the institutional bases of what it is possible to know, and its openness
to querying whose interests are served by the circulation of academic
'knowledge'. Yet feminism has been seriously remiss in largely
declining to examine the material preconditions of its own knowledge
and the institutional circuits for feminist scholarship's rapid dissemination. Precipitating such debates promises not only to cast new
light on feminism's own historical development and the variety of
its contemporary manifestations, but simultaneously to further the
original feminist project of seeding the study of women in all academic
disciplines. In this instance, such disciplines are contingent fields in
actuality deeply marked but – in their self-conception – seemingly
barely touched by feminist analysis: book history, publishing studies
and the cultural politics of the book.

4
Collective Unconscious: The Demise of Radical Feminist Publishing

I've watched the rise of what I call 'Failure Vanguardism' – the philosophy that if your group falls apart, your personal relationships fail, your political project dissolves, and your individual attitude is both bitter and suicidal, you are obviously a Radical. If, on the other hand, your group is solidifying itself (let alone expanding), if you are making progress in your struggle with lover/husband/friends, if you have gained some ground for women in the area of economics, health, legislation, literature ... and if, most of all, you appear optimistic – you are clearly Sold Out. To succeed in the slightest is to be Impure. Only if your entire life, political and personal, is one plummet of downward mobility and despair, may you be garlanded with the crown of feminist thorns. You will then have one-upped everybody by your competitive wretchedness, and won their guilty respect. Well, to such a transparently destructive message I say, with great dignity, 'Fooey'. I want to win for a change.   .

Robin Morgan, 'Rights of Passage' (1977: 13)

During the course of the 1990s, Britain's two highest profile feminist publishers – Virago Press and The Women's Press – both celebrated twentieth birthdays with a flurry of promotional material and with befitting self-congratulation on their publishing achievements to date. For a critique of feminist publishing these anniversaries hold particular significance, given the media debates that they both generated around feminist publishing's socio-literary impact and its continued relevance to the multinational-dominated publishing industry (Bennett, 1993; Macaskill, 1993; Griffey, 1998a; Steel, 1998). Simultaneously the publicity had the unfortunate effect of encouraging an overly simplistic conflation in the public mind of these two individual presses with the phenomenon of feminist publishing as a whole. Reducing a widespread movement to an

126

emblematic pair of presses invites critical reassessment because it effectively casts to the periphery of critical attention the radical, collectively run women's liberation presses burgeoning during the same period. It is this more radical segment of the second-wave feminist publishing spectrum that this chapter explores in order to disrupt the overeasy popular conflation of Virago and The Women's Press with a publishing movement of which they are but two of the many manifestations. The fact that these two publishing houses have now achieved a degree of mainstream recognition and assimilation should not obscure the fact that many of the most politically engaged and radical rationales of feminist publishing emerged from the separatist wing of the 1970s women's liberation movement.

Scholars would be amiss to interpret the demise and subsequent collapse of the radical women's publishing sector during the 1980s and 1990s as necessarily an indictment of the movement's ideas. For, at the same time that collectivist feminist presses largely disappeared from the commercial marketplace, radical women's publishing has proven the seedbed of influential developments in feminist thought. The fact that mainstream booksellers now devote prominent portions of their shop-floor displays to books of 'gay and lesbian interest', and that a corporate publisher such as Routledge annually produces a glossy catalogue of gender studies titles on topics as diverse as the politics of sexuality, the nature of lesbian identity and the construction of motherhood testifies to the percolation of radical feminist discourse into mainstream culture.[1] Radical feminist publishing is thus in the curious position of being rendered conspicuous as much by its presence as by its absence: the *content* of its ideas has increasingly been embraced, yet the *context* in which it propagated those ideas is dismissed as unworkable. As a result its influence appears, paradoxically, to be both everywhere and nowhere.

The central tenet of radical feminist publishing – and that which places it in contradistinction to corporate feminist presses of the Virago or The Women's Press models – is its conviction that women's entry into the sphere of cultural production involves the complete transformation of *process* as much as it does of *product*. Radical women's presses were characterised by non-hierarchical, collectivist structures, an emphasis on political engagement over profit generation, and a heightened self-consciousness of their position *vis-à-vis* the corporate mainstream. In Britain prominent radical feminist publishers have included the 'radical feminist lesbian' (1997 promotional leaflet) press Onlywomen (established in 1974), Leeds-based Feminist Books (established in 1974), Scottish feminist publishers Stramullion (established in 1979), influential pro-lesbian multiracial collective Sheba Feminist Publishers (established in 1980), and Afro-Caribbean and South Asian British women's press Black Woman Talk (established in 1983). The writing that emerged from these presses is crucial to an analysis of the kind undertaken here, in that it frequently marks out cutting-edge publishing territory subsequently popularised by corporate feminist and multinational houses – thus illuminating the dynamic by which mainstream publishing feeds upon and transforms vibrant subcultural genres. Furthermore, British radical feminist publishers reiterate and rework manifestos of radical feminist press activism emerging from the US women in print movement of the early to mid-1970s – in particular from writers associated with Daughters, Inc. (established in 1973) and the San Francisco-based Women's Press (Arnold, 1976; *Workforce*, 1975; Shelley, 1976). Contextualising British radical feminist publishing within the broader scope of international women's liberation media theory highlights the specificities of the UK movement, in particular the ways in which its financial resources and racial profile differed in important respects from those of its US, Canadian or Australian counterparts. The decline in British radical feminist media thus derives both from a repudiation of separatist feminist activism, which was experienced internationally, as well as from political, economic and literary trends specific to the domestic scene.

The politics versus profit conundrum, which both plagues and energises other varieties of feminist publishing, is no less prevalent among radical feminist presses, although the issue operates upon the far left of the alternative publishing sector in specific ways. The underlying dilemma is exacerbated by a combination of external and internal factors. Throughout the 1980s and 1990s, British feminist publishers suffered under the economic rationalist cuts to public spending of the Thatcher, Major and, later, Blair governments and were forced to seek alternative sources of funding in the wake of these governments' abolition or restructuring of grants-awarding bodies such as the Greater London Council (GLC) and the London Arts Board (LAB) (Shah, 1987: 99). Yet, contemporaneous with the contraction of the public sector across Western democracies and recession within the publishing industry internationally, radical imprints were also negotiating the contradictions inherent in their structure as politically committed organisations trading in the commercial sphere. The feminist priorities of political engagement, staff consciousness-raising, skills-sharing and the development of theoretical analysis pulled in the opposite direction from the quick decision-making, editorial individualism and financial opportunism that constitute prerequisites for survival in the competitive publishing realm (Shah, 1987: 96). As a spokeswoman for Melbourne's Sybylla Co-operative Press encapsulated the issue, it is 'the question of to what extent being a small business contradicts our feminist politics' (*Co-operator*, 1985: 10).

As proved to be the case with feminist publishing enterprises throughout the last decades of the twentieth century, the tensions that stem from condemning the gender policies of the mainstream media and setting up alternative media to challenge its marketshare can be crippling. To exist simultaneously outside of a system ideo-logically, while needing to co-operate with it for the practical purposes of distribution, sales, finance and sheer survival, is an exercise in political acrobatics and labyrinthine self-justification which severely taxed the energies of the separatist print movement. Radical feminist publishers' dilemma in this regard, and the costs in terms of individuals' life experience, warrant sympathy and an informed understanding. But this discussion discerns two fundamental assumptions in 1970s radical feminist thought which hamstrung women's attempts to create a strong alternative media base: firstly, an underexamined allegiance to non-hierarchical organising; and secondly, an undisguised suspicion of profit-making and the commercial imperative. These two assumptions account for a large share of the failure, self-recrimination and personal animosity that is the unfortunate legacy of much radical women's media activity. Anyone who has interviewed women centrally involved in this publishing scene will recognise the glazed-eye, head-in-hands, disil-lusioned response that the question 'what is your experience of collective organising?' invariably provokes (Gerrard, 1995b; Butterworth, 1998; Hennegan, 1998). The dominant tone – a mixture of bafflement and despair – echoes testimonies to be found in the periodicals of the 1970s women's liberation movement: disgruntled and genuinely questioning personal testimonies, which ask how attempting to put feminist politics into practice could result in such dismaying counterproductiveness (dell'Olio, 1970; Freeman, 1970; Winant, 1975). In a contribution to Polly Joan and Andrea Chesman's *Guide to Women's Publishing* (1978), a co-founder of Canadian non-sexist children's books publisher Before We Are Six articulates the contradictions of this experience. According to Susan Shaw

Weatherup, the presumed benefits to feminists of working collectively and of downplaying the profit motive are largely illusory:

> It has been hard, as our political beliefs have often brought us together, but once there we have found that attempting to run a business & survive with many of those beliefs takes twice as much work. Yes, I often feel discouraged. How much easier it would be to view Before We Are Six strictly as a business with the only motive being profit ... (quoted in Joan and Chesman, 1978: 116)

The archival material, articles, books and interviews that comprise the primary source material for an analysis of radical women's publishing indicate that these publishers were cognisant of critiques of collectivism emerging from the US and UK women's movements, and were predisposed to subjecting personal experience to theoretical analysis. Yet, despite these tactical advantages, radical women's publishers have manifestly failed in their aim of developing a robust, financially and organisationally autonomous women's communications network, and have frequently proven unable to sustain even individual women's publishing enterprises for periods sufficiently lengthy to constitute anything approaching a threat to the corporate mainstream. That the individual women involved in such projects were not lacking in commitment to radical publishing ideals is proven beyond doubt by contemporary sources. Thus feminist media critics are forced to shift their focus to re-examine the movement's central goal – that of institutional autonomy. The chill conclusion suggested by such analysis is that the collective separatist model and profitable publishing are, in practice, mutually exclusive options.

The implications of such a conclusion are clearly of significance to contemporary feminism, its modes of organisation and its understanding of its own history. Yet such academic discussion of feminist publishing as does exist tends to shy away from directly addressing the failings of the collective experiment (Spender, 1981; Spender, L., 1983a, 1983b; Gerrard, 1989; Duncker, 1992; Butalia and Menon, 1995). Considered at the level of theory, this critical silence is problematic because of the women's movement's insistence that political analysis be constructed in dialectical relation with personal experience. For feminist media studies to ignore a wealth of publishing experience on its own doorstep – however uncomfortable the implications of that evidence – amounts to an indefensible intellectual inconsistency on the part of feminism. Moreover, in practical terms, feminists would be well advised to make use of the much media-heralded 'death' of feminist publishing to mount a timely review of the radical print movement's achievements and failings. For women now embarking on professional careers in the media or reaching their prime as media commentators and consumers, such critical re-evaluation is especially pressing as feminism searches for strategies to ensure the continued visibility of feminist ideas within ever more powerful multinational media conglomerates. Given that market economics and multinational media moguls show no sign of retreating from the publishing sphere, the obligation on feminist critics must be to resist the overly dichotomised 1970s view of authentically 'radical' publishing as by its very nature diametrically opposed to the mainstream industry. Rather, the onus is on such critics to articulate theoretical analyses attuned to the changed politico-economic circumstances in which feminist publishing finds itself. Such analyses should eschew the neat dogmatism of endorsing a single variety of feminist print endeavour while decrying all others as irredeemably tainted by mainstream collaboration. For it is not purity but *survival* that has come to constitute feminist publishing's uncongenial reality, and flexibility based on market diversity and tactical interaction with the mainstream is likely to prove its optimal survival strategy.

COLLECTIVE VERSUS CORPORATE FEMINIST PUBLISHING

In any analysis of radical feminist publishing the question of what exactly constitutes 'radical' press activity presents itself as an initial definitional challenge. The notion of radicalism is, in the broad sense of the term, fundamental to *all* feminist publishing enterprises, for they all seek to redress a perceived absence in mainstream publishing practice and to amplify the voices of women marginalised from the centres of literary discourse. Hence, in the general sense of the word as outlined by Raymond Williams, Virago might be said to have constituted a 'radical' endeavour in that it was founded to challenge mainstream publishing's under-representation of women writers (Williams, 1983: 251–2). It is crucial, however, to distinguish this generalised use of the term 'radical' from its more specific sense in which it denotes a particular limb of second-wave feminist activism that eschewed the reform agenda of liberal feminism and favoured withdrawal from the existing structures of social power (Freeman,

1973: 33). The radical feminist agenda – in publishing as in its more activist political manifestations – viewed withdrawal of support for capitalist and established political systems as a necessary prerequisite to a more fundamentally subversive political manoeuvre: the creation of alternative women-centred systems that, it argued, would precipitate the downfall of the status quo (Echols, 1989). In this sense, radical feminist organisations claimed to serve both prefigurative and directly revolutionary ends.

In the sphere of feminist print activity, radical presses are identifiable less by their self-description (for individual presses analysed in this chapter may not necessarily embrace the political connotations of the term) than by their internal structure; collectivist organisation, non-hierarchical operating practices, job rotation, skills sharing, and a low prioritorisation or even disregard for profit-making commonly characterise radical feminist publishing endeavours. Yet this discussion resists the academic predilection for airtight classi-fication in its handling of the term 'radical'. As the migration of radical feminist ideas towards the lists of mainstream publishing houses over the last three decades attests, there is a certain ambiguity and fluidity at the heart of the concept. If radicalism is deemed to inhere in the content of a publishing house's list, rather than in its organisational set-up, then a press funded by corporate finance and run hierarchically but which nevertheless publishes innovative lesbian fiction would, for the purposes of the definition, be deemed 'radical' – an outcome that would seem to miss certain nuances inherent in the broader usage of the term. Furthermore, corporate feminist publishers with large print runs and high sales figures might with some justification argue that their radicalising influence on the book-buying public at large outweighs that of collectivist presses publishing for an already card-carrying political minority. Hence this discussion utilises the term 'radical' in a shifting sense, remaining alive to the nuances, ambiguities and terminological relativism that have accreted to the word over 30 years of feminist history. This discussion proposes as the term's core meaning the collectively run, low-budget, all-women publishing houses that predominated – in terms of numbers though not necessarily in terms of press coverage – during the 1970s and early 1980s. However, in an industry as unstable and as subject to shifts in cultural politics as publishing, definitions can only ever hope to be provisional and to err on the side of inclusiveness.

Varieties of British Radical Women's Publishing

Onlywomen Press

The British feminist press that might be read as adhering most closely to the pattern of a radical women's publishing outfit is Onlywomen Press, founded in 1974 from a meeting of radical women interested in developing feminist alternatives to the dominant print culture and still publishing under the description 'independent feminist lesbian book publishers'. A crucial aspect of Onlywomen's operations, which distinguishes it from the corporate-backed publishers Virago, The Women's Press[2] and Pandora Press, was its foundation as both a printing *and* publishing operation. The interpenetration of printing and publishing was understood by press founder Lilian Mohin and the other members of the original four-strong Onlywomen collective as serving both the political end of ensuring complete control over all stages in the chain of cultural production, as well as the practical economic end of subsidising publishing activity with periodic commercial printing work.[3] The underlying conviction in all of Onlywomen's self-descriptions is, however, an insistence on the political centrality of separatist organising by radical women, a position that castigates others' attempts to reorient mainstream structures towards feminist ends as, at best, political self-delusion:

> Being part of the Women's Liberation Movement has meant to us not only recognising our own oppression, but resolving to overthrow it and, therefore, to withdraw support for any of its systems that we could by establishing on our own. (Cadman, Chester and Pivot, 1981: 33)

In the twenty-first century, the picture for Onlywomen has changed in response to dramatic shifts in global economic activity and in organisational fashion. Onlywomen is now essentially run by Lilian Mohin from her west London flat, although vestigial remains of the original collective are found in the loose advisory group that meets periodically to discuss submissions and policy directions. The list has also evolved in line with literary fashion: Onlywomen's 1970s lesbian poetry anthologies such as its first title, edited by Lilian Mohin, *One Foot on the Mountain* (1979), have been overtaken by currently fashionable genres such as lesbian theory and literary criticism, crime fiction, feminist sci-fi, lesbian historical romance, and – with recent titles Jay Taverner's *Something Wicked* (2002) and Helen Shacklady's

The Stolen Crate (2002) – corporate thrillers (Onlywomen promotional leaflet, 1997; Chester, 2002: 198). Currently, Onlywomen's output stands at around three titles per annum. Compared to the slick, populist repackaging that Virago engineered in 1997, Onlywomen remains steeped in the back-to-basics, anti-Establishment politics of mid-1970s lesbian separatism. The press may have nudged its publishing programme in the direction of lighter, feel-good feminist genres in recent years, but in basic orientation, practice and rhetoric it adamantly resists the tide of feminist fashion.

Sheba Feminist Publishers

In contrast with Onlywomen Press, the radicalism of Sheba Feminist Publishers inhered not so much in rejecting co-operation with the mainstream but in the dynamics of its internal organisation. From its origins in London in 1980 to its eventual demise in 1994, Sheba operated as an all-woman collective, generally with a membership in the region of seven to ten women, although the actual composition of the collective was subject to constant change (O'Sullivan, 2003: 29). By the time of Sheba's establishment, Virago and The Women's Press already occupied distinct niches of the feminist book-buying market with their respective historical and contemporary list foci. Sheba's avowed aims in seeking to distinguish its list from those of the more established women's imprints were to seek out new feminist readerships and to see 'both more and a greater variety of publications committed to feminism in bookshops and libraries everywhere' (Cadman, Chester and Pivot, 1981: 37). That Sheba went some way towards demonstrating the existence of untapped markets for writing by black women, for lesbian-feminist erotica, and for feminist humour in the form of cartoon collections is borne out by its posthumous influence on the lists of progressive independent and mainstream publishers. The Sheba Archive in London's Women's Library confirms the general impression gleaned from contemporary press reports that the house suffered from chronic undercapitalisation throughout its active life (Bardsley, 1982; Fritz, 1986a; Loach, 1986).[4] This fact suggests that it was financial underdevelopment rather than a misreading of the auguries for future trends in feminist thought that led to the press's demise in early 1994.

Although Sheba described itself in its published books as 'a racially mixed feminist publishing cooperative', it in fact operated on a modified collective pattern; decisions about commissioning and manuscript selection were conducted by consensus, but individuals within the group specialised in editorial, production, rights and marketing (Lorde, 1987: 76). Sheba regarded itself as a publisher rather than as a print production co-operative, subcontracting printing and binding to outside firms rather than training collective members to undertake these tasks in-house. Nor did Sheba suffer qualms over dealing with mainstream distribution channels in order to guarantee its books were displayed in the high street: its most successful title, a collection of feminist cartoons entitled *Sourcream* (1980) was carried by WH Smith, thereby selling in sufficient numbers to spawn a sequel, *Sourcream II*, the following year. The success of these titles, of black women's writing such as *A Dangerous Knowing: Four Black Women Poets* edited by Barbara Burford (1984), of the poetry of American writer Audre Lorde, and of the fiction of Barbara Burford, suggests that had Sheba not encountered the severe public spending constriction of the Thatcher period, and had it confronted and resolved the conflicts endemic within its collective, it might have profited from its often astute publishing decisions – rather than serving as the shock troops for a more cautious mainstream publishing culture.

Silver Moon Books

A doubtfulness as to what can be achieved via shoestring budgets and volunteerism characterises the foundation of a very different enterprise: London's Silver Moon Books (SMB). Sue Butterworth and Jane Cholmeley were among the small group of women who in May 1984 founded what long purported to be Europe's largest women's bookshop, Silver Moon, in the central London book-retailing district of Charing Cross Road (Cornwell, 2001: 12; Spender, 2003). In late 2001, pending rent hikes on their West End shopfront, Silver Moon reconstituted as 'an in-store area dedicated to books by and for women' within long-running independent bookshop Foyles, across the road from its former premises (*Guardian*, 2001: 8; *Independent*, 2001: 12; Paton, 2001: 9; Murray, 2002: 2). Like Onlywomen, Sheba and many other radical cultural organisations of the early 1980s, the original Silver Moon bookshop was also a recipient of the GLC's Arts and Recreation Committee subsidies, and the shop also operated for a brief four months on a non-hierarchical job rotation basis (Cholmeley, 1991: 219–27; Paton, 2001: 9). This practice was, however, quickly abolished in favour of more standardised job demarcation once it became clear, in Sue Butterworth's words, that continuing collective practices would be tantamount to committing 'financial suicide' (Butterworth, 1998). She maintains that collectives suffer on account of the varying political and personal commitment levels of what are, theoretically, equally responsible members. Co-founder Jane Cholmeley, in her 1991 overview of the venture, 'A Feminist Business in a Capitalist World: Silver Moon Women's Bookshop', emphasises the inevitable business stresses aggravated by adherence to 'the dogma associated with collectives' (1991: 229): muddled workspaces; erratic ordering and stocktaking; customer confusion; and a generalised, pervasive 'crisis of communication and accountability' (1991: 226). In contrast to this chaotic situation, Butterworth observes dryly that having one's house on the line if the business folds 'clears the head wonderfully' (Butterworth, 1998).

Out of retailing success and a determination to capture the mainstream market, Butterworth and Cholmeley in 1990 created Silver Moon Books, an imprint that undertakes little commissioning but which purchases UK and Commonwealth rights to foreign (usually US) fiction titles, especially in the areas of lesbian detective fiction, romance and erotica. Perceiving that this 'gap in the market' had been successfully tapped in North America by the Florida-based Naiad Press, SMB bought rights to a number of Naiad titles and boasts a backlist of over 30 self-proclaimedly 'schlocky' novels and 'Friday night reads' (Butterworth, 1998).[5] While benefiting from what was – for a feminist publisher – the near unique position of having their own retail outlet for the sale and promotion of house titles, SMB also distributed to major bookselling chain Waterstones, a firm that in terms of general trade represents a significant retailing competitor. Interdependence, rather than autonomy at all costs, best encapsulates SMB's attitude towards the contemporary book publishing and retailing market: their oppositionality lies in the *content* of their books rather than in the *context* of their production. In fact, if anything, the political subversiveness of SMB's lesbian fiction list derives from its rejection of explicit politicality as the hallmark of lesbian writing – a familiarly twenty-first-century disassociation of lifestyle politics from the convictions of earlier lesbian feminist subcultures.

Clear-eyed financial pragmatism and an informed appraisal of when it is advantageous to interact with the mainstream and when, on the other hand, political commitment necessitates independence, accounts for the fact that SMB demonstrated steady growth and consolidation between its foundation and Butterworth and Cholmeley's exit from the book business in 2001. In this it far outlasted the majority of British radical feminist print organisations: Sheba Feminist Publishers ceased trading in 1993 and declared bankruptcy the following year;

Onlywomen has dwindled to a front-room mail-order operation with low publicity and slow turnover; Stramullion Press and Feminist Books folded within a few years of their respective foundations; the north London SisterWrite Bookshop was wound up in 1985; and the *Spare Rib* magazine collective disbanded in acrimony in March 1993. The perusal of this dismal roll-call of failed radical initiatives prompts speculation that it is adherence to the collective principle and its oft-encountered corollary of financial myopia which so compromised commercial feminist endeavours. Initiated with robust idealism and tremendous energy, radical feminist presses all too frequently imploded through naive adherence to organisational principles fundamentally incompatible with the surrounding politico-economic reality. As Ellen Messer-Davidow summarises, collectives 'found themselves buffeted by a shortage of dollars and a surplus of discord' (2002: 132). The devastatingly ironic result is that, for all its sophisticated political rhetoric and potentially large market base, radical feminist publishing never constituted anything resembling a serious commercial or political threat to the mainstream; more commonly it managed to engineer its own spectacular and rapid demise.

Radical Feminist Media Theory: Communicating a New Reality

The rapid proliferation of feminist publishing houses during the early years of the women's liberation movement sparked a commensurate proliferation of feminist media criticism – both responses to the mainstream media's relentless trivialisation of the movement, and arguments for an independent women's communications network. Key manifestos of the women in print movement frequently originate from the United States, notably June Arnold's landmark essay for lesbian-feminist periodical *Quest*, 'Feminist Presses & Feminist Politics' (1976), Alexa Freeman and Valle Jones's more multimedia-focused 'Creating Feminist Communications' (1976), and the Female Liberation group's 'From Us: Thoughts on the Feminist Media' (1974). In addition to these important radical feminist media manifestos from across the Atlantic, Britain harboured an indigenous separatist media critique, often developed by feminist media practitioners themselves and benefiting from a close interrelationship of theorising and individual experience (*Women's Report*, 1974, 1979; *Spare Rib* collective, 1979; Wallsgrove, 1979; *Spare Rib*, 1982).

A leitmotif of 1970s radical feminist media theory is a deeply ingrained suspicion of the multinational corporate publishing sector. Chiefly, this intense distrust stems from radical women's awareness that capitalism rather than political commitment powers the corporate mainstream, hence women would be deluded in thinking that Madison Avenue corporate giants would promote texts subversive of the capitalist, patriarchally endorsed status quo. According to June Arnold's analysis – one honed during her years at the helm of feminist press Daughters, Inc. – the relationship between the radical fringe and the corporate centre can never be one of interdependence and cultural negotiation, but is instead structured by a logic of implacable opposition:

> The finishing press [Arnold's term for the publishing mainstream] is the hard-cover of corporate America and absolutely does not want the independent women's presses to survive. Each time he takes a feminist book from us he weakens us all. (Arnold, 1976: 25)

The fear of co-optation stemmed from mainstream publishers' demonstrated interest in the women's movement as a social phenomenon capable of generating bestseller sales figures. In search of the elusive bestseller that would serve as *the* indispensable vade mecum to the women's movement, publishers variously promoted titles such as Betty Friedan's *The Feminine Mystique* (1963), Germaine Greer's *The Female Eunuch* (1970) and Kate Millett's *Sexual Politics* (1970), prompting feminist critics to remark caustically that 'they will publish some of us – the least threatening, the most saleable, the most easily controlled' (Arnold, 1976: 19).[6] The outright hostility of radical theorists to enterprises 'cash[ing] in on the sales value of feminism' (Arnold, 1976: 24) was motivated by awareness that women, carrying little policy-making weight in the managerial echelons of corporate publishing, risked having their writing co-opted and subsequently dismissed as commercially passé as soon as the feminist 'trend' was deemed to have peaked (Ehrlich, 1973: 268). As literary agent Anne McDermid cautioned, the power to consume is by no means necessarily coterminous with the power to determine: 'I'm afraid we are not more in control of it than we were before, they've just decided that we are a market ... If they decide to cut it off, that's it. We should be in control from beginning to end' (quoted in Cadman, Chester and Pivot, 1981: 26).

The rigorous separatism of radical feminist communications theorists created a dilemma for feminist-identified authors: should they reap the financial and promotional benefits of mainstream publication, or was it politically preferable to exemplify their pro-women rhetoric by publishing – almost certainly without an advance – with a small-scale, woman-run operation? Heated debate on the issue in feminist periodicals levelled charges of 'selling out' the movement at feminist literary luminaries who were, it was alleged, manipulating a grassroots women's movement for personal celebrity and – somewhat paradoxically – in the hope of patriarchal endorsement (Arnold, 1976: 22–3; Desmoines and Nicholson, 1976: 128). Women purchasing feminist titles from mainstream publishers and bookshops were also directed to analyse the financial implications of their actions in cutting down the potential market share of radical presses (cf. Douglas 2000). Such arguments tend to propound a brand of ethical consumerism that, since taken up by organisations such as Fairtrade, Community Aid Abroad and The Body Shop, has a familiarly twenty-first-century ring to it, although the reader guilt-tripping is highly characteristic of right-on 1970s publications:

> [mainstream] publishers have been more than happy to cash in on the women's market, even though they worry each year that 'the wave is peaking'. Many have been clever enough to employ feminists. But this still amounts to no more than tokenism ... The fact is that, for any one feminist title on the list, dozens of sexist books still pour into the market. So, for committed feminists, purchasing a book from a commercial publishing house may feel a bit discomforting: not too different from eating iceberg lettuce or wearing cotton from textile mills in which the workers suffer from Brown Lung 'epidemics'. Even if the quality is all right, you know where it came from ... (Moberg, 1974: 16)

Unable and unwilling to be accommodated by the corporate publishing sector on its own terms, radical feminists chose instead to subvert the corporate communications network through tactics of non-co-operation, rhetorical assault and wholesale replication. Only a communications system controlled entirely by women's movement adherents and funded by its supporters could, they argued, withstand the insidiously corrupting influence of the established media: 'We must look beyond male-created mass media and create our own forms and designs of feminist communications. Only in this way can we assert uncompromising control over the content and distribution of our message' (Freeman and Jones, 1976: 4). Radical feminism envisaged that revolution in media ownership would prove the catalyst for a revitalisation of media formats in line with qualities valorised as specifically female; a heightened 'mutuality' in women's media would manifest itself in responsiveness to reader interests and in greater managerial openness (Freeman and Jones, 1976: 5). The championing of new literary forms – 'the art and politics of the future' – would initiate a groundswell in women's cultural consciousness, which was itself conceived of as inherently political (Arnold, 1976: 20). Thus new genres would herald new political realities – a seductively easy slippage between the vocabulary of literary criticism and mass-movement politics, which betrays the mid-1970s women in print movement's increasing flight towards a politics of 'women's culture' and away from the difficult struggle for a culture of women's politics.

The radical women's publishing movement, inheriting its automatic mistrust of corporate involvement from the new left, fatally over-estimated the degree to which any commercial operation in the developed world – regardless of its political hue – can insulate itself from capitalist processes. It thus failed to develop a responsive critique of the crippling organisational problems individual feminist presses faced as they strove to generate profit from women's books. Instead, the silence of thinkers such as Arnold, Freeman and Jones, and Desmoines and Nicholson on the issue implies that individual failure rather than theoretical oversimplification underlay the collapse of feminist businesses. Without women-run banking networks, distribution chains, accountancy firms, printeries and bookshops of national strength and profile, Arnold's battlecry that support must be withdrawn 'from any woman who is still trying to make her name by selling out our movement' (1976: 26) penalised feminist presses while leaving the giants of Madison Avenue unscathed and pleasantly oblivious.

New Structures for a New Society

The early women's movement was pushed towards embracing collectivism because, when so much that characterised mainstream society appeared irredeemably tainted by patriarchal modes of thought, these equality-based group structures had at least recently been revitalised by the left, and thus were seen as more compatible with women-centred theories than Establishment-propagated hierarchies. Further prompting this choice were the recent experiences of many radical women within the ostensibly democratic structures of the rigidly hierarchical socialist left. Here the gap between policy and practice, rhetoric and reality, became painfully apparent to women, who were commonly relegated by the machismo leaders of the new left to organisational, sexual and domestic inferiority

(Freeman, 1973: 37–8; Wandor, 1990: *passim*). As early women's liberation activists cuttingly expressed it, even the revolution seemed to need its handmaidens.

Despite qualms over its application in male-centred groups, the non-hierarchical model was nevertheless sufficiently politically modish for the majority of 1970s women's presses to establish themselves along collectivist lines. This was in spite of the fact that their antecedents in the first-wave women's suffrage presses – such as the Women's Social and Political Union's Woman's Press – owed much of their financial strength and political leverage to their elaborate systems of administrative subdivision and clear lines of editorial authority (Murray, Simone, 2000b). Movements that conceive of themselves as revolutionary are, however, inclined to prioritise innovation over precedent. The radical women's movement conceived of its revolutionary programme as one not only of action but also of structure. Thus rejection of the Pankhurst-style model of military command was indivisible from the movement's rhetoric of women's equality. Political conviction merged, in any case, with organisational fashion to endorse the collectivist model: as Martha Shelley remarks of the establishment of the San Francisco Women's Press Collective in 1970: 'we started off being a collective because that was the thing to be' (1976: 121).

Apart from its innovative quality, collaborative working also secured strong approval among feminist activists because it harmonised with certain assumptions about women's nature then propounded by radical wings of the women's movement. With the perversion of patriarchal social encoding removed, radical second-wave feminists believed that women's consultative, peaceful, non-domineering and consensus-seeking attributes would come to the fore, fundamentally transforming the tensions and rivalries of individual behaviour that had traditionally divided progressive social groups. Such sisterly *esprit de corps* was (perhaps in spite of evidence to the contrary) much heralded at the first major British second-wave feminist event, the 1970 Women's Liberation Conference at Ruskin College, Oxford (Wandor, 1990). The women's movement's valorisation of small group processes is crystallised in literary form in the poem 'Councils' by influential contemporary feminist writer Marge Piercy, in which Piercy insists that 'women must learn to dare to speak' (1982 [1973]: 117).[7] Political working in a psychologically supportive, non-competitive environment would, it was believed, transform women's psyches in tandem with transforming the concept of the political.

Radical feminist presses were simultaneously infused with a related and complementary desire: to demonstrate by example that the corporate mode of production was neither inevitable nor desirable. Rather than treating publishing as an industry 'turning out products like hotdogs', radical publishers envisaged a politically and creatively synthesised working environment in which theoretical development would take place in constant dialectical relationship with publishing practice (Cadman, Chester and Pivot, 1981: 35): as Onlywomen co-founder Sheila Shulman observed, 'to us women's printing and publishing wasn't about a job or a career; it was about politics. We would both be doing the feminist revolution by writing and printing and publishing, and we would be furthering it by the work we were getting out' (quoted in Jackson, C., 1993: 46). Surveying the US radical feminist press scene in 1978, Polly Joan surmised in optimistic vein that the direct democracy model had worked, and that it constituted radical feminist publishing's international common denominator:

> Women's publishing has accomplished in a very short ten years what the male norm in publishing has always maintained couldn't be done. Whatever the differences between feminist women in publishing, this rejection of hierarchies is the strong thread that links all of us together. (Joan and Chesman, 1978: 110)

Yet, even within non-hierarchical, all-women consciousness-raising and political groups, competitive behavioural patterns proved difficult to eradicate, as feminists' lived experience stubbornly refused to comply with the rhetorical ideal of sisterly co-operation and group-mindedness. In the late 1960s, the radical New York women's group The Feminists instituted a mode of anti-hierarchical political organising that aimed for total equality, including an attempt to equalise the amount of time for which any participant could speak at group meetings by means of a 'disc system':[8] 'Every member is given 15 to 20 chips at the beginning of the meeting. Each time someone speaks, she throws a disc in the middle of the room. When your chips are used up, you can no longer participate in the discussion for the remainder of that meeting' (Atkinson, 1974: 70). The Feminists' policies for controlling group discussions implicitly acknowledge the existence of de facto varieties of hierarchy, for example of rhetorical skill or of political status, which exist even in the most avowedly 'leaderless' of groups. Although this policy was not followed in the publishing realm that is the specific focus of this discussion, it nevertheless heralds an incipient awareness of the contradictions belying collectivism's professed equality; it points, in an oblique way, to the enormous tensions to which collective working experiences give rise. It was the failure to examine thoroughly the causes of these tensions and to develop strategies to combat them that sent collective women's publishing down the painful path to disbandment, acrimony and financial failure.

Feminist Critiques of Collectivism

A movement as politically self-conscious as feminism might be expected to examine its theoretical principles in the critical light of its experience. From the early 1970s, the women's movement did produce such a critique of collectivism's tendency to entrench unacknowledged elites by its very claims to openness and equality. A central text of this debate, Jo Freeman's powerful and much reprinted essay 'The Tyranny of Structurelessness', was first published in 1970, but was circulating within the US women's movement in mimeographed form for some time prior to that date. Basic to its argument is the assertion that ostensible 'structurelessness' in fact serves as a smokescreen for covertly hierarchical groups whose elites remain unaccountable because of group members' inability to prove that power inequalities actually exist within the organisation. Thus a crucial double-standard emerges supporting an officially sanctioned de jure equality and disguised de facto power relationships:

> Thus structurelessness becomes a way of masking power, and within the women's movement is usually most strongly advocated by those who are the most powerful (whether they are conscious of their power or not). As long as the structure of the group is informal, the rules of how decisions are made are known only to a few and awareness of power is limited to those who know the rules. Those who do not know the rules and are not chosen for initiation must remain in confusion, or suffer from paranoid delusions that something is happening of which they are not quite aware. (Freeman, 1970: 21)

That the oftentimes uncomfortable criticisms articulated in Freeman's essay were the subject of debate within British publishing and bookselling circles is evidenced by a series of articles that subsequently appeared detailing the internal tensions of the *Spare*

Rib collective (*Spare Rib* Collective, 1979; Wallsgrove, 1979; *Spare Rib*, 1987), of an (anonymous) bookselling collective (*News from Neasden*, 1979), of a collective editing the anthology *No Turning Back* (1981) for The Women's Press (Feminist Anthology Collective, 1981), and in the minutes of Sheba's fraught collective meetings throughout its active life (Sheba Feminist Publishers Archive, 1980–94).[9] In only its second year in operation, Sheba members recorded a lengthy debate about the failings of their modified collective, perceiving that their operating problems were at least as attributable to factors intrinsic to the group model itself as to personal, Sheba-specific failings: 'This is not an excuse, but we are attempting to be both a successful publishing house and a successful part-time collective with all the problems (individually and together) those two facets involve' (Sheba Feminist Publishers Archive, 1981, box 2.3).

Yet, despite their political sophistication with the issues involved, the practical publishing regimen of deadlines and budgets caused British commercial collectives to perceive the failings of their operating systems without constructing strategies of the kind formulated by Freeman for containing non-democratic tendencies (1970: 25, 42). In this sense, feminist collectives experienced the worst of both worlds: they endured the enervation of political disenchantment (at least partially) with the collective status quo, yet they were unable to disavow an ideal to which the group had so publicly nailed its colours. The recorder of the minutes at a 1981 Sheba collective meeting bemoaned this inability of the group to act upon the feminist maxim that 'the personal is political' by restructuring the purportedly structureless model that was so compromising the press's effectiveness. The consciousness-raising/activist ideal had, she despaired, degenerated into 'all swapping info on business and floundering towards decisions' (Sheba Feminist Publishers Archive, 1981: box 2.3).

COLLECTIVE ORGANISING: EFFECTING EQUALITY OR AFFECTING QUALITY?

When the Political is Personal

Dutch media theorist Liesbet van Zoonen observes in her essay 'Feminist Perspectives on the Media' that 'a constant feature of radical feminist media has been internal conflict about organization and editorial policy' (1991: 37). It is possible to trace the origins of this organisational problem to the pre-eminent value ascribed to 'sisterhood' and solidarity in the women's liberation movement, a subtly enforced egalitarianism that tarred those women who advanced 'individualist' solutions with the brush of elitism (dell'Olio, 1970: n.p.; Freeman, 1970: 21–3). Although the consciousness-raising model certainly perceived itself to be open, unthreatening and prepared to challenge all orthodoxies, the ultimate unchallengeable orthodoxy tended to be the group model itself. Reflecting on this phenomenon 20 years after the Ruskin College meeting, British historian Sheila Rowbotham concludes that 1970s feminists' 'faith [in] and enthusiasm for participatory democracy' led inevitably to the tyranny of the majority. As in the ancient Greek *polis*, 'when people disagree the only thing you can do is to ostracise' (quoted in Wandor, 1990: 41).

Further aggravating this incipient tension for radical women involved in the production of literature was the nature of the writing process as it has evolved in Western societies. The isolated individualism of fiction writing clashed fundamentally with the group ideal, yet writing penned by collectives tended to lack the dynamism and tone of personal authenticity crucial for achieving critical success and high sales. For collectives engaged only in the publication – as opposed to the writing – of feminist literature, the individualist problem nevertheless persisted, as individuals' literary critical judgements on texts submitted for publication were, invariably, at odds. Elaborate consensus models for arriving at group decisions were implemented, but as the Lesbian Writing and Publishing Collective involved in editing a 1986 anthology for the Women's Press (Canada) confessed, 'it is hard to make any generalizations about why a piece of fiction worked for one of us and not another' (1986: 8). A collectively written statement of the group's editorial policies was adopted in this instance as a way of consciously acknowledging value judgements – even if not all the individuals involved actually subscribed to them (see also Feminist Anthology Collective, 1981: 2). But the subsumption of personal response within a system of literary collective responsibility is inevitably uneasy: 'No one wants to talk about the egotism involved in authorship. No one wants to talk about the innately non-collective nature of the impulse to write … How the fuck are you supposed to fit *that* into feminism? *Please*' (Hennegan, 1998).

In the pressured environment of a commercially oriented collective such as a publishing house, this subordination of individual opinion to the group will created especially acrimonious outcomes. Essentially, if – as the feminist slogan has it – the personal is political then, inevitably at some point, the political is also personal. For Boston's Female Liberation group, disbanding in 1974, it had already become so: 'We are separating because we are unable to work together effectively as a single political unit, since we cannot agree on priorities or political perspective' (*The Second Wave*, 1974: 2). Lamenting that 'for the last two years most of our energy has been absorbed by conflicts within the group' (1974: 2), the authors of the Female Liberation statement acknowledged that the problems with their working methods had become so acute as to silence the media outlet they built to proselytise feminist ideas. There is a devastating political irony here – that the collective medium that was to be a major component of the message should itself function to silence the message.

Conflicts over production reached particularly divisive levels during the mid- to late 1980s as they intersected with pre-existing debates within feminism around black women's oppression and racism within the women's movement. The already fragile fiction of group solidarity was further wrenched by women of colour's accusation that feminist publishing itself perpetuated society's 'racist fabric' (Lesbian Writing and Publishing Collective, 1986: 13). Black British women, such as the members of the press Black Woman Talk, felt forced to decide between white feminist racism, on one hand, and the tokenising interest in black women's writing of mainstream publishers on the other. Refusing a false choice between equally compromising options, they decided to work outside of both systems and to establish a publishing collective of their own (Black Woman Talk Collective, 1984b: 28). Sheba Feminist Publishers, becoming conscious of its all-white, middle-class origins, in a 1982 newsletter expressed 'aware[ness] ... of our privileged position' (Sheba Feminist Publishers Archive, 1982: box 2.3), and through the feminist media solicited for 'Asian and Afro-Caribbean women to join what is at the moment an all-white collective' (Bardsley, 1982: 36). Yet, for the members of the Women's Press Lesbian Writing and Publishing Collective (Canada), such multiracial organising proved insolubly divisive. A prominent five-page statement entitled 'Notes About Racism in the Process' was appended to the collectively written introduction to *Dykeversions*, prompting a sobered *mea culpa* from the three white members of the collective, which was also included in the volume's preliminaries (1986: 11–15). Yet the vociferousness of the criticisms aired renders the black women's avowal 'to stay in the collective because of our commitment to lesbian of colour writing' (1986: 13) less an approach towards resolving the problem than a deferral of inevitable fracture.[10]

A strong emphasis on group solidarity and a low tolerance for dissent characterises not only the early women's liberation movement, but in fact many groups still in an emergent phase in which they must galvanise support, determine policy and radicalise potential group members. Yet radical feminism in particular has been historically ready to level allegations of 'false consciousness' at those who would take issue with basic tenets of group policy, as an early second-wave list of 'resistances to consciousness-raising' disturbingly highlights. These 'wrong' opinions include thinking that 'individual solutions are possible, your man is the exception, Women's Lib is just therapy, some women are better than others, and women are already equal' (quoted in Rosenwasser, 1972: 47). It is the combination of such aggressively unexamined egalitarianism with the self-proclaimed openness and receptivity of the early women's movement that appears most intellectually unsustainable, and that effectively alienated many potential women's movement sympathisers (see dell'Olio, 1970: n.p.; Randall, 1987: 256). For women already active within the movement, the tensions sparked by underexamined principles of direct democracy tended more often to burn with a long fuse (Lynch, 1998). As an ex-member of the Manchester-based Moss Side Community Press neatly summed up: 'The worst thing about working in a co-op is that nobody can criticise each other, because you're all meant to be operating on goodwill, and goodwill doesn't always work at 8 o'clock in the morning' (Cadman, Chester and Pivot, 1981: 65).

The Paradox of Leaderless Dictatorship

In an insightful article entitled 'The Agony of Inequality' (1979), Jane J. Mansbridge enumerates several forms of de facto power within avowedly 'leaderless' organisations, developing Jo Freeman's earlier critique with more explicit reference to sociological and organisational group models. Whether it be the superior status of a group founder over that of recently joined members, the power accorded those whose verbal fluency or command of complex political terminology grants them a demagogic role, or the subtle and perhaps unconscious distinctions based on race, class background or sexual orientation, power discrepancies in self-proclaimedly democratic groups are a reality over which collectives all too frequently implode. As Mansbridge sagely observes, the common outcomes of a collective's self-destructive 'big bang' are 'orgies of self-blame and recrimination' (1979: 194). When these very real inequalities of status remain unacknowledged, the result is often a serious erosion of faith in the professed ideals of the organisation, a pattern confirmed in the minutes of fraught collective meetings from Sheba's later years (Sheba Feminist Publishers Archive, 1990–93). The file of resignation letters contained in the Sheba Archive cites with a depressing frequency communication problems and resentments at being ignored or overruled as grounds for members' decision to leave (box 8.5). There are complaints over inequitable divisions of labour, of other members' unreliability or lack of commitment to the general cause, of being overworked, of lacking assistance, of feeling an outsider at collective meetings and of having no chance to work or plan 'any of the things that Sheba is "really about"' (Sheba Feminist Publishers Archive, 1981: box 2.3).

Magnifying the stresses inherent in any poorly funded collectivist project was the suspicion harboured by individual Sheba members that the collective structure was being manipulated by a powerful but unacknowledged majority. This they understood as giving rise to a group authoritarianism of the kind delineated by both Freeman and by her contemporary movement critic, Anselma dell'Olio: 'It was me being afraid to say what I thought about Sheba. Afraid, for God's sake – in a women's group' (Sheba Feminist Publishers Archive, 1983: box 8.5). The issue of dictatorship by the majority crystallised especially in the 'agonising' process of voting on submissions (Bardsley, 1982: 36). This was a system of consensus publishing, with provision for a 'no' veto, but without a corresponding 'yes' veto – with the result that a manuscript to which one collective member felt passionately committed could be effectively relegated to oblivion by a non-unanimous vote. On this issue Sheba collective members faced the inverse of the usual problem encountered in attempting to reconcile publishing practice with feminist politics. For, habitually, arriving at a decision of the whole membership is too time-consuming for the group to move sufficiently quickly to sign a promising author or to seize a publicity opportunity with the short deadline print and electronic media. Here, by contrast, is a plea for a more extended discussion period when deciding on submissions and publishing policy directions. The feminist objective of discussing 'issues raised by the material submitted' pulled in the opposite direction from prompt, commercially astute decision-making, thus further exacerbating the existing tensions between group members (Bardsley, 1982: 36). As Freeman observed, with bitterness unmistakably derived from her personal experience of women's movement organising, political self-reflexiveness – however admirable in a theoretical sense

– is no substitute for administrative efficiency: 'Unstructured groups may be very effective in getting women to talk about their lives; they aren't very good for getting things done' (1970: 24).

The Personal Cost of the Political

It is a safe presumption when analysing radical feminism to assert that no one joins a women's publishing collective out of financial self-interest. The reality of the collective experience is that, while it may provide a congenial, politically engaged environment in the company of like-minded women and a welcome relief from workplace sexism, it offers minimal or no pay, no job security, long hours, no sick leave, no pension schemes or holiday pay, often cramped, underheated and unsafe working conditions, little or no prospect of advancement, and (either a positive or a negative value, depending upon individual perspective) low-class status in the eyes of the mainstream media (*Co-operator*, 1985; Shah, 1987; Brown, 1998; Lynch, 1998; Poland, 2001). In an era of economic rationalism and the dismantling of the welfare state, the decision to live out one's personal politics by joining a women's publishing collective is a triumph of political idealism over financial pragmatism – a fact that has contributed significantly to the decline in such operations' numbers.

The extent of the economic detriment borne by individual publishing collective members becomes apparent when the costs aside from low remuneration are examined. Initial start-up costs for press outfits are significant, and the expenses of hiring premises and purchasing business hardware are almost always met out of the founders' own pockets. For example, a member of the lesbian Women's Press Collective, active in printing and publishing in San Francisco from 1970, recalled the crippling expense of purchasing their first printing press, 'an ancient German press you couldn't get parts for in the U.S.' (*Workforce*, 1975: 7). Even once a publishing house is operational, accumulated funds are rarely sufficient to cover production expenses. Thus the paper, ink, illustrating and binding costs of each title must be borne on a book-by-book basis, and the period between capital outlay and recoupment from sales is frequently long and arduous. It is during this uncertain period that inexperienced and financially precarious presses most frequently collapse into bankruptcy. Catering only to a coterie readership, they can implement no economies of scale, and thus remain trapped in the vicious financial cycle of small print runs generating limited sales capital:

> Each book has its own financing. Often the [Women's Press] Collective borrows money to buy the paper. Everyone keeps track of the number of days worked a month. When the money comes in from sales, the collective deducts overhead for the shop, pays what can be paid for the graphics and writing, pays off debts, and individuals take a bare subsistence wage (about $6.00 a day). (Joan and Chesman, 1978: 180)

Characteristic of the movement is the (US) Women's Press's policy of relegating staff wages to the lowest budgetary priority – a commonplace in feminist publishing as women's enterprises have commonly relied upon a stream of voluntary labour in order to remain operational (Pitman, 1987: 106). Many feminist publishing collectives operate entirely on unpaid labour, some – like Sheba from 1981 onwards – employ semi-waged workers who are paid minimal wages but each of whom puts in a required day or half-day of unwaged labour per week, and some – like Silver Moon bookshop in its embryonic period around 1984 – pay subsistence wages. Feminists active in press collectives are, understandably, forthcoming about the financial sacrifices they make in order to promote a passionately held political conviction: again the Women's Press Collective in California assert, 'we're not making money, not anything near the minimum wage' (*Workforce*, 1975: 8); a spokesperson for Onlywomen in 1986 confided in an interview that the press was paying only 'minimal salaries to the few working members of the collective' (Fritz, 1986a: 17); Brenda Whisker, an Onlywomen member from 1977, recalled in 1993, 'I don't know where all the money from the printing jobs went to … but I never made an income' (quoted in Jackson, C., 1993: 52). It is acts of faith that, in the final analysis, support non-mainstream feminist publishing enterprises and bestow upon their overworked and underpaid workers the righteous glow of the politically committed as some compensation for their very real financial hardship. Martha Shelley, of the US Women's Press Collective, asserts that it is this hidden substratum of unwaged labour that alone makes many alternative women's publications possible:

> What kept the press going, however, was not equipment but thousands of hours of woman labor – hand collating, hand stapling, women caring enough to put in hours and hours of time with no pay in order to get the word out. To a large extent we still rely on that kind of caring – either in the form of voluntary labor or

donations – women believing in the writing and also in the graphics. (1976: 120–1)

It remains an open question, however, whether the exploitation of women's unpaid labour in the name of a feminist communications network is any more ideologically defensible than women's utilisation as an unpaid labour force within the domestic sphere. While early second-wave feminists were adamant that the institution of the housewife epitomised just such a damaging representation of women's labour as somehow 'non-work' in order to justify the economic subordination of women (Friedan, 1963, 1976; Greer, 1970; Oakley, 1976 [1974]), feminists in general have shied at confronting unpaid women's labour in their own movement on the same terms. To the best of my knowledge, only London's The Women's Press declines to take on unpaid labour because of a conviction that women's work has for too long been exploited under the rubric of volunteerism. But this high-principled decision is (as collective feminist presses are quick to point out) made possible by The Women's Press's guaranteed overdraft from businessman Naim Attallah's Namara group. This is a principle, in other words, they have the corporate-cushioned luxury of being able to espouse.

There may, in addition, be a detrimental aspect to unpaid or minimally paid labour for the collective as well as for the collective member. For a feminist enterprise paying at or below subsistence wages effectively guarantees a self-selecting, middle-class membership – no boon to organisations publicly committed to representing the variety of women's voices. In a sociologically informed analysis entitled 'Conditions for Democracy: Making Participatory Organizations Work', Joyce Rothschild-Whitt concludes that paying at market rates weakens an alternative organisation, hence such operations 'should be structured so that it is *not* economically rational for staff members to seek a career in them' (1979: 225). This surprising contention, perhaps reflecting the article's origins in the more economically buoyant 1970s, encapsulates much of what is financially self-defeating about the collective mentality as it has been embodied in feminist publishing. For it in effect stipulates that membership of a collective will, as a matter of principle, be economically detrimental to the individual. In its fatalism and unexamined suspicion of profit, it echoes Robin Morgan's diagnosis of 'Failure Vanguardism' in the women's movement: the perverse belief that only commercial and personal failure win an activist the badge of political martyrdom –

'the crown of feminist thorns' (1977: 13). Any press enterprise that is incapable of generating a profit, or that is reluctant to pay its staff at competitive market rates even if it is solvent, damages not only the morale and security of its workforce, but also jeopardises its own professed cause. It is blatantly hypocritical for any press to pledge commitment to improving the status of women while lowering the living standards of its own staff.

An early second-wave press in Pittsburgh, Pennsylvania, which published as KNOW, Inc., constitutes an exception among radical feminist publishers in its disavowal of the destructive anti-profit mentality. Opposed to the innately exploitative volunteerist ethos, KNOW, Inc. paid all of its collective members, and prioritised profitability as a key step in ensuring its own survival:

> Our immediate goals are to make working for KNOW a viable alternative for a feminist who needs to earn a living. We feel that there must be a way to keep us from being constantly near doom and/or losing our skilled people because they must survive and our wages are not survival-oriented. We feel that it is important for KNOW and crucial to the Feminist Movement to keep going. (Joan and Chesman, 1978: 146)

The exceptionalism of KNOW, Inc. on this issue is attributable to its origins within the Pittsburgh branch of the hierarchical liberal feminist organisation, the National Organization for Women (NOW), a lobby group of considerable political stature, and one whose sympathies for the exhaustive metagroup analyses of collectivism are limited (Joan and Chesman, 1978: 146; Frank, 1982: 101–2). The damaging failure to accept the capitalist nature of the publishing industry and to transform it for feminism's own interests effectively doomed many radical publishing initiatives once government funding for such projects began to be drastically curtailed. In the face of the ruthless economic rationalist ethos of 1980s British publishing, the radical feminist press sector clung for too long to the misguided belief that commitment and credibility would ride out uncongenial politico-economic reality. The collective medium was indeed a significant element of the women's movement message, but radical feminist publishing may have fatally overestimated its centrality. In a statement that, analysed retrospectively, reads as a succinct and prescient reading of the auguries, Margie Wolfe surveyed the 1980s Canadian women's publishing scene:

Though it is clear we must continue publishing in the 1980s it looks as if it's going to be more difficult ... In the 1980s dedication and commitment are not, it seems, going to be enough. We'll have to become more business-minded if we are to survive. (1980: 14)

STAYING CREDIBLE/STAYING SOLVENT

Suspicion of Profit-Making

The left has historically harboured a deep-seated suspicion that profit-making is inimical to political credibility and that to make money from popularising an oppositional political cause is, inevitably, to dilute the purity of that cause. Radical feminists of the 1970s commonly recoiled from profit-making initiatives, which they regarded as attempts to cash in on the women's movement, in the same way that music and clothing companies had earlier exploited the 1960s counter-cultural ethic. A further complicating issue for committed feminists eager to establish sustainable women's business enterprises was the inconsistency of radical feminism's views about the publishing industry. As has been noted, one of feminism's key contributions to media theory has been its exploration of the ways in which ownership of a medium characterises its content and perspective. Early second-wave feminism's tendency was to emphasise the inherently ideological nature of publishing by elucidating the ownership links between multinational industrial conglomerates and high-profile publishing firms. June Arnold wittily dismissed all Madison Avenue publishers generating profits for their corporate heavyweight parent companies as 'Random House', highlighting their interchangeable sameness from the alternative press perspective (Harris, 1993 [1976]: xxxii). Backed by the likes of 'Kinney Rent-a-Car, Gulf and Western, and RCA', they are, according to Arnold, 'the intellectuals who put the finishing touches on patriarchal politics to make it sell' (1976: 19). Such is the commercial disapproval encoded in radical analyses that the profit-generating nature of the cultural industries is presented as though it constituted revelatory knowledge: 'It is a fact which is disagreeable to many feminists that to produce any commodity, including books, in large quantities, it is necessary to become immersed in the aforementioned patriarchal and capitalistic world of business' (Cadman, Chester and Pivot, 1981: 29). Presses owned by the mainstream, which could be discredited as 'ripping off' the women's movement, were clearly profit-seeking enterprises. But, by a curious argumentative lacuna, radical feminists consistently failed to confront the uncomfortable fact that *any* feminist operation that continued to publish was *also* – inescapably – a profit-seeking enterprise.

The unfortunate corollary of radical feminism's failure to seize propagandising opportunities by embracing capitalist principles was a movement that declined to give whole-hearted support to the founders of its own print enterprises. Frequently staff of such undertakings were showered with praise for their 'sisterly' commitment, but cold-shouldered as movement 'freeloaders' once they asked for the requisite financial support and for demonstrations of consumer loyalty. Occasionally, articles expressing profound discontent at this self-defeating situation emerge in specialist media. A case in point is an article by Cinema of Women's Jane Root entitled 'Distributing *A Question of Silence*: A Cautionary Tale' (1985), in which she describes the obstructions her British feminist film distribution collective experienced when trying to encourage feminists to part with their cash in the interests of having a Dutch feminist film on public release in selected London cinemas: 'some feminists and aficionados of independent film share a particular antipathy for "proper" cinemas like the Screen on the Green [in Islington, north London] and what might be seen as exploitative attempts to cash in on "fashionable feminism"' (1985: 63). The question such experiences necessarily provoke is: do radical women want to see feminist enterprises succeed to the extent that they are prepared to support them – perhaps at some personal cost – even when those enterprises are simultaneously reaching into the mainstream to attract new, as-yet-unconverted audiences?

Fran Winant, founder of the New York lesbian-feminist publishing company Violet Press, believes that in any such conflict between ideological purity and hip-pocket nerve, radical feminists display a tendency to appease the latter by scurrying under the cover of the former. Her 1975 article 'Lesbian Publish Lesbians: My Life and Times with Violet Press' is a remarkable *cri de coeur* from a woman mired at the treacherous intersection of feminist politics and profit; it may be significant that it appeared in the leftist US cultural periodical *Margins* rather than in a women's movement paper such as *Sinister Wisdom*, *off our backs* or *The Second Wave*. The radical wing itself, she implies, bears prime responsibility for the decay of alternative feminist media:

I hadn't yet learned to ask how much women who want to read Violet Press books or see a press like this continue are willing to contribute to its support. I had created another 'movement freebee', like the many other women's 'alternative institutions', [sic] (food co-ops, women's schools and centres, groups putting on non-oppressive women's dances – groups in which I also freely gave my labour), who didn't know how to insist that their sisters pay enough to insure the group's survival. (1975: 62)

Two obvious ways to fund an alternative press such as Violet Press are, aside from requesting charity-type donations, to amass revenue from sales either to already converted feminists or to women who are not already self-declared feminists but who might be receptive to feminism's message. This policy – the underpinning of Virago Press's mainstream market penetration – derives from the commercial knowledge that only an expanding readership can underwrite an expanding budget for feminist book production (Owen, 1998b). Publishers engaged in preaching only to the converted are, conversely, condemned to ever diminishing returns. In attempting to sell Violet Press titles 'at women's get-togethers that I would have gone to anyway' (Winant, 1975: 62), Winant experienced the uncritical anti-capitalist ethos prevalent in 1970s radical feminist circles: 'I was treated as a peddler, out to get other women's money. One woman asked me if I was living on the money I made from the books' (1975: 62).

Addressing this question of potential revenue from outside sales, contemporary feminist media critics are long overdue to confront directly radical feminism's astonishing inability (or unwillingness) to be financially self-sufficient. As van Zoonen has commented, feminist media – especially periodical media – tend to serve primarily a 'ritual' function (1991: 37), addressing principally a coterie readership with their defensive, highly oppositional tone, abstruse terminology and tendency to sign articles with first names only (carrying the implication that readers will be sufficiently *au fait* with movement personalities to identify the author of the piece from this clue alone – see, for example, Freeman, 1970: 20; Desmoines and Nicholson, 1976: 129). Spreading the feminist message is everywhere trumpeted by such magazines as crucially important, yet their very tone and specialist distribution tend to militate against the goal of populism. Thus preoccupied with the task of reiterating policy to the already converted, and cocooned within their own oppositionality, radical feminist media have too frequently averted their gaze from the inescapable equation that profitability = longevity = audience (Fairweather, 1993: 12). This fact in itself paints an ominous picture of the wing's political future. Yet in reading accounts such as Winant's and Root's, critics cannot but be aware of the enormous personal cost to feminists in setting up cultural enterprises only to be disowned by the political movement that spawned them.

Government Funding: 'Non-Political' Money

A third obvious source of finance for radical women's presses (obvious, at least, in the 1970s) was public arts funding in the form of local government grants – a source of start-up capital upon which alternative feminist publishing initiatives relied heavily. Two problems arose from these presses' public funds dependency: firstly, a tendency to regard this income as speciously 'non-political'; and secondly, a failure to predict the rapidity with which government funding could be reallocated or could evaporate altogether. The first of these issues is essentially ideological, and highlights the manner in which radical feminism's economic analysis was capable of being clouded when money was acting in the movement's own interests.

Antonio Gramsci's theory of cultural hegemony was widely influential within the 1970s Marxist-inflected British left. The influence of the Italian thinker is discernible in feminist theorists' willingness to investigate the economic bases for specific cultural phenomenon, for example feminists' attribution of the 1950s cult of the 'happy-housewife-heroine' (Friedan, 1965 [1963]: 30–60) to the economic interests of the post-war consumer industries (Oakley, 1976 [1974]). Yet while the radical wing of feminism was eager to illumine the industrial substructure of multinational publishing corporations, there was a disinclination to subject the origins of local government arts grants to comparable political scrutiny. While public money could validly be argued to comprise roughly 50 per cent women's taxes, the political bodies distributing this funding were (like all political institutions of the period) overwhelmingly male and frequently as hostile to the demands of their female employees as was the private sector. Given the manifestly unequal position of the women's presses, arguably their best-advised action would have been to take the money regardless of its political ties. This is precisely what most presses did; the minutes of the Sheba collective's original meeting, for example, list 'Grants' prominently under the heading

'Sources of income for Sheba' (Sheba Feminist Publishers Archive, 1980: box 2.3; *Co-operator*, 1985: 10). It nevertheless reads as politically inconsistent to brand as freeloaders entrepreneurial women attempting to sell copies of their books without similarly asking what political leverage local government might stand to gain from granting funds to women's groups. Vested interests undeniably exist on both sides, and deserve equally rigorous examination.

A further negative aspect of government grants funding is as prosaically practical as the foregoing is abstractly theoretical: namely, the time-consuming nature of feminist presses' search for sources of public funding. The hours lost from in-house work by the need to complete application forms, and to write reports on the manner in which grants money had been spent, amounted to a drain on the already scant labour resources of feminist presses. The minutes and daily logbooks contained in the Sheba Archive again testify to precisely how time-consuming such foraging for financial sustenance could prove for a small press already critically understaffed (Sheba Feminist Publishers Archive: box 2.3). Furthermore, government funding was fraught with insecurity both in the short term, where grants were commonly one-off and inevitably subject to review, and in the longer-term, where the victory of the British Conservative Party at successive general elections soured the political and economic climate for radical independents.[11] Founded in the earliest months of the first Thatcher government, the Sheba collective may not have predicted how devastating an impact that government's later abolition of the GLC and its slashing of the arts budget were to have on their publishing enterprise. Margie Wolfe, however, observing a similarly right-wing drift in Canadian federal politics, foresaw that the 1980s would sound the death-knell of generous state subsidies for the arts: 'Many feminist publishers began and sustained themselves on grants. These days are over: "women" are no longer a priority' (1980: 14). Bad political timing, exacerbated by a lack of practical financial acumen, saw radical feminist enterprises decimated by the 1980s' increasingly market-driven climate. But could not radical publishers have availed themselves – Virago-like – of commercial opportunities to expound their message? It is a question that strikes at the heart of the radical press agenda, for the pragmatist's argument that the end justifies the means was inevitably to prove unpalatable to a movement which had long maintained that means and ends were, in fact, indistinguishable.

Autonomy/Oppositionality/Separatism:
The Perspective of Radical Lesbian Publishers

The Achilles heel of radical feminist publishing has, since its inception in the late 1960s, consistently been money and the appropriate attitude to adopt towards it. The complex issues at stake were, in the case of radical lesbian publishers, given particular urgency by the confluence of 1970s debates around feminist entrepreneurialism with a contemporaneous schism over lesbian separatism (Echols, 1989: 269–81; McDermott, 1994: 34–5, 77–8). Radical feminists proposed that the significance of financial power for feminism lay in its ability to guarantee independence from male-defined and -dominated systems. Only a press that was financially self-sufficient or that could derive its income from sources not controlled by the mainstream could, it was argued, guarantee its own operating methods and ensure the uncompromisingly oppositional tone of its message. Onlywomen Press, in an early manifesto statement, articulates these central concerns of the radical wing by insisting that 'communication should not be controlled by business considerations or, in some instances, by bookshops' (Onlywomen Press, c. 1977). For radical publishers still in operation at the time of The Women's Press resignations débâcle in 1991 (in which managing director Ros de Lanerolle and senior staff resigned over the male owner's interference with list direction and commissioning), the interconnected nature of press freedom and press funding could not have appeared clearer. Yet long prior to this concrete demonstration of an unsympathetic owner's power to gag a feminist publishing operation, awareness that such an hypothetical risk shadowed any non-independent press had already been articulated. In their media manifesto, 'From Us: Thoughts on the Feminist Media', Boston's Female Liberation group stipulate that the first criteria of genuinely feminist alternative media must be that they are 'media controlled and *owned* by women' [my italics] (1974: 2).

The Boston Female Liberation group's cagily mistrustful tone is echoed by Britain's sole radical lesbian publisher, Onlywomen, which stipulated that if women's words were vulnerable to the processes of co-optation and subsequent commercial rejection, how much more vulnerable were the voices of lesbian women? The particular history of lesbian literature and mainstream publishing bears out Onlywomen's suspicion at the motivations of the corporate presses, for lesbian love stories and semi-pornographic pulp novels had been a publishing subgenre throughout the 1950s and 1960s, and had frequently been penned by lesbian writers. But the imperatives of a heterosexual-dominated industry required that lesbianism be portrayed as a tortured, unfulfillable condition, hence the preponderance of the 'dilettante-dyke-returns-to-her-husband' plot and the ubiquity of the suicidal lesbian protagonist – a direct descendent of *The Well of Loneliness* model of the 1920s (Koski and Tilchen, 1975: 42; Adams, 1992). Because of this experience of image distortion and literary ventriloquism, lesbian presses of the 1970s were commonly at the vanguard of the separatist media movement, asserting that the goal of developing 'political analysis unhindered by patriarchal values' required the establishment of 'our own culture' (Cadman, Chester and Pivot, 1981: 29). Because the 'double oppression' model commonplace in radical lesbian theorising from the early 1970s posited lesbian women as two-fold victims of a sexist *and* heterosexist society (Myron and Bunch, 1975), lesbian presses tended to articulate their concerns over co-optation as a more heightened form of the anxiety prevalent among feminist presses generally. It is an analysis that, viewed in retrospect, reads with a certain irony. For lesbian fiction and theory constitute a valuable niche market for mainstream publishers, and only the most hardline of 1970s lesbian separatists could construe the contemporary visibility of lesbian identity within mainstream culture as politically inimical. Literary separatism, such a publishing dynamic suggests, may more profitably serve as a temporary tactic than as a steadfast ideological conviction.

RESISTING MAINSTREAM/ALTERNATIVE BINARIES: A POLITICS OF PROVISIONAL SEPARATISM

If the foregoing discussion of profit and politics paints an oppressively bleak picture of radical feminist publishing's fortunes, the gloom of commercial failure and political retreat may be alleviated somewhat by outlining an alternative model of lesbian publishing, the success of which may point towards future reinvigoration of the alternative press sector. The long-running US publishing house Naiad Press has previously been best known across the Atlantic as the originator of much of Silver Moon Books' list. While SMB was innovative in its own right in vigorously marketing its books through its 'highly visible' central London Silver Moon women's bookshop, in addition to mainstream outlets, much of SMB's sales success and market distinctiveness must be traced to its US partner (Cholmeley, 1991: 217). Of the SMB fiction backlist only two titles – Jane Thompson's *Still Crazy*

(1994) and *Diamonds and Rust* (1996) – were originated by the London firm. Former SMB director Sue Butterworth aimed to commission several original titles each year, yet she freely acknowledged that the imprint's financial and literary substructure derived from buy-ins of the 'better' titles from the Naiad list (Butterworth, 1998). Naiad's concentration on previously undervalued feminist genres – in particular lesbian romance, erotica and detective fiction – unearthed a market of women anxiously seeking respite from second-wave feminism's often high moral tone in escapist lesbian easy-reads. The distinctiveness of Naiad *vis-à-vis* other lesbian presses arises from the fact that the firm did not emerge from a consciousness-raising group or political meeting, but from a 1973 agreement struck between lawyer Anyda Marchant and lesbian writer and critic Barbara Grier (author of fiction published under the pseudonym Gene Damon). Marchant provided the necessary financial backing while Grier, with literary connections from long involvement with lesbian periodical *The Ladder*, and the input of two other partners, Muriel Crawford and Donna McBride, recruited authorial talent and managed press administration (Marchant and Crawford, 1976; Frank, 1982; Hermes, 1992).

Naiad has always operated separately from mainstream publishing, but in its relatively sanguine conception of the commercial industry's ideological function it differs radically from contemporareous US presses such as Daughters, Inc., Violet Press or Diana Press – or from their closest British counterpart, Onlywomen Press. These committedly separatist presses conceive(d) of the multinational-dominated sphere of corporate publishing as not only hostile to lesbian-identified books in the present instance (as exemplified by their insistence that positive lesbian portrayals were not commercially viable) but as *inherently* inimical to lesbian texts because of the industry's saturation with patriarchal values. As a result of this conviction, the rhetoric that emerged from the separatist limb of feminism advocated women-only distribution chains, total disassociation from male literary institutions, and a near conspiracy theory that the extinction of lesbian publishing featured strongly on the agenda of the mainstream 'finishing press' (Moberg, 1974; Arnold, 1976; Desmoines and Nicholson, 1976). The conceptualisation of radical feminism's relationship to the mainstream as one of implacable opposition bound these presses into a binary ontological pattern of embattled political virtue versus nefarious institutionalised power:

Every genuinely feminist work of art is a blow at the heart of patriarchal reality. When lesbians control our own publishing and our own printing and our own distributing of our own words, we're directing those blows to the target. (Desmoines and Nicholson, 1976: 127)

The constricting nature of such a position became starkly manifest in an increasingly conservative political and economic climate. Faced with the collapse of alternative lesbian feminist institutions, separatist feminists too often retreated into escalating glorification of radical failure as visionary self-sacrifice – the self-deluding martyrdom diagnosed by Robin Morgan as 'Failure Vanguardism'. By conceiving of the mainstream as an antithetical Other, rather than as a powerful socio-political force with which lesbian feminist politics maintains a shifting, always contested relationship, separatist feminists in effect burnt their theoretical bridges. Ineluctably precluded from rapprochement with the mainstream, the collapse of radical feminist institutions permitted escape only through spectacular – but politically defeatist – rhetorical self-immolation.

The absolutist radical feminist theoretical model stands in marked contrast to the remarks of Naiad Press's Anyda Marchant, for whom lesbian literature represents more an end in itself than a preliminary step in an ongoing political revolution. She, too, bemoans the paucity of strong, well-written lesbian novels and is convinced that 'this scarcity is due at least in part to the obstacles in the way of publication', but the press's remedy for this lack has been to supply 'good quality' and 'veracious' lesbian works rather than rhetorically to rehearse the downfall of the mainstream industry (Marchant and Crawford, 1976: 117). Intriguingly, Marchant's indictment of 'the strangling effect of the market conditions that dominate the large commercial presses' (1976: 117) still allows for the construction of the mainstream not as inherently oppositional to lesbianism, but as only empirically so at specific historical junctures and in specific geographical spaces. That Naiad was 'brought into being to protest' (1976: 117) against this strangling effect allows for the possibility that, should the attitude of the mainstream undergo a political sea change and should it embrace lesbian literature, Naiad-style presses may be rendered culturally redundant. It is a manoeuvre that appears to presage the quintessentially 1980s redefinition of the 'political' away from an encompassing socio-economically determined reality towards a cultural politics of representation. Were more quality lesbian titles produced via mainstream press channels, such a relativist argument implies, lesbian-run separatist operations may cease to serve their distinctive cultural purpose.

Discernible in the statements of Naiad Press, and constituting a profound shift from the manifesto statements of radical separatist women's print operations, is such a concept of *provisional* separatism – namely lesbians operating their own presses until such time as the mainstream recognises the value of their work and begins to imitate it. It is an argument that, admittedly, lends itself to assimilationism and remains far from unproblematic. There is a risk that the absorption of lesbian literature into the lists of mainstream houses may not be paralleled by a similarly rapid elevation of lesbian employees into the managerial structures of such firms – resulting in a tokenising discrepancy between cultural profile and political power of the kind that bedevils black women's writing. Moreover, even within women-run houses such as Virago, the prioritorising of lesbian literature – commissioned and edited *by* lesbians – is subject to commercial fluctuation: amid the directorial instability of Virago's board in 1995, the distinctively branded Virago Lesbian Landmarks series was culled for being insufficiently profitable (Pitman, 1995; Hennegan, 1998).

Yet Marchant's position offers a way out of self-defeating binary structures, which lesbian publishing should not disregard lightly. The position can be read as backing a tactical interrelationship with the mainstream, in which independent lesbian presses exist to cut the radical edge of new writing, while the mainstream industry remains doggedly a few paces behind, observing the directions that prove profitable and advancing accordingly. Just such a dynamic has been at work in, for example, Naiad's publication of erotic lesbian anthologies with suggestively marketable titles such as *Diving Deeper* (1993) and *The First Time Ever* (1995). In the wake of proven commercial success of such titles from feminist houses – including Sheba's influential collection *Serious Pleasure* (1989) – mainstream publishers began in the 1990s to enter the market for women's erotica, publishing profitably in the area (for example, *The Penguin Book of Erotic Stories by Women* (1996); *The Mammoth Book of Erotica* (2002); and *The Best American Erotica* (2002). As Joanna Briscoe marvelled in her review of *The Penguin Book of Lesbian Short Stories* (1993), 'who would ever have dreamed, in those early days at Virago, that Penguin would calmly produce a collection of lesbian short stories and wrap it up in Sapphic hard sell?' (1993: 9). This present publishing reality is a long way from the New Jerusalem of an autonomous and dominant radical women's communications network. But the fact that Naiad has enjoyed financial growth and expansion of market share while trenchantly oppositional collectives have withered on the vine indicates that strategic interventionism may signal the publishing and political future for lesbian presses.

Discernible in recent statements from Naiad's directors is the belief that mainstream publishing has not yet eclipsed the need for independent lesbian-run enterprises. In mid-2000, Naiad Press founders Grier and McBride sold their backlist and the majority of their author contracts to Bella Books, a woman-run publisher in Michigan, and scaled back the Naiad list from 34 titles per annum to four.[12] Presenting the press downsizing 'as a way to protect our authors, our bookstores, our readers', Naiad acknowledges the mainstream's interest in lesbian books, and the vast resources available to multinational firms aggressively targeting such audiences, but reserves a segment of that market for lesbian-run publishing enterprises (Howell, 2000: 12). It is a plausible means to balance the personal exhaustion of operating a press for many years on virtual 'slave labor', and the founding ideological commitment to controlling the publishing process (Frank, 1982: 105). Viewed in broader perspective, Naiad's decision encapsulates in microcosm the debate within the lesbian, gay, bisexual and transgendered (LGBT) book sector: whether to celebrate the migration of LGBT titles towards mainstream industry outlets as the culmination of political battles for recognition, or whether participation in mainstream book channels signals political dissipation and risks corporate misrepresentation. Such 'glass half empty or half full' debates parallel and intersect with mainstream/margin debates in the academic feminist publishing sector, highlighting how cumbersome and manifestly inadequate inherited opposition/collaboration frameworks have become to describe twenty-first-century book industry cultural politics (Abbott, 2001: 33).

CONCLUSION: ASSIMILATING LITERARY SEPARATISM

In the course of interviewing women involved with feminist publishing, I have been struck by the frequency with which they speak of the 'next wave' of young women whom they anticipate will move into feminist publishing, invigorating it with fresh insights and enthusiasm (Callil, 1996; Butterworth, 1998; Mohin, 1998; Owen, 1998b; Brewster, 2003; Spender, 2003). Should this third wave gather force – and there is some evidence in Virago's 1997 relaunch that it has already done so – its innovations will inevitably be in part a reaction against the perceived failings of its publishing predecessors. It appears crucial, therefore, to initiate debate on the legacy of second-wave radical publishing, a movement that appears now to have drawn to a close. Because of overwhelming changes in international economic circumstances, in publishing industry structures, and in social attitudes towards feminism, the vast majority of 1970s and 1980s radical women's publishing ventures have folded or have dwindled to essentially single-person operations. Rightly credited with revolu-tionising the *content* of publishing lists across the industry, their rhetoric of *political* revolution appears increasingly travestied by the actuality of their demise. The invigorating 'new blood' in the women's publishing sphere cannot begin to make itself generally felt until the pros and cons of a previous era's record are calculated – a fact that makes feminist media criticism's overly respectful silence on the fate of radical women's publishing not only puzzling, but inhibiting.

In a thought-provoking essay on a related topic, 'Gay Fiction R.I.P.?', Viking New York's senior literary editor Jonathan Burnham argues that gay culture has now achieved sufficient mainstream recognition that the classification 'gay fiction' has a ghettoising rather than a self-affirming effect: 'In a world where gay writing has emerged from the ghetto, grown up and significantly broadened its frame of reference, the continuing segregation of gay fiction is puzzling' (1998: 33). Without attempting to collapse the gay male literary experience into the quite distinct heritage of lesbian writing, the gist of Burnham's argument nevertheless translates well to debates around feminist and lesbian publishing. The overlapping literary spheres of feminist and lesbian publishing have been – like gay men's writing – previously marginalised by the mainstream yet – again like gay fiction – they too have migrated markedly towards the centre of Western cultural consciousness. Yet, whereas Burnham's article propounds a largely assimilationist framework with which to conceptualise gay male writing, this discussion advocates for radical feminist writing and publishing a more strategically flexible position located on the outer margins of the mainstream – akin to it, but not of it, as it were.

The 1970s and 1980s feminist press boom demonstrated incon-testably that there existed a public appetite for politicised publishing. The dilemma confronting contemporary feminists now becomes how meaningfully to integrate a consumer demand for *culturally* oppositional texts into a movement founded to initiate concrete *political* change. Feminist publishing, because of its obvious alignment with the cultural – as opposed to the activist – feminist sector has always struggled against this threatened tendency towards consumerist containment: namely, the risk of diluting political ideas through their very commodification and dissemination in book form. If anything, the 1990s drift towards an amorphous politics of sign and representation threatened to amplify this pre-existing problem. A potential resolution of the dilemma may lie in appropriating the all-woman workplace practices of radical presses, so as to ensure political investment by those producing the literature, but repositioning these presses on the margins of the cultural mainstream. According to such an argument, radical women's presses would be fully acknowledging the ubiquity of mainstream culture, but acknowledging also the permeability of its discursive boundaries. By pushing its margins and destabilising its certainties, radical women's publishing can capitalise upon its heritage of oppositionality, but from a position sufficiently close to the mainstream to attract new readerships. Attitudinal changes, which must underpin any such reconfiguration, would include the rejection of ostensibly democratic group models that are, in reality, powerless to check oligarchical tendencies, the renunciation of the destructive anti-profit mentality, and an unembarrassed exploration of ways in which modern marketing techniques may be employed to proselytise feminist ideas. This is not to argue that feminists must abandon critical reflection on mainstream developments, but rather that they should be open to appropriating mainstream tools for feminist ends. Audre Lorde's oft-quoted observation that 'the master's tools will never dismantle the master's house' would seem to militate against such a co-optational strategy by feminism (1984: 112). But the statement belies the fact that Lorde's words were themselves disseminated only through feminist intervention in that historical bastion of male cultural hegemony – the publishing industry.

Radical women's publishing has always felt itself to be straddling a chasm: one foot in the righteous realm of marginal politics and the other in the polluting world of mainstream profit. By the twenty-first century, radical presses are in the advantageous position of being able to reconceptualise their split nature as a tactical advantage: closer to the ground-level issues of women's politics, and benefiting from an enhanced political credibility in the eyes of consumers, they can specialise in cutting-edge writing, constantly pushing at the margins of mainstream respectability and compounding their earlier successes in championing new literary forms and idioms. Their smaller size and independence grants these presses the manoeuverability to pursue riskier publishing opportunities than their mainstream competitors, while successes – if well marketed – can crystallise public perception of a specialist brand identity. Unquestionably, it is uncertain, little-charted territory, which may involve, as Silver Moon Books found, working tirelessly to launch new writers only subsequently to see them jump ship for the larger advances and promotional packages on offer from mainstream competitors (Butterworth, 1998). Politics and profit may yet be far from synonymous terms. But if feminist publishing is to envision a future it is imperative that these concepts evolve from the diametric opposites they represented for many second-wave radical women. Accustomed as 1970s feminists were to thinking in dialectics, it is long since time that the publishing houses they spawned appreciated the interdependency and mutability at the concept's heart.

5

'This Book Could Change Your Life': Feminist Bestsellers and the Power of Mainstream Publishing

> In general the [women's] movement's relationship with fiction was uneasy. 'Authenticity' required either poetry (with its minimal readership and consequent freedom from commercialism) or the straight talk of non-fiction. In terms of sexual politics *The Female Eunuch* was generically sounder than *Fear of Flying*.
>
> John Sutherland, *Bestsellers: Popular Fiction of the 1970s*
> (1981: 83)

Within the second-wave women's movement, literature always existed in a state of troubled ambiguity – valued for its proselytising potential and communicative power, yet simultaneously regarded with wariness as in some sense an indulgence, sapping revolutionary action by the isolating, individualist nature of its production and consumption. Some 30 years since feminist theory began its bid for entrenchment within the discipline of literary studies, lingering doubt is still discernible in writings of selected critics as to whether the reading, criticism and teaching of literature represent sufficiently *political* engagements with the cause of women's rights (Wolf, 1993; Eagleton, 1996b; Stanley, 1997; Walter, 1999 [1998]; and see also Robinson, 1978: 52). As John Sutherland's observations in his 1981 study *Bestsellers: Popular Fiction of the 1970s* attest, such debates over the political value of feminist literary-critical activity are not a recent phenomenon. Yet the assumption implicit in the passage cited above – that non-fiction publication represented a less politically fraught manoeuvre for women's liberationists than did fiction publication – warrants critical re-examination in the light of mainstream publishers' unabated fascination with the feminist bestseller.

As explored in the preceding chapter, the risks contingent upon feminists' collaboration with mainstream fiction publishers gave rise to impassioned theoretical debate in the early to mid-1970s over the merits of separatist print organising. However, when the generic classification of the text to be published shifted from feminist fiction to feminist non-fiction, these debates were not necessarily allayed in the manner that Sutherland's statement suggests – if anything they were in fact further aggravated. For if fiction publication with the mainstream carried implicit risks of containment and political distortion, how much greater were those risks when the theoretical manifestos of the movement were themselves subject to the ideological whim and commercial imperative of the mainstream publishing industry? Having struggled to articulate an oppositional critique in the teeth of social conditioning and Establishment disapproval, feminists found themselves made doubly vulnerable at exactly the point where they sought to communicate their message to a wider public. If, according to Marshall McLuhan's dictum (2001 [1964]: 7–23), the medium is indeed the message, feminists' commercial impotence *vis-à-vis* mainstream publishers was tantamount to political silencing.

The chapter that follows explores the mainstream publishing industry's ambiguous treatment of feminist ideas in the period both prior to and since the emergence of the modern feminist press movement. In any examination of feminism and publishing politics such a discussion is crucial, for it confronts directly the issue of separate women's publishing houses which has energised – and which currently preoccupies – the feminist press movement. The market successes enjoyed by feminist publishers and examined in the foregoing chapters have been interlaced with, and sometimes compromised by, seemingly endemic structural problems in a greatly undercapitalised and organisationally chaotic feminist press sector. These recurrent problems prompt renewed consideration of feminist presses' original separatist conviction: now that mainstream publishers have successfully promoted feminist titles to diverse readerships, have the women's presses witnessed the erosion of their very *raison d'être*? In the analysis that follows, this discussion argues for an attitude of critical circumspection in approaching the specious phenomenon of the 'feminist bestseller'. For the mainstream industry has not been a neutral medium for the communication of feminist ideas, but has crucially *mediated* those ideas through its commissioning, packaging and marketing of feminist texts. Only by analysing the corporate publishing industry's modulation of feminist thought can interested observers hope to arrive at a prognosis of feminist publishing's future. The machinery of the feminist bestseller potentially foreshadows the brave new world of an industry in which independent, women-run alternative presses have been commercially eclipsed.

The discussion that follows centres upon five texts spanning almost 40 years of modern women's political activism. In their diverse cultural reference points they testify to the variety of influences upon second- and third-wave feminist thought: Betty Friedan's *The Feminine Mystique* (1963); Kate Millett's *Sexual Politics* (1972 [1970]); Germaine Greer's *The Female Eunuch* (1970); Naomi Wolf's *The Beauty Myth* (1990); and Germaine Greer's 'sequel' to *The Female Eunuch*, *The Whole Woman* (2000 [1999]). Each of these texts is a 'bestseller' in the commonly used sense of the term, having figured among the industry's top 10 or 15 highest selling non-fiction titles in its year of publication.[1] Moreover, in the case of all five works, commercial turnover has been paralleled by critical inclusion in the canon of feminist books commonly discussed within academia and the wider literary community. Their status as feminist 'classics' has been repeatedly hailed in contemporary reviews and further underlined by subsequent critical commentary. Indeed, this sample feminist canon is in many ways self-sustaining: later books in the group frequently refer explicitly or rely implicitly on analyses and methodologies proposed in earlier titles – Wolf, for example, reformulates Friedan's earlier critique of women's magazine culture for a 1990s audience, while Greer's *The Whole Woman* consciously mimics the chapter structure, page layout and mode of address utilised by its famed predecessor.

In selecting these works as analytical foci, this discussion does not attempt to reinscribe the concept of a hegemonic feminist canon, one incapable of radical critique or impervious to changes in feminist politics. Rather, by siting these texts within their institutional, commercial and industrial contexts, this discussion aims to interrogate the role of the publishing industry in constructing the category of the 'feminist classic', thereby calling into question the rarefied aura that surrounds the term. If 'classic' status inheres at least partially in the pre- and post-publication history of an individual text, then potentially *other* texts and *other* feminist authors could equally, depending on their individual publishing histories, have laid claim to 'classic' status. The deployment of the terms 'classic' and 'bestseller' in this discussion betokens primarily publishing industry endorsement and promotion rather than any innate metaphysical or even intellectual superiority. Other politically engaged female critics – among them Eva Figes, Juliet Mitchell, Ann Oakley, Suzanne Moore, Susan Faludi, Katie Roiphe and Natasha Walter – could alternatively have been included in this chapter's sample cross-section of texts. Indeed, by highlighting the extent to which canonical inclusion is the arbitrary outcome of publishing industry intervention and media serendipity, this discussion aims vigorously to problematise, rather than to buttress, the notion of canonicity itself.

Acknowledging the mainstream book industry's crucial role in engineering feminist bestsellerdom may prove highly discomforting to those interested in the production of feminist knowledge. Firstly, the idea that marketing and not pure merit may be instrumental in denoting feminist classics casts a veil of further complication between the texts of the feminist canon and their contemporary readerships. For now readers are obliged to factor into their interpretations not only developments in feminist thought subsequent to the book's original appearance, but also the *nature* of the book's initial marketing and reception, and the effect that this may have had on its subsequent publishing (and academic) fortunes. It is destabilising, to say the least, to recognise that the publishing and commercial interests of which feminism has rightly been critical may themselves have crucially determined the landmark texts of feminist thought. The net effect is to add a powerful variable to an already complex literary-political equation.

Moreover, the concept of publishers as prescribers – rather than mere purveyors – of feminist theory casts an unflattering light on feminism's previous methodologies. Outspoken in its analyses of women's interaction with all aspects of society and culture, feminism would seem simultaneously to have maintained an analytical blind spot with regard to the *publication* of those findings. To return to the argument with which this volume began, can feminist scholarship be as culpable of ignoring the publishing industry as publishing studies has frequently been guilty of ignoring gender issues? Feminists here risk at best intellectual sloppiness, at worst unconscious political collusion.

The complex interface of feminist thought and mainstream publishing is best explored by tracing the production of a feminist bestseller through the industry's institutional apparatus. Such a publishing-centred analytic model conceptualises the text not as finished artefact but rather as ongoing process, originating with a text's research and writing by the author, passing through industry-demarcated departments such as contracts, design, marketing and publicity, and subsequently to the text's public release, reviewing, sales and initiation into the canon of feminist thought. This method-ological framework recommends itself because of the light it throws on the immensely complex and labour-intensive processes by which authorial creation is transformed for public consumption. Literary-critical feminism has illumined the material and cultural factors governing the writing (or non-writing) of literature by women, as well as the subtle means by which women readers decode those literary texts. It might, therefore, look upon such a publishing-centred analysis as a critical missing link. Publication is *the* indispensable intervening event by which writers and readers are brought into relation with each other. It is the linchpin that makes feminist literary criticism as it currently stands simultaneously possible and problematic.

While such a product-based framework may appear novel, its use is justifiable in that it impresses feminist analysis with the dynamics of the commercial publishing industry. Rather than merely adding publishing terminology and processes to a standard literary-critical analytic framework, leaving that framework substantially unaltered, such a modified approach has the advantage of radically infusing an academic mode of criticism with industry processes – allowing the latter to transform the usual paradigms of the former. Because this discussion argues that industry exigencies crucially influence the production of feminist knowledge, it appears important explicitly to factor these exigencies into the construction of *this* critique. Those alleging myopia in other critical schools are well advised to ensure their own critical *modus operandi* is at least explicitly acknowledged.

Radical feminist media theorists of the early 1970s were inclined to view the publishing industry's capitalist ethos as implacably opposed to the revolutionary zeal of feminist consciousness. The industry's opportunistic interest in feminism was viewed as tantamount to a repressive tolerance, which aimed to anaesthetise feminist dissent by publishing 'the least threatening, the most saleable, the most easily controlled', while commercially exploiting a convenient niche market (Arnold, 1976: 19; Ehrlich, 1973). Yet, with the advent and expansion of an independent feminist publishing culture, the lists of mainstream houses have not been populated by a merely token feminist presence (as early radical theorists feared). Corporate-owned imprints have sponsored pioneering works responsible for major developments in feminist thought. If anything, the rhetorical positions of publisher and purchaser may have become reversed, with publishers increasingly offering radical treatises to an apparently satiated and apathetic public. In a jaded 1990 editorial, the *Independent on Sunday* adumbrated the tedium of a 'radical new look at the oppressions of women' being offered to the public 'almost every autumn', with 'the publisher (if no one else) hail[ing] the book as revolutionary' (*Independent on Sunday*, 1990: 21). Far from the corporate mainstream censoring feminist books outright, publishers appear to have annexed feminism's rallying power to their pre-Christmas publishing schedules.

Yet the fact that the most dire predictions of separatist feminist media theorists have failed to eventuate should not tempt feminists into the opposite response – an unduly sanguine embrace of the mainstream in the belief that multinational publishers represent the optimal means for disseminating feminist ideas. Such an assertion is vulnerable precisely because it confuses the publishing industry's interest in feminism with what is in feminism's own best interests. Only through critically examining the means by which the corporate mainstream commissions and promotes 'classic' feminist texts can critics be alert to the industry's filtering power. For behind the received canon of feminist intellectual development there stands a spectral apocrypha of texts unwritten or, if written, largely unpromoted, unreviewed and untaught. The publishing industry, in its role as de facto gatekeeper of feminist knowledges, urgently needs to be incorporated into the formulations of feminist thinkers. By elevating the publishing industry from the status of an implicit to that of an explicit element in its theorising, feminist criticism stands to gain a heightened awareness of the conditions of its own intellectual and material production.

THE PRE-PUBLICATION PHASE

Research, Writing and Literary Agents

The means by which authorial inspiration is transformed into written text is a process upon which feminist critics have long trained their attention, producing subtle and culturally nuanced readings of the paths taken by texts from original idea to bound volume. Whether these readings are produced under the rubric of biographical criticism (tracing the circumstances of individual authors that were conducive to, or that inhibited, literary production) or of cultural and intellectual history (analysing the broader cultural environment of historical periods and their influence upon creation of literary texts), the fundamental critical insistence has been on contextualising individual works within an historically grounded societal framework. The species of materialist-cultural criticism advanced here of necessity draws upon the productive insights and methodologies of existing feminist readings, but it moreover focuses specifically on the *institutional* contexts from which feminist texts derive. In particular, a publishing-focused analysis concentrates upon the points at which individual authors enter into the machinery of publication and promotion, initiating the communication cycle that achieves completion once their text is consumed by readers – only to begin again with other readers and with the writing of still other texts. The benefit of such an approach is that the basic unit of critical analysis shifts from the lifespan of a single book, or of multiple books by a single author, to an emphasis on the channels through which published books move, and the manner in which the success of earlier books influences the publication and reception of later, generically related titles. This approach attempts to balance the cumulative category-driven marketing tactics of the bookselling industry against the specifics of an individual title, formulating an analysis that is alive both to the generic pattern and to the surprise bestseller.

An industry-focused analytic technique is particularly productive for a reading of perhaps the second-wave's earliest bestseller: Betty Friedan's *The Feminine Mystique*. Because the text has been commonly regarded as a magnificent exception to the general malaise of mid-century feminist inertia, critics have tended to overlook the ways in which *The Feminine Mystique* reworks pre-existing discourses and genres to introduce feminist arguments under the guise of adjacent disciplines. Viewed in this light, the text emerges not as a towering achievement isolated from its contemporary literary context, so much as a sophisticated collusion with an often reluctant publishing industry to introduce feminist analysis to a mainstream audience.

For author Betty Friedan, writing in the immensely conservative climate of suburban America in the early 1960s, few models for feminist non-fiction came readily to hand. Simone de Beauvoir's *Le Deuxième Sexe* (1949) had been translated into English and published as *The Second Sex* in the United States by Alfred A. Knopf in 1953, but Beauvoir's text served Friedan both as prototype and as unwelcome fellow traveller. *The Second Sex*'s dangerous reputation as a sexually explicit book was, in the post-McCarthy United States, compounded by Beauvoir's explicitly socialist political convictions. In any case, Beauvoir's audience of philosophically informed, left-wing Europeans differed radically from the implied audience envisaged by Friedan for her more populist work (Dijkstra, 1980; Murray, 2000c).

The means by which Friedan sought to ensure her book a large readership among the suburban heartlands of commuter-belt America was by appropriating the audience for mass-market women's magazines and by utilising their accessibly non-academic writing style to convey a politically radical conception of women's role. Friedan extrapolated from her experience as a journalist on titles such as *McCall's* and *Ladies' Home Journal* to mount an influential critique of the role of women's magazines in socialising American women into low academic expectations, domestic careerism and vicarious achievement. Yet, ironically, it was Friedan's existing magazine publication record and industry connections that ensured invaluable pre-publication publicity when extracts from *The Feminine Mystique* were published in these same magazines to coincide with the book's February 1963 publication by W.W. Norton & Company. The surprising decision of these magazines' editors marks a triumph of circulation boosting over editorial consistency:

> The letters I got came not only from those who had bought the book itself, but also from those who had read excerpts of it printed simultaneously – in unprecedented inexplicable defiance of custom – by the major competing women's magazines whose feminine mystique I was attacking, the *Ladies' Home Journal* and *McCall's*, and earlier, *Mademoiselle* and *Good Housekeeping*.[2] In this fashion, I suppose the book reached five times the 3,000,000 or so who actually bought it.[3] The unprecedented passion of their response was such that later that year *McCall's* asked me to do an article about the letters. (Friedan, 1976: 19)

The generic hybridity of *The Feminine Mystique* was much remarked upon in the reviews and publishing industry comment that the book generated in the wake of its 1963 publication, hinting at a formal radicalism about which later critics have tended to remain silent. The book's critique of Freudian theory and the American psychoanalytic establishment's obsession with individual adaptation ensured it coverage among psychological and sociological journals such as *Contemporary Psychology*, *American Sociological Review* and *Social Forces* (Engel, 1963; Fava, 1963; Higgins, 1964). These original reviews tended to focus on Friedan's charge that graduate women lacked professional opportunities, understanding the work as a study of 'the distorted image of today's woman' (*PW*, 28 January 1963: 184) written in the style of 'a magazine article [which] got out of hand' (Higgins, 1964: 396). Friedan's publisher appears to have identified the college-educated social sciences audience as the book's primary market. The slipcover of the original hardback edition features bold-type quotes from writerly celebrities such as Pearl S. Buck in an attempt to buttress the book's reputation with the force of intellectual prestige (Friedan, 1963). Yet Norton's attempt to pitch the book upmarket perhaps underestimated the lure of its accessibility for domestically isolated housewives. The sales figures in *Publishers Weekly*'s 1963 'Best Sellers' list indicate that sales tended to rise dramatically in the wake of Friedan's 'personal appearances on radio and television' (*PW*, 28 January 1963: 184). A publicity announcement in *Publishers Weekly* on 29 April 1963 that 'the author will make personal appearances in Chicago, Detroit, St. Paul and Cleveland early in May' (226) is followed within weeks by the industry update that 'sales are especially good in Chicago, Norton reports' (*PW*, 27 May 1963: 98). Mainstream media channels such as *McCall's* and the *Ladies' Home Journal*, coupled with radio and television promotion, ensured that Friedan's book targeted an audience largely bypassed by academic journals. Norton's advice to booksellers in *Publishers Weekly* that 'over 40,000 copies' had been sold and that 'nation-wide advertising will continue' (23 September 1963: 90) is an early instance of a feminist bestseller receiving mainstream media attention, despite the fact that the mainstream media constitute a central target of the book's cultural critique. Viewed optimistically, this could be interpreted as proof of the publishing industry's openness to radical innovation; viewed more circumspectly it suggests tolerance for radicalism only within the rigorously circumscribed boundaries of commercial profit.

Friedan's remarks on the publication history of *The Feminine Mystique* evoke a media industry initially as sceptical of the book's intellectual credibility as of its commercial viability. An earlier article-length version of the book's central thesis was rejected for publication or extensively subedited to support entirely opposite conclusions by three mainstream women's journals, leading Friedan to withdraw the article from submission in the somewhat naive belief that book publishers would be more responsive to her unconventional agenda (Friedan, 1976: 17). This sanguine view of the book industry was promptly dispelled when Friedan's 'then agent refused to handle the book when it was finished, and the publisher [Norton] only printed several thousand copies' (Friedan, 1976: 18). Such initial publishing industry indifference had been foreshadowed during the book's writing when Friedan endured the disparaging comments or outright disapproval of those in her immediate environment: the scorn of fellow researchers at the New York Public Library for devoting herself to such a quasi-intellectual topic; the conflicting demands on her time in running a household for a husband and three young children in suburban Rockland County, New York; and the moral reproaches of her housewife neighbours for stealing time for the project from the presumed higher calling of household management. Recalling graphically in *It Changed My Life: Writings on the Women's Movement* how she 'chauffeured, and did the P.T.A. and buffet dinners, and hid, like secret drinking in the morning, the book I was writing when my suburban neighbors came for coffee' (1976: 14), Friedan evokes an air of feared disapproval reinforced by an absence of feminist writerly models or publishing industry precedent.

Commissioning Feminism

The point in the book production process at which a would-be feminist author comes into contact with a publishing house may be mediated in a variety of ways, though it is a relationship almost invariably characterised by discrepancy in the status of the parties. At the lowest level of authorial helplessness is the unsolicited manuscript, submitted to a commissioning editor in the hope of its gaining acceptance for publication. Significantly, none of the five major feminist bestsellers analysed in this chapter achieved publication via this channel. Yet between the status of the commissioned 'star' author and the writer of the unsolicited submission is an intermediate category of authors whose work has already been produced for non-commercial (usually academic) purposes, and which is subsequently taken up by the publishing industry for commercial ends. Kate Millett's landmark radical feminist text, *Sexual Politics*, enacted this translation from the academic sphere to the mass market, though its translation was characterised by industry hesitancy and confusion as to how such an explicitly oppositional text might secure a mainstream audience. The notoriety gained by Millett during the book's publicity campaign, and the misrepresentation attempted by publisher Doubleday in marketing the title, highlight the dangers of disproportionate book industry power for the dissemination of feminist ideas.

In its theoretical self-consciousness and academic prose style, Millett's *Sexual Politics* reflects its origins as the author's dissertation for her doctorate in comparative literature at New York's Columbia University. With the disingenuousness of the newly famous, Millett revealed to *Life* in a September 1970 interview that 'all it is is my goddamn Ph.D. thesis' (Wrenn, 1970: 16). Yet, despite the casualness implied by this remark, the text was in fact painstakingly assembled over a period of five years, and then written up, in white-hot anger over the author's dismissal from a teaching post at Barnard College, between February 1969 and March 1970 (*Time*, 1970a: 17). Millett's isolation from academic structures during the time *Sexual Politics* was written significantly contributed to the radicalism of the text. Her teaching contract having been abruptly terminated because of her unrepentant support of the 1968 Columbia student strike, Millett was able to write without the pressing need for institutional approval commonly experienced by postgraduates in teaching positions. As a result, the text emerged from its writing phase relatively unmarked by academic institutional preferences – it was, Millett remarked in a 1995 interview, 'a much braver thesis than I might otherwise have done' (Mitchell, 1997: 237). Though the published text remains footnote-laden and is subdivided into an obvious thesis structure, Millett's original dissertation was in fact slightly rewritten for commercial publication: Millett records in her autobiographical work *Flying* that US publisher Doubleday paid her an advance of $4,000 to fund the rewriting process (1976 [1974]: 76). Even taking into account inflation since the early 1970s, the relative paucity of the 'tiny sum' suggests that Doubleday was aiming Millett's book at only a moderate-sized, predominantly tenured academic audience (Mitchell, 1997: 237), with perhaps a crossover market among laypersons interested in the then embryonic women's movement.

Publisher expectations for the title were clearly limited, as Doubleday did not include the book among its eleven frontlist titles in the 1970 fall announcements issue of the US book industry organ, *Publishers Weekly* (31 August 1970). A glance at the cumulative bestsellers of 1970 goes some way to illuminating this curious lack of prescience on the part of Doubleday: the year's top-selling non-fiction titles, such as *Everything You Always Wanted to Know About Sex But Were Afraid to Ask* by David Reuben and *The Sensuous Woman* by the enticingly anonymous 'J', bespeak a market preoccupied with the sexual revolution rather than women's liberation (Hackett and Burke, 1977). The presence of the word 'politics' in Millett's title was the cause of considerable author–publisher conflict, as Doubleday foresaw problems in marketing a self-declaredly political analysis to an audience seeking books about sex rather than sexism. In the discord between author and publisher that followed over the proposed cover design, latent conflicts between political and marketing priorities crystallised. Proposing a design with 'two arms arm-wrestling – one brawny male and one fragile female' (Mitchell, 1997: 239), Doubleday met with Millett's implacable opposition to a design that reduced her subtle political analysis to a misleading symbol of fatally unequal physical strength. Moreover, the cover's clichéd sex war spin on women's movement politics partook of the ubiquitous media tendency to encapsulate feminism as a prize fight between heavyweight individual combatants. As the marketing hype for Norman Mailer's execrably written anti-feminist polemic, *The Prisoner of Sex* (1971), swaggered pugnaciously:

> In this corner, the Pulitzer Prize-winning author, journalist, mayoral candidate, film-maker, and self-confessed PW (Prisoner of Wedlock). In the other corner, Kate Millett, Betty Friedan, Bella Abzug, Germaine Greer, and the armies of Women's Lib. (*PW*, 29 March 1971: 8)

Sexual Politics's vast post-publication publicity campaign, consisting of coast-to-coast lecture tours, television appearances and press conferences – recorded by Millett in *Flying* as a destabilising whirl – escalated only once sales of *Sexual Politics* had already taken off. Having paid Millett a derisory sum to transform an academic dissertation, Doubleday perceived that they had – almost inadvertently – stumbled upon 'the bible of the women's movement', a text with the theoretical rigour and historical scope to provide the polemical backbone for an emergent social trend. Though published on 31 August 1970 with minimal publicity, by mid-October 1970 the book was selling '6,500 copies a week, for a total so far of about 50,000' in the United States (*PW*, 12 October 1970: 86). Two months after its hardback publication, *Sexual Politics* peaked at number six on the *Publishers Weekly* listing of non-fiction bestsellers (2 November 1970: 94). In short-term sales rankings, this represents a higher turnover for Millett's academic tome than for Friedan's book of accessible journalese seven years earlier. Given serendipitous political timing, even an intimidatingly dense text written in 'mandarin mid-Atlantic' academese could secure a mainstream audience, a fact that a bemused (though hardly displeased) publishing industry noted, and accordingly added to its arsenal of marketing tactics (Millett, 1990 [1974]: ix).

It is during the years 1970 and 1971 that the phenomenon of the feminist blockbuster emerges in its contemporary guise: the book whose cover confidently purports to change women's lives, to revolutionise social thinking and to provide a blueprint for liberation.[4] The superlatives that predominate in marketing hype around feminist non-fiction in these years implicitly characterise feminism as essentially a one-book movement, although the claim that subsequently produced books represented *the* definitive text was, of course, endlessly repeatable. The marketing oversimplification of the one-book movement aroused the ire particularly of independent 1970s feminist publishers, who perceived that mainstream presses of the period had no interest in nurturing a multiplicity of women's perspectives and a diversity of feminist interpretations (Arnold, 1976; Desmoines and Nicholson, 1976). Definitive pronouncements have a tendency to quash intellectual developments within radical movements, a rigidifying tendency about which women's liberationists, themselves frequently fugitives from the 'false consciousness' dogma of the new left, were highly cynical. The publishing industry's publicity motivated star system was thus directly at odds with the non-hierarchical communalism espoused by the women's movement:

> Now that Women's Liberation has become a subject upon which each publishing house must bring forth its book, much as it must upon such pressing topics as contract bridge or the techniques of modern marketing, the struggle for the liberation of women is being mistaken for yet another battle of the books. Each publishing house backs its own expertise to identify the eventual bible of the women's movement, characterising it as a religious cult in which one publisher will corner the credibility market, sending the world's women rushing like so many lemmings after a book. The hapless authoresses of the books in question find themselves projected into the roles of cult leaders, gurus of helpless mewing multitudes … The penalty is to find oneself reviled by one's sisters as a self-styled leader, a lady don who cannot know the perils and endurance of the front upon which the battle must be fought. (Greer, 1971c: 355)

Intriguingly, this quotation is taken from an article penned for the *Listener* in March 1971 by Germaine Greer, herself perhaps the prime example of the celebrity feminist, her fame meticulously constructed – with Greer's avid participation – by the machinery of book publicity. In the course of Greer's article 'Lib and Lit.', the author proceeds to belittle *Sexual Politics* as 'basically a literary and pedantic enterprise' (1971c: 355), a far from neutral statement given that Greer's competing text, *The Female Eunuch*, had been released in hardback in Britain in October 1970 by publisher MacGibbon & Kee. Moreover, in the spring of 1971 Greer was due to embark upon a mammoth US publicity tour to promote her work as *the* indispensable distillation of contemporary feminism, a publicity blitz with an initial advertising budget of $25,000 (*PW*, 25 January 1971: 205). Hence, in a manner that has continued to plague Greer throughout her subsequent public career, her acute insight on one hand and her desire for self-promotion on the other are fundamentally at odds. While she is undoubtedly correct in diagnosing the publishing industry's desire for the definitive feminist book as an intellectually inhibiting fixation on singularity, she here appears blind to the fact that, by reviewing Millett's book negatively, she is – implicitly – nominating her own publication for the title of feminist vade mecum. Indeed, it is plausible that this is the specific reason Greer was commissioned to write the review. Alert to the politics of the publishing machine, she yet opts to remain conveniently oblivious to her own collaboration with its commercial agenda. Greer's charges against Millett's US-centric perspective, her overly academic prose and the American author's thorough attack on patriarchal exponent Norman Mailer carry as their implicit corollary a plug for Greer: Australian expatriate and UK resident, writer of wittily accessible prose, and high-profile feminist who will grant *Playboy* an interview (Greer, 1981) and debate Mailer publicly in New York Town Hall.[5] As ever, when hoist on the petard of her seeming self-contradiction, Greer pleads strategic necessity over ideological consistency. Ten years into her post-*Female Eunuch* international fame, Greer stated, 'I'm against the cult of personality, too, but I think we have to use whatever weapons we've got' (Greer, 1981: 335).

The accessible nature of Greer's prose is inextricably interlinked with questions of commissioning and marketing, for Greer's *The Female Eunuch* was commissioned by her Cambridge University contemporary, Sonny Mehta, then head of Granada's newly launched trade paperback imprint, Paladin. While Dr Greer, holder of a PhD in Shakespearean drama, could doubtless have written in the heightened academic prose of Millett, it was her journalistic experience in writing iconoclastic feature articles for satirical underground magazines such as *Oz* that made her Mehta's choice of author. For the nascent paperback imprint Paladin, a wittily written title with cross-market appeal on the most pressing social question of the day was crucial for establishing its market identity, and for demonstrating to its parent house, Granada, that trade paperback publishing harboured lucrative possibilities. Significantly, Greer was a member of no organised women's group in Britain in the late 1960s, nor was she involved in the period's emergent feminist media. Her occasional membership of the loose advisory group that in the early 1970s assisted Virago's directors was due more to personal friendship with fellow Australian Carmen Callil and others in the group than to ideological commitment (Callil, 1996). It was in fact Callil who, in an intriguing demonstration of the connections between feminist and trade publishing, co-directed the 1970 British launch publicity for Greer's *The Female Eunuch*, an event that she later pinpointed as the inception of a dynamic new collaboration between feminism and publishing: '*The Female Eunuch* was the beginning of a marketing as well as a female revolution, with Germaine one of the first to present herself as writer and media star' (Callil, 1995: 8).

Critic Maggie Humm asserts that the style of *The Female Eunuch*, one of 'simple paraphrase [rendered] into a contemporary everyday vocabulary' was 'dictated by [Greer's] commissioning editor' (1986: 32). This would appear to cast Greer in the mould of a passive publishing industry creation. A striking feature of the 1970–71 *Female Eunuch* campaign is Greer's adroit and self-conscious presentation as spokeswoman for a movement that, in its more radical wings, vigorously rejected the concept of spokeswomen. Hence, Greer's public metamorphosis into the icon of women's liberation was paralleled by a grassroots activist disaffiliation from her brand of feminism – rendering Greer susceptible to attack from both proponents and opponents of women's liberation (Dreifus, 1971; Spongberg, 1993). Significantly, in a 1998 interview Greer parried a question about her emblematic role in 1970s feminist debates with the claim: 'I was a fairly ordinary, badly dressed, pale, badly-coiffed then and badly-coiffed now person. And not particularly a feminist' (*Uncensored*, 1998a). The issue encapsulates a troubling ambiguity at the heart of feminism's conceptualisation of the media. For Greer's *The Female Eunuch*, a number one bestseller in America in August 1971 (*PW*, 2 August 1971: 104), created a groundswell of public support for feminist ideas, which could not be channelled by any single group into concrete political action. Such decentralisation of political power may represent a grassroots activist ideal, but it carried with it the problematic corollary that feminism's public image increasingly came to be defined by the commercial media rather than by a public of politicised women.

Like Greer, third-wave feminist author Naomi Wolf honed her writing skills within academia, first as an English literature under-graduate at Yale and later as a Rhodes Scholar at New College, Oxford. Her familiarity with communicating feminist issues in academic prose is demonstrated by her numerous references to her Oxford doctoral dissertation (as yet unsubmitted), a discussion of female hysteria in nineteenth-century literature, which explicates the socially constructed nature of medical disorders (Wolf, 1991a: 198, 220–2, 224; Mitchell, 1997: 193). Hence Wolf's commitment in *The Beauty Myth* to writing in 'a language that a smart 15-year-old could understand' (Viner, 1997: 4) represents an admirably self-conscious attempt to broaden the audience for feminist writing, particularly given that the subject of the book is the cultural pressure upon adolescent girls and young women to conform to an impossible physical ideal. It is more especially remarkable given that, in the period between Greer's book and the appearance of Wolf's, feminist thought increasingly retreated into the academy, in the process clothing itself in a prose style so opaque and terminologically dense as to be unintelligible to the majority of women (see also Wolf's subsequent book, *Fire With Fire*, 1994 [1993]: 123–6). By reviving the concept of the mass-selling feminist polemic, Wolf harks back to a more activist age of feminist consciousness. Yet the political ambiguities involved in harnessing the mainstream media for radical ends – politically treacherous waters earlier traversed by both Millett and Greer – have in the intervening 20 years grown in direct proportion to the mass media's steadily accreting power.

In the late 1980s, Wolf's synopsis for *The Beauty Myth* was auctioned among numerous publishers by her New York agent, and was secured for British publication by Chatto and Windus with a £30,000 advance (Mitchell, 1997: 194–5) – 'pretty unusual for an unknown name with no particular track record', as Sally Brampton cuttingly remarked in the British press (1990: 17). Following a two-year publicity campaign, much of which lingered reverentially upon the author as a third-wave feminist messiah, the book achieved hardback release in Britain in September 1990, to a spread of mixed-to-poor reviews. The chief criticism of the book – that what it heralded as a radical breakthrough in feminist thought had in fact been previously explored by Beauvoir, Greer and in particular by Susie Orbach in *Fat Is a Feminist Issue* (1978) – engenders the suspicion that Wolf's media profile depended more upon her skills as an articulate populariser and moderniser of feminist ideas than upon her intellectual originality (Brampton, 1990: 17; Heller, 1990: 33; Smith, 1990: 22). Reviewing the book for the *Independent*, Zoë Heller adumbrates the extent to which pre-publication publicity can condition a book's reception, counterproductively triggering a satiated response among the reading public:

Wolf's publishers have chosen, a little rashly, to herald *The Beauty Myth* as 'a cultural hand-grenade for the Nineties'. Fatally over-estimating the book's radical import, they have laid their author open to irritable scoffing and charges of arrogance. (1990: 33)

The contradiction underpinning the reception of *The Beauty Myth* is that its author, even prior to the publication of this, her first, book was being hyped by the industry as a compelling feminist theorist. Wolf and her public persona would seem to epitomise the publishing industry dystopia predicted by early 1970s radical feminist theorists such as Arnold: having appropriated and neutralised feminism as an activist politics, the commercial mainstream continues to manipulate its appeal as a hollow bookselling category. Yet, conversely, one of the central targets of Wolf's analysis is the mass media itself, which she castigates for normalising impossibly underweight and dangerously passive stereotypes of femininity through the medium of glossy women's magazines. That Wolf's cultural import was being hailed by publicists and marketing managers *prior* to the book's actual production – let alone its reception by reviewers and other feminist theorists – suggests that feminism has become so detached from any specifically political analysis that the term is freely appropriable by any interested party. This is perhaps inevitable, given that since the mid-1970s activist feminism has increasingly dissipated into a far more politically ambivalent cultural politics. Paradoxically, this process is itself an example of exactly the species of political anaemia that Wolf's polemic deplores. *The Beauty Myth* is, therefore, a product of the system it indicts: deriding the manipulation of ostensibly 'emancipated' female images by a cynically profit-driven media, the book calls for a new wave of grassroots activism. Yet it articulates this battle-cry having bypassed almost completely any vestiges of feminist community. Greer's *The Female Eunuch* was criticised as a book dissociated from contemporary feminist organising; Wolf's book is avidly promoted in an age virtually devoid of any such women's activism. Thus Wolf's corporate publishers are placed in the anomalous position of themselves calling for oppositional feminist resurgence.

THE POST-PUBLICATION PHASE

Cover Design

If publishing and bookselling constitute realms comparatively unexplored by academics and feminists, then the politics of cover design surely constitutes this realm's dark continent.[6] Formerly considered only as a peripheral publishing concern, cover design and its effects on book sales are issues that the book retailing industry has only come to appreciate fully in the wake of the trade paperback revolution of the last 20 years. Book Marketing Ltd (formerly the Book Marketing Council), Britain's provider of statistical analyses and market research for the publishing and book retailing sector, in its reports takes cognisance of the power of packaging to influence consumer purchasing trends. In one of the earliest British investigations of the subject, *Impulse Buying of Books* (1982), the Book Marketing Council demonstrated publishers' underdevelopment of their design departments in the face of the finding that 19 per cent of 2,908 impulse book purchasers sampled were 'solely influenced by the cover of the book and the accompanying blurb' (1982: 6). Yet the Book Marketing Council's surveys are – by their very nature and financing – concerned with how to increase bookshop turnover and not with the political ramifications of cover design. Book marketing and design may not at first glance appear likely candidates for the commonly applied adjective 'political', yet their power to mediate between authorial-driven content and reader reception of a given text can register a significant impact on sales. Considering that financial considerations largely determine whether texts do or do not achieve publication in the contemporary industry, any factor significantly determining a book's financial success – and thus the likelihood of further publications in the area – should properly be regarded as an important variable in an overarching *political* equation. The size and commercial leverage of design and publicity departments in contemporary mainstream publishing bear testimony to marketing's centrality to the modern book industry.

The feminist bestseller phenomenon of the last 30 years has spawned cover designs that have metamorphosed into iconic representations of the women's movement. A case in point is Abacus's manipulation of political rosettes into the classical male and female symbols for the cover of its 1972 paperback edition of Millett's *Sexual Politics*. Millett, however – having already wrangled with Doubleday over the US cover – confesses in her autobiography to finding the British cover dishearteningly 'hideous' (1976 [1974]: 2). By contrast, the female flesh-corset hanging from a pole on the cover of Germaine Greer's *The Female Eunuch* has become so indelible a visual shorthand for the commodification of women described in the book that in

February 1998, when Greer announced a forthcoming sequel – significantly titled *The Whole Woman* – much of the newspaper coverage featured the original paperback cover, with satirical suggestions as to how it might be adapted for a modern sequel (Viner, 1998: 4; Sorensen, 1998: 5; *Australian Financial Review*, 1998: 55). Although it is now culturally entrenched, the famous *Female Eunuch* cover was in fact British artist John Holmes's second attempt at a visual condensation of Greer's pungent political thesis. The original, rejected, artwork featured a sexless torso recognisable (at least from the neck upwards) as Greer herself, her mouth fused into silence and a mound of bizarrely detached breasts piled in front of her (Callil, 1995: 8; Wallace, 1998 [1997]: 192). Given that the paperback publishers of the text, Paladin, planned a glamorous, personality-centred campaign with promotional pin-ups of Greer distributed in selected British broadsheets, it seems likely that Holmes's proposed cover design was dismissed for erring too far on the side of the literal.

The success of the revised *Female Eunuch* cover design was predicated upon its ability to attract the audience most likely to purchase the title: middle-class women with disposable incomes interested in feminist issues. It managed to combine a seeming sensuality with what was in fact a searing critique of conventional male views of women. Such a seamless blend of cover design and target readership is often achieved only after initial mismatches. The original hardback slip-cover of Naomi Wolf's *The Beauty Myth* featured an Old Masters female of Rubensesque proportions, her hands bound before her and her eyes cast melodramatically upwards in an imploring expression. Partly on the basis of mixed reviews and partly, I suggest, on account of this classical, highbrow, Rape of Lucretia-style cover, sales were respectable but in no way comparable to the bestseller status achieved by the 1991 Vintage paperback. This repackaged edition featured Clare Park's recognisably contemporary photograph of a painfully thin model, gagged, bandaged and uncomfortably constricted in a crouching position. Coinciding with an early 1990s paperback design trend for artistically photographed female nudes (Souter, 1995: 47), the cover effectively imitated *The Female Eunuch*'s encapsulation of a polemical position in an arresting visual image.

Yet, as always in feminist analyses of the publishing industry, the most revealing examples occur where the commercial imperatives of the industry are demonstrably in conflict with the political nature of a book's content. It is at such points that a fault line emerges between the industry's tectonic plates of politics and profit. The cover

Figure 4   Abacus struggles for a visual encapsulation of Kate Millett's revolutionary new concept 'sexual politics', combining political rosettes with classical male and female symbols. Note which gets to be on top. (Reproduced by kind permission of Abacus, a division of Time Warner Books UK.)

of Hamlyn's paperback edition of Susie Orbach's *Fat Is a Feminist Issue...: How to Lose Weight Permanently – Without Dieting* (1979) engineers a subtle redirection of the text away from feminism/women's studies towards the dieting/self-help sector. Its cover depicts a naked female torso reminiscent of classical sculpture, which has been cut into cross-sections of ever-decreasing size – a visual representation of precisely the school of self-minimising body hatred that Orbach attacks in her critique of the cult of thinness. The suggestion encoded in the visual – that within all overweight women there exists a 'true' thin self struggling to break free – directly contradicts Orbach's central thesis: that once women break their compulsive relationship with food and hunger they will regain their natural body size. For Orbach (enunciating a critique since recapitulated for a 1990s readership by Wolf), eating disorders are political entities in that they represent capitulations 'to sexist pressure in contemporary society' (1979: 14). The reasons underlying such misrepresentation of the book's perspective appear cynically commercial: a Euromonitor survey published in the same year as Hamlyn's paperback records that 17 per cent of all non-fiction books purchased by women in Britain could be categorised under the labels 'food' and 'cookery'. Books falling under the heading of 'feminism' or 'women's studies' did not constitute a large enough category to be listed separately and were comprised within the 'other' category (Mann, 1979: 27). Given that the Euromonitor survey predates the exponential sales growth of dieting and self-help books during the 1980s, Hamlyn's design decision may be seen as a prescient, if unscrupulous, attempt to market feminism in less blatantly oppositional guises. It is conceivable that Orbach's readership may have expanded as a result of this cynical design disguise, which may be said to amount to a progressive political outcome. But considerations other than sales may here give feminists pause: firstly, in what ways does cover design affect the genre classification of feminist books, determining their display and shelving in bookshop layout, influencing reviewers, and thereby nominating evermore self-selecting readerships? Secondly, what conclusions can be drawn about the power relationship of authors *vis-à-vis* publishers given that in-house designers are usually briefed only sketchily regarding a book's content, rarely if ever reading the text themselves, and that authors have at best only a right of refusal on draft cover designs at mainstream houses? Finally, it is important to consider the ways in which readers' responses to texts are conditioned by the decisive medium of book packaging. A poorly chosen or misleading design is capable of contradicting or even subverting insurgent authorial intention.

Chatto and Windus's design and packaging of Naomi Wolf's third title, *Promiscuities: A Secret History of Female Desire* (1997a), illustrates how such a disjunction between content and format may problematise public reception of feminist work. In a manifestation of book marketing's increasing sophistication and cultural cachet, Chatto and Windus in April 1997 sponsored a reading by Wolf from her latest release as part of the 'Platform' literary series at London's National Theatre (1997b). Intriguingly, in that the forum juxtaposed the author with a representative of the book's commercial backers – Chatto and Windus's deputy publishing editor, Alison Samuel – the event raised significant, though perhaps unanticipated, issues in relation to cover design. Both Chatto and Windus's hardback slip-cover and the B-format softcover of *Promiscuities* feature Terry Whiteman's arresting photograph: a naked female torso pictured in profile, spine arched suggestively backwards, 'no cellulite, nice hard nipples, a little armpit hair to add danger' as the *Guardian*'s Katharine Viner observed wryly (1997: 4). Questioned about the packaging of the UK edition by an audience member, Wolf observed amusedly that no depiction of female nipples would be permitted in American mainstream book retailing, and then, more significantly, that she was not altogether satisfied with Chatto and Windus's choice of cover image. She wished that the model depicted was 'carrying another 10 to 15 pounds' and feared that the design risked contradicting the polemical position advanced in her first book, *The Beauty Myth* (Wolf, 1997b; Coleman, 1998). *Promiscuities*, like Wolf's earliest book, catalogues the powerful social pressures brought to bear on adolescent girls to conform to idealised body types and socially normatised sexual behaviour. Given this polemical position, Chatto and Windus's cover for *Promiscuities* risks undercutting not only Wolf's rhetoric contained within the volume, but also the authorial persona constructed by Wolf in her previous works. Here the design/content discrepancy of Hamlyn's Orbach cover (in which cover contradicts content) has multiplied, complicating reader reception not only of the book in hand, but also – retrospectively – of other texts by the same author. Publisher Alison Samuel's reassurances that much thought had gone into the *Promiscuities* jacket and that 'all the women I showed it to found [the image] very powerful and sexy', clearly failed to alleviate entirely the author's qualms on the subject, providing a rare public glimpse of the conflicts and contested priorities latent in the author–publisher relationship (Wolf, 1997b; Coleman, 1998).[7]

The cover of the 1998 Vintage UK paperback edition of *Promiscuities*, adapted from the title's original US cover design, appears set to inflame rather than defuse debate over the packaging of this particular title. Fanning wider media debates about the prescriptive power of media depictions, the Vintage edition's cover utilises Will van Overbeek's photograph of a young teenage girl, perhaps 14, with a cigarette hanging seductively from the corner of her mouth. Callowly aping adult sexual behaviour, the girl's image is a fitting visual depiction of the book's key theme – the hothouse socialisation of adolescent female sexuality. The ire the cover doubtless provoked among anti-smoking lobbyists would perhaps be better channelled into enhancing public recognition that broader issues than health policy are at stake in book design. In an increasingly consumer-driven society, feminism – itself now perhaps as much product as political philosophy – can ill afford to remain blind to the apparatus of its own commodification.

Selling Feminism/Selling Out: 'Wrestling ... in Medialand'[8]

The key factor that distinguishes feminist books nurtured within the independent women's publishing sector from those launched by the mainstream is marketing: in its scale, financial clout, multimedia penetration and image-making power, the mainstream publishing sector largely dictates public opinion as to what feminism *is*. The development of contemporary feminism since Knopf's relatively modest US$15,000 launch of Beauvoir's *The Second Sex* – an 'important Spring title' publicised predominantly by bookshop circulars (*PW*, 31 January 1953: 524) – makes the creation of a feminist bestseller *without* saturation marketing virtually inconceivable. A powerful dilemma is thus created for feminists: the mass media as it is currently composed frequently patronises women and satirises feminism with overt hostility, yet in order to broadcast an oppositional message to the largest number of women feminists' collaboration with the mainstream media remains an inescapable necessity. Focusing upon utopian ends, feminists have long sullied their hands with less-than-ideal means. Seizing whatever communicative opportunities were available in their marginalised position, early second-wave feminists of liberal, socialist and occasionally also radical tendencies opted for clear-eyed engagement with the mainstream media. Friedan, critic of the anti-intellectualism of domestic women's magazines, nevertheless harnessed their circulation to her political cause by

Figure 5   Chatto and Windus's female nude cover design for the first UK edition of Naomi Wolf's *Promiscuities*. While striking in its explicit sexuality, the picture risks undercutting the author's reputation as a campaigner for realistic female body images. (Used by permission of the Random House Group Limited.)

Figure 6   The subsequent Vintage UK paperback cover for Wolf's *Promiscuities* adapts the original (nipple-free) US cover design. Callow adolescence replaces assertive female sexuality as the volume's key image. (Used by permission of the Random House Group Limited.)

writing accessible feature articles for the same publications. Germaine Greer, scathing critic of teenage girls' pulp romances (1993 [1970]: 193–205), was and still is in other modes content to pose for lifestyle spreads and television interviews, and to discuss details of her personal history (*Sunday Times Magazine*, 1981; *Uncensored*, 1998a). Naomi Wolf, thorn in the side of the cosmetics and beauty industries, nevertheless authorises use of a widely circulated Random House publicity photograph, which would not be out of place in one of her chief targets – *Cosmopolitan* (see Mitchell, 1997: 179). Without a vibrant network of large-scale, independent feminist media, no feminist non-fiction title can hope to achieve top ten bestseller status except by participating in what Maureen Freely scathing dubs the circus of 'commercial feminism' (1994: 9).

For Friedan, Millett and Greer, publication of a first book with a commercial press was necessitated by the complete or – in the case of Millett and Greer – relative absence of alternative feminist presses. To castigate these authors for a perceived failing of sisterly solidarity would be to overlook the historical fact that, from the demise of the suffrage movement until the early 1970s, no such independent women's publishing sector existed. The embryonic women's presses that were in existence by 1970 could not have hoped to mount a multimedia campaign as effective and well co-ordinated as the marketing juggernauts for *Sexual Politics* and, especially, *The Female Eunuch* (Griffin and Wilson, 1982: 83). Moreover, such titles were important catalysts for the establishment of alternative women's publishing – both because of the inflammatory nature of the ideas they expressed, and because the cultural critiques they articulated armed women with sufficient intellectual tools to question the publishers' packaging of the books (Ehrlich, 1973). The book that 'could change your life' (as publishers' cover stickers enthusiastically claimed) could also empower readers to query the motives behind such a claim.

For feminist non-fiction authors of the post-1970 era, however, the decision to publish with a mainstream imprint is qualitatively different, as it now constitutes a decision *against* a feminist print alternative. Natasha Walter, author of the much hyped 1998 British title *The New Feminism*, stipulates that her decision to publish under the Little, Brown colophon rather than between the familiarly branded covers of its subsidiary Virago, was prompted by the desire to escape a ghettoised niche market: 'I didn't decide *against* Virago, I decided *for* Little, Brown because I wanted the book to hit a mainstream audience – and with its title, I felt I already had the Virago readership' (Griffey, 1998a: 5).[9] Such reasoning attempts a difficult reconciliation of capitalist process with oppositional politics, displaying a determined optimism that feminist subversiveness can elude commercial containment. But as Millett notes in her revealing account of feminist stardom and its brittle superficiality in *Flying*, any such position is fraught with political ambiguity and personal uncertainty: 'For a good while I imagined I was using a diseased system to attack exploitation itself in advocating radical ideas. A tricky proposition' (1976 [1974]: 92).

The debate between practical politics and ideological purity is a crucible for all oppositional movements attempting to proselytise and expand in capitalist, media-saturated societies. Yet for the women's liberation movement of the late 1960s and early 1970s, the usual dilemmas were overlaid with a further layer of ideological complexity: how could feminism, an ideology asserting the collective identity of women, collude with the Western media's insistence on organising news coverage around individuals? It appeared to amount to a conversation at cross-purposes, an attempt constantly to wrestle with 'the media's insane reduction of all issues to personalities' (Millett, 1976 [1974]: 214). Attempting to straddle this contradiction, early 1970s women's groups often opted for the half-way measure of the collective statement, issued to the press by an unnamed spokeswoman. The aim was to satiate the eagerness of women in the suburbs to learn of movement events, but to frustrate the media's relentlessly individualist focus. Publishers with a feminist author to promote are, however, rarely so politically scrupulous or so ready to draw attention to the mechanisms by which the public receives and processes information. The remainder of this chapter proceeds, therefore, to detail the marketing campaigns around three high-profile feminist titles of the last 30 years – *Sexual Politics*, *The Female Eunuch* and *The Beauty Myth* – to investigate how individual feminists attempted to balance media co-optation with espousal of an oppositional critique – and the internal stresses and contradictions that may result from such a project.

Kate Millett: 'Has Anyone Ever Gone Mad from Media Before?'[10]

Sexual Politics, perhaps more than most books, began as a highly individualistic exercise. The dissertation component of Millett's PhD, *Sexual Politics* was not only researched in the usual claustrophobic isolation of postgraduate study, but was written in a period of intense concentration: between February 1969 and March 1970, the entire period of composition, Millett claimed to have had '2½ days off' during the most frenetic eight months – throughout which time she wrote for '14, 16, 18 hours a day' (*Time*, 1970a: 17). By the time of its August 1970 publication, Millett had been involved in women's political groups for several years, having in 1967 published a report on the curricula of women's colleges, *Token Learning*, for the New York chapter of NOW. Yet because of the academic gestation and original scholarly purpose of *Sexual Politics*, Millett understandably resisted movement demands that the text – dubbed the women's movement's bible upon publication – be left unsigned and that Millett should not refer to it as 'her' work or retain royalties from its sale (Millett, 1976 [1974]: 77, 252). It appears an impossible position: unable to take credit for consciousness-raising prompted by her book, Millett was nevertheless obliged to accept personal responsibility for its shortcomings, be they political or textual. Reviewers, true to the individualist ethos of the literary community, were united in attributing such faults as they found in *Sexual Politics* specifically to Millett's theorising (Messer-Davidow, 2002: 135–8). Mary Ellmann, author of the important early second-wave *Thinking About Women* (1979 [1968]), proved surprisingly unsympathetic to Millett's project in the third part of *Sexual Politics*, in which Millett reads the works of individual male authors as 'instances of sexual politics' (Millett, 1972 [1970]: 3). Dubbing *Sexual Politics* 'a dull but significant book' (1971: 590), Ellmann adds her voice to those of other critics who queried Millett's conflation of author with fictional narrator (Kaplan, 1986: 24), and who baulked at Millett's conception of literature as a sociological tool (*Times Literary Supplement*, 1971: 410). Acclaimed by the likes of *Time* as the movement's theoretical guru (*Time*, 1970a: 14), Millett was rather its lightning conductor – targeted for her conspicuousness by hostile outsiders just as she was castigated for the crime of her star status from within.

The first section of *Flying*, Millett's account of events between August 1970 (when *Sexual Politics* appeared in hardback) and late 1971 (when the wave of media interest in her began to abate) is entitled 'Vertigo'. It is a powerful stream-of-consciousness account of the psychological invasion Millett experienced in the 'vulgar insanity' of the media's frenzy to find a women's movement spokesperson:

> It is all a mistake. The nightmare months of folly. Microphones shoved into my mouth ... 'What is the future of the woman's [sic]

movement?' How in the hell do I know – I don't run it. Every day in winter more ignorant, weaker. Chicanery of press conferences, interviews, lectures at universities. All arranged. Don't spoil the arrangements. Tired and I don't know any answers. The whole thing is sordid, embarrassing, a fraud. The same questions always. Boring. Repetition of old stuff, no new work. Have I lost faith? If I am bored am I a traitor? They ought to shoot me. Made into a leader. We're not supposed to have leaders. I will be executed in some underground paper, my character assassinated sub-terraneously. (1976 [1974]: 12–13)

The early high point of this isolating fame was the now famous 31 August 1970 cover of *Time*, in which 'Kate Millet of Women's Lib' appeared (without authorisation) in a painting derived from a photograph – a form of personal promotion that Millett insists she had explicitly refused, instructing *Time* reporters to use a photograph of crowds of women marching on the streets of New York City in that week's Women's Strike for Equality (Mitchell, 1997: 237). Her gestures towards collectivity ignored, Millett was further manipulated by *Time* in December of the same year when she acknowledged her bisexuality at a movement forum. The statement was picked up and run as a scintillating exposé, 'bound to discredit her as a spokeswoman for her cause', as *Time* slatheringly pre-empted (*Time*, 1970b: 41). 'Out[ed] in Timese', as Millett later bleakly summed up the event (1976 [1974]: 18), the author and her media image became emblematic of yet another acrimonious debate beginning to fracture the movement: the question of whether lesbians should agitate in their own political interests, or whether gay women's liberation must remain closeted within feminism until initial battles for mainstream acceptance had been won. In this manner, *Sexual Politics* and its marketing ignited a debate within feminism about degrees of oppression, specifically whether divergence from the white, middle-class and (relatively) media-friendly image of NOW would taint the feminist campaign with what Friedan, first president of NOW, memorably dubbed the 'lavender menace' (Echols, 1989: 212, 214–15).

The impact of these debates on sales of Millett's work suggests a disheartening slavishness on the part of the US book-buying public to the homophobic judgements of *Time* and its media cohorts: in the week after *Time*'s 31 August cover, *Sexual Politics* was first flagged by *Publishers Weekly* as a candidate for future bestsellerdom (7 September 1970: 94); it peaked at number six on the non-fiction list by 2 November 1970 (94); yet by December and the week of the 'lesbian exposé', Millett's book had slipped permanently out of the top 10 non-fiction listing.

The marketing campaign for *Sexual Politics* and the media storm it generated might properly be regarded as the first recognisable instance of celebrity feminism. Friedan had achieved significant public profile in 1963, but the lack of synchronicity between the initial appearance of her book and a widespread public women's movement tempered the media's portrayal: Friedan was depicted chiefly as a housewife and took pains to couch her radicalism in the less threatening language of US liberal humanism. Millett, on the other hand, symbolised several aspects of an already (by 1970) prevalent feminist stereotype. The December 1970 article outing Millet is illustrated with an *Esquire* cartoon of a bra-waving, pendulous-breasted, bespectacled, scowling feminist, a crude stereotype inviting association with the earlier depiction of Millett in *Time* as free-living, plump and bookish (*Time*, 1970a: 14–19; *Time*, 1970b: 41). Millett thus represented an ideal candidate for the vertiginous experience of what in Australia is termed the 'tall poppy syndrome': rapid media-generated celebrity and acclaim followed by a swift descent into personal attack and public opprobrium. As a media creation, Millett's integrity was capable of being destroyed at the media's whim – her newsworthiness was all.

The fickleness of mainstream media interest in feminism should rightly give critics pause. Firstly, because of its devastating personal impact on individual, highly articulate and intellectually productive feminists, as evidenced by Millett's account in *Flying* of her media-induced near breakdown. More broadly, the feminist star system may be politically counterproductive, in that it reduces the breadth and complexity of a political movement to a single identity – a precarious point unable to support the weight of ideological baggage piled upon it by media speculation. Thirdly, the inherent selectivity of media feminism should alert consumers to the arbitrary manner in which the media sets the parameters of public debate. In heralding the oppositional as radically innovative, the media disingenuously disavows its own filtering function as the gatekeeper of public discourse. Elevation of a thinker such as Millett to media prominence, followed swiftly by her relegation to public notoriety, are events orchestrated by the media, and are important to it not so much for their outcome (be it eventual celebrity or infamy) but as *process*. By hailing and then denouncing individual feminists, the mainstream media have a reliably two-pronged story, coverage that in media parlance has 'legs'. Accordingly, as maintained by Millett, the process is not a mere commentary on contemporary developments within feminism, but the *instigator* of those events: 'The truth of the media is that first you're exploited and manipulated until you become this big balloon, which later they puncture. And puncturing me was supposed to puncture feminism' (quoted in Mitchell, 1997: 238). The wider issue of why a declaration of bisexuality should necessitate banishment from the media pantheon and the discrediting of a movement is glossed over in the fact of the publicity itself. Any political movement concerned with the formulation of public knowledge can only enter such a realm of media power with reservations so deep-seated as to risk negating the tactic of mainstream media engagement.

Germaine Greer: 'The Brand-Name Feminist'[11]

The marketing of a political movement such as feminism cannot be understood solely by reference to promotional campaigns for individual titles, for the nature of publicity is to operate cumulatively – the success of one feminist bestseller providing impetus for the launch of others. The extended promotional tour of the United States undertaken by Germaine Greer in the spring of 1971 to launch the American edition of *The Female Eunuch* can thus only be comprehensively understood as a response to the previous year's media interest in Millett. The publicity campaign engineered by US publisher McGraw-Hill was at the time the most extensive feminist book promotion ever undertaken, with public lectures, interviews, book readings, television talk show appearances, a *Life* magazine cover (7 May 1971), public debates with Norman Mailer and a film of the tour all feeding interest in Greer herself as much as in her book. Greer was in many ways an ideal candidate for feminist celebrity. *The Female Eunuch* had received generally enthusiastic reviews upon its British publication by MacGibbon & Kee in October 1970 (James, 1970; Tomalin, 1970; *Times Literary Supplement*, 1970). The sales potential of Greer herself was early demonstrated in events such as a January 1971 call-in programme on BBC Radio 4, in which Greer fielded questions from occasionally hostile members of the public with fluent logic and witty aplomb, the programme's controller congratulating her on air at the session's close for 'a virtuoso performance' (Greer, 1971b: 82). Hence, even before glowing reviews of *The Female Eunuch* appeared in the mainstream US press – the *New York Times* titled its review 'The Best Feminist Book so Far' – the essential lineaments of Greer's media profile had already been drawn: she was the amusing, flirtatious, bawdy face of the women's liberation movement – in the words of a fawning 1971 *Life* magazine cover story, a 'Saucy Feminist That Even Men Like!' (Bonfante, 1971).

Greer's media positioning as the attractive face of feminism in contrast to an uncompromising Millett was made explicit early in the book's marketing campaign. Christopher Lehmann-Haupt's assertion in his *New York Times* review that *The Female Eunuch* 'is everything Kate Millett's book is not' (1971: 45) established a conveniently Manichaean conception of feminism. It was one that McGraw-Hill's 15 March 1971 cover advertising in *Publishers Weekly* was eager to reinforce with the headline 'So Far You've Only Heard Half the Story: Germaine Greer'. In addition, Greer's contempt for the 'unliberated' woman, which recurs throughout *The Female Eunuch* (as, for example, in her lofty dismissal of the tedious faculty wives to which her academic career had exposed her), suggested to the mainstream media that Millett's unsettling notion of patriarchy might be replaced by the less discommodious concept of women's complicity in perpetuating their second-class status. Such demonstrable lack of sympathy for women trapped within the mentality of the 'female eunuch', in addition to Greer's non-membership of any organised feminist network, won her few adherents among organisers of the British or, especially, the US women's movements (Wallace, 1998 [1997]: 214–17). But this fact barely dented her mainstream media canonisation as the epitome of a contemporary social trend – the emancipated woman. The impact of her personal popularity on book sales was not lost on McGraw-Hill, which dubbed the film of Greer's US tour (self-deprecatingly titled *Germaine Greer Versus the USA*) 'the best 60-minute book commercial ever made' (Greer, 1975: 332). In fitting recompense for McGraw-Hill's initial US$25,000 advertising outlay (*PW*, 25 January 1971: 205), the American public bought the book at a peak rate of 89,000 copies per week, with the result that for two weeks in August 1971 *The Female Eunuch* was the US's number one bestselling non-fiction title (*PW*, 2 and 9 August 1971: 104 and 82 respectively).

The match between Greer's promotable personality and the media need of a feminist superstar to fill the vacuum created by their character assassination of Millett was too neat not to provoke criticism from second-wave feminists. Claudia Dreifus in her 1971 review of *The Female Eunuch* for *The Nation* recapitulated a familiar critique of

Greer in dubbing her the facile 'big femme lib superstar', a mere puppet of 'the high priests of publishing':

> Miss Greer was everything those messy American feminists were not: pretty, predictable, aggressively heterosexual, media-wise, clever, foreign and exotic ... Her philosophy, as outlined in *The Female Eunuch*, could be expected to appeal to men: women's liberation means that women will be sexually liberated; feminism equals free love. Here was a libbie a man could like. (1971: 728)

The first half of Dreifus's criticism is striking in its similarity to Greer's own earlier lukewarm review of Millett's *Sexual Politics* for the *Listener* (25 March 1971). Greer, who had herself diagnosed cynical publishing competition for 'the eventual bible of the women's movement', had in a mere three months moved from the role of expositor to that of the subject of feminist media critique. It is salutary in analysing Greer's media blitz and the problematic ramifications such publicity may have for feminism to highlight two specific concerns: firstly, the tendency of marketing campaigns to dilute or even contradict a book's content; and, secondly, the trivialising and depoliticising influence of the media spotlight.

The major premise underpinning *The Female Eunuch* is that biological differences between the sexes are minimal, hence the vast sexual discrepancies discernible in contemporary society are attributable almost exclusively to socialisation into highly constructed gender roles. These, as the creation of human society, are capable of being recast in ways more conducive to female intellectual and social fulfilment. In outlining this incremental distortion of the female sex away from spontaneity, emotional reciprocity and individual ambition towards the artifice, impotence and passivity of 'the female eunuch', Greer does not hesitate to indicate where socio-political responsibility lies – with the system of male control she terms patriarchy. Because Greer's thought is sufficiently nuanced to distinguish between the role of individual men and the operations of this overarching political superstructure (radical poet William Blake, to cite only one example, is quoted approvingly throughout the text), an argument evolves whereby Greer can be seen to praise individual men while castigating the social system from which they profit. Feminist philosophy from Mary Wollstonecraft onwards has conscientiously insisted upon this individual/patriarchy distinction, but Greer's vocal heterosexuality and attractive appearance made her marketable as the 'feminist that even men like' in a way less practicable with other second-wave polemicists.

The media spectacle provided by Greer was thus one of guilt-free voyeurism: here was an articulate and spirited woman speaking plainly upon the most controversial social issue of the day, but without (in her media persona) necessarily attributing blame for oppressive patriarchal behaviour to individual men. Titillation rather than accusation allowed Greer's brand of feminism access even to that previously sacrosanct *Kaaba* of American machismo – Hugh Hefner's *Playboy* magazine – which reassured readers: 'Men can read the same book and likewise admire – even desire – its author, while at the same time not feel compelled to burden themselves with guilt for the crimes against women discussed therein' (Greer, 1981: 328).

In the years since Greer's publicity tour, feminist thought has evolved to the point that simplistic anti-male rhetoric is now regarded as perhaps the least credible or compelling variety of feminist discourse. Yet it is fair to argue that any movement in its initial consciousness-raising phase ought, for rhetorical and political expedience, clearly to denominate its enemies. What price then Greer's slippage from her position in *The Female Eunuch* to marketing-driven sloganeering along the lines that sexual liberation for women in itself heralds social liberation. Conveyed simplistically in media soundbites, Greer's cheerful promotion of the joys of (heterosexual) promiscuity veered dangerously close to the trenchantly sexist 'libertarianism' of the new left. 'The difficulty', as Claudia Dreifus observed testily, 'is that many feminists have been to that movie before' (1971: 728).

For all its endless self-regard, the sole topic in which the mainstream media demonstrates an emphatic lack of interest is itself – if defined as the means and processes by which it selects and moulds presentation of the 'newsworthy'. The second salient element in the media trivialisation of Greer's sexual politics critique is its problematic omission of Greer's own scathing media analysis. In *The Female Eunuch*, Greer develops the argument that the media, by projecting intellectually unchallenging and physically unattainable images of women, distracts them from the collective *political* nature of their oppression, creating a smokescreen of all-consuming – though essentially trivial – personal concerns (1993 [1970]: 192–212). As substance for this position Greer analyses the cult of heterosexual romantic love, which is the central preoccupation of teenage girls' magazines, the photostories of which Greer deconstructs much as Friedan had earlier critiqued the 'Happy Housewife Heroine' magazine narratives of

1950s America (Friedan, 1965 [1963]: 30–60). In the personality-centred marketing of the feminist bestseller, however, critiques of socialisation centrally indicting media imagery are sacrificed in favour of the cult of the remarkable individual:

> Who is Germaine Greer? The most loveable creature to come out of Australia since the koala bear? A feminist leader who admittedly loves men? A brilliant writer, 'extraordinarily entertaining'? Great Britain's Woman of the Year? The author of a perceptive, outrageous, devastating book on women? Germaine is all of the above. (quoted in Spongberg, 1993: 409)

The reduction of a social movement to the appealingly packaged media celebrity 'Germaine' – no matter how eagerly complicit Greer may have been in this process – signals a troubling trend towards intellectual diminution and political containment. Hence *The Female Eunuch*'s cumulative worldwide sales of over 1 million, its translation into twelve languages (Viner, 1998: 4), and its canonical inscription as a feminist classic have been achieved via collaboration with a media industry pursuing goals perhaps only tangentially related to those broadly understood as feminist. A certain degree of commodification may be essential to 'sell' feminism via the corporate-owned media, but only the most optimistic of feminists would claim that the means used to bring about this result may not substantially alter the ends at which feminism originally aimed. Greer herself gives no indication of retiring from a now more than 30-year media reign: the publisher Doubleday saturated media outlets in the build-up to the March 1999 release of Greer's *Female Eunuch* sequel, *The Whole Woman*, seeking to reprise a 1970s-style female insurgency with its promotional tag line; 'it's time to get angry again'. Greer's comments in recent years on the ambiguous status of female poets do, however, stand in interesting counterpoint to her own public career. Speaking of the figure of the poetic muse, Greer asserts that 'most of the women [poets] now are at the mercy of the people merchandising them; and they're actually being prostituted in a way'. Hence the poet – and conceivably even the bestselling feminist author – are 'at the mercy of the male literary establishment, who will exploit her in any way they find convenient' (Greer, 1995).

Naomi Wolf: 'There is No Right Way She Can Look'[12]

The marketing of the feminist blockbuster reaches its current apotheosis in the persona of American author and iconic figure of third-wave feminism: Naomi Wolf. Of all the feminist writers who might be considered to stand at the vanguard of contemporary public debates around gender, Wolf is the media-appointed spokeswoman-in-chief, a position she occupies on the basis of her thoroughly marketable books and public persona. The underlying tenet of the marketing for Wolf's first book, *The Beauty Myth*, was that in Wolf feminism had found living rebuttal of the hardened stereotype of the ugly, overweight, strident feminist. Wolf's youthfulness (at the time of *The Beauty Myth* campaign she was 27), physical attractiveness and record of academic success appeared to give the lie to the resilient myth of feminist undesirability. Yet Wolf's approach to the media has been and remains fundamentally compromised: highly critical of the media's representation of women, she yet – in the marketing of her books – becomes complicit in its standard tactics. The big-budget media campaigns orchestrated by Wolf's British hardback publisher, Chatto and Windus, effectively isolated Wolf in an impossibly self-contradictory rhetorical position: criticising the highly artificial media construction of femininity, Wolf must nevertheless adhere strongly to it, if only to prove her non-membership of that still less desirable caste of media untouchable – the 1970s-style feminist.

The contradiction between media cynicism and media savvy that dogs Wolf's public career prompts analysis of three problematic issues: her relationship to the cult of the feminist superstar; the charge of unoriginality to which her marketing campaigns render her vulnerable; and the dilution of Wolf's political analysis through cross-genre marketing of her works, specifically their packaging as women's self-help manuals. The first of these issues – Wolf's position as cultural spokesperson for contemporary womanhood – both replays the collective versus individual debates of the early 1970s, while at the same time fundamentally transforming them. As spokeswoman for feminism in the 1990s, Wolf speaks without the background of a broad-scale radical social movement. Indeed, her first work was compiled out of a deep unease with the *absence* of such a movement, Wolf claiming 'I wrote [*The Beauty Myth*] to prove the need for a feminist resurgence' (1991b: 19). Hence it is in some sense inevitable that Wolf, child of the 1980s cult of individualism and self-styled instigator of a revitalised feminist consciousness, should find herself at the focus of her marketing campaigns. But, like earlier feminist spokeswomen such as Greer, Millett and Gloria Steinem (with whose career Wolf's shares interesting parallels), Wolf renders herself vulnerable to arguments that her personal experience and outlook cannot encompass the diversity of women's perspectives. She is, it is argued, generalising on the basis of her own life experience in order to promote her career – operating self-servingly, the allegation has it, under the guise of gender politics. In *The Beauty Myth* and in her second publication, *Fire With Fire: The New Female Power and How It Will Change the 21st Century* (1993),[13] Wolf takes up a median position between the social activist's rhetorical extremes of isolated individualism, on one hand, and the submergence of the self in the collective, on the other. Her speaking position is that of the social instigator, a writer channelling already discernible dissent and giving voice to the silently disaffected. She is careful to argue in *The Beauty Myth*'s conclusion for the creation of a 'peer-driven feminist third wave' (1991a: 281), of which the book itself represents both herald and product: a 1990s women's movement 'would need to analyze the antifeminist propaganda young women have inherited, and give them tools, including arguments like this one, with which to see through it' (1991a: 281). The speaking position here is one of masterful adaptability: it ensures that Wolf is sufficiently radical and innovative to warrant the immense publicity she receives, while at the same time being wholly representative, merely the theoretical formulator of young Western women's inchoate disgruntlements and insecurities.

Such protean instability is the essence of Wolf's marketability and the prime cause of her publishing success. It is nowhere more apparent than in Wolf's own media-savvy exploitation and defence of her personal appearance. In writing *The Beauty Myth*, Wolf need only have cast the most cursory glance over the careers of Greer and Millett to realise that her appearance would constitute a central factor in the book's reception – a media preoccupation in relation to feminism multiplied a hundred-fold by the fact that Wolf's book was about the very issue of women's speech being evaluated according to the speaker's appearance. Intriguingly, concerns of the kind usually left to a marketing campaign director here spill over into the content of the book itself – evidence that book marketing is now such a vital component of the publishing equation that it pervades pre-publication as well as post-publication phases. Astutely forecasting the 1990s media's correlation of beauty with feminist worth, Wolf encapsulates the debate that has since both plagued and buoyed her career:

> For a woman to speak about the beauty myth (as about women's issues in general) means that *there is no right way she can look*. There

is no unmarked, or neutral, stance allowed women at those times: They [sic] are either called too 'ugly' or too 'pretty' to be believed. (1991a: 275)

Wolf's prescient, pre-emptive strike indicates a tactical clear-sightedness about media priorities, as three of the four initial British reviews of *The Beauty Myth* made reference in some way to its author's appearance (Davenport-Hines, 1990: 1097; Picardie, 1990: 39; Smith, 1990: 22). Given such a media environment, Wolf's handling of the repeated author tours, endless personal promotions and glitzy publicity shots can be variously read either as a brilliantly parodic subversion of mainstream media methodologies or as a hoodwinked capitulation to their power. In this ambiguous positionality, Wolf is representative of a familiar post-modern quandary: at what point does a stance of self-serving ironic detachment cease to have any oppositional value and begin in fact to buttress the ideological status quo? Wolf, veteran of four international publicity tours, has by the early twenty-first century reached the point where promotion has so blended with media-denominated 'radicalism' for the two to have become virtually indistinguishable – a dark reflection upon the mainstream media's near-insuperable power to appropriate and neutralise dissent. How is feminism to operate in an ideological schema where media support may be as politically debilitating as media silence? This analysis cannot hope to offer final judgement on such a complex issue. But by critiquing the concept of the feminist bestseller, this discussion suggests that feminism, in order to remain at all credible as a contemporary political theory, urgently needs to mount more rigorous analysis of its *own* construction through the lens of the twenty-first century's dominant ideological force – the mainstream media. Suzanne Moore, a British feminist commentator who has repeatedly touched upon the need to instigate such debate (1992: 16), perceives the issue in microcosm in Wolf's posing – back-lit, taped and vaseline-lensed – for the questionable feminist affirmation of women's glossy magazines:

It is wonderful that she is so attractive and photogenic but isn't it just a little strange that a woman whose success was predicated on deconstructing The Beauty Myth should then choose to have herself pictured using all the tactics of the trade that she denounced? (1993: 10)

Two further issues raised by Wolf's iconic feminist status – the question of her work's originality and its marketing as therapeutic self-help – are best dealt with in conjunction, for the marketing exigencies of the latter illuminate debate around the former. Given Wolf's current prominence, what is striking about the first reviews of *The Beauty Myth* in 1990 is their generally lukewarm tone, and the frequency with which they dispute the book's claims to originality. In a representative review, Zoë Heller argues that 'Wolf's discussion of the feminine beauty cult clearly isn't breaking "an uneasy silence" or confronting a "final taboo"' as 'a rich tradition of feminist analysis [including] Simone de Beauvoir, Germaine Greer and Susie Orbach' has already opened this argumentative territory to political analysis (1990: 33). Feminist author Joan Smith equally queries Chatto and Windus's claim that *The Beauty Myth* 'breaks the silence of centuries', given that 'the imposition on women of an ideal of beauty which is not their own is a subject which has exercised the women's movement for many years' (1990: 22). Admittedly, Wolf in the acknowledgements section of *The Beauty Myth* marks her indebtedness to 'the theorists of femininity of the second wave, without whose struggles with these issues I could not have begun my own' (1990: 292). But in Chatto and Windus's two-year pre-publication publicity campaign for the book, the mantra of radical innovation had been so often repeated that it, rather than the book's actual content, came to condition public response to the book – a characteristic example of a book's media hype eclipsing its actual political contribution. Heller again remarks that 'it seems harsh to damn a book on the basis of its publicity blurb' (1990: 33) yet, surfeited with hype, this is what British reviewers almost to a woman proceeded to do (Brampton, 1990; Picardie, 1990; Smith, 1990).

Chatto and Windus's confusion of quality with ubiquity in constructing its promotional campaign may have backfired, but its decision to promote *The Beauty Myth* less under the bookselling category of feminist theory than as a women's self-help manual heralds a significant marketing development for feminist titles in general. The 1970s consciousness-raising slogan that 'the personal is political' had insisted upon the centrality of personal experience to any genuinely radical political consciousness, but the end at which the slogan aimed was, nonetheless, the broader social landscape of public, activist politics. In line with the near-complete marginalising of activist politics (aside, perhaps, from environmental movements) during the 1980s, feminist bestsellers were restyled not as blueprints for social revolution, but as guidebooks for personal reformation. The women's liberation movement's erstwhile role model, Gloria Steinem, encapsulated this retreat from broad canvas agitation to personal reinvention in her title *Revolution from Within: A Book of Self-Esteem* (1992). The ever-present potential for consciousness-raising to degenerate into narcissistic self-communion was recognised early in the history of the women's movement (Freeman, 1970: 24–5, 1973: 47). However, the immense commercial investment at stake in mainstream publishing has greatly facilitated slippage between analysing 'political' problems and providing personal consumer solutions, not least in that texts about dieting and female body image comprise a major subsection of the booming self-help publishing market. Because of this encompassing commercial reality, Wolf's *The Beauty Myth* (like Orbach's *Fat Is a Feminist Issue* before it) was easily marketable as a corrective for *personal* misapprehensions rather than for *societally structured* oppressions. In its discussion of the author's teenage battle with anorexia, her enculturation within northern California's cult of the body beautiful, and her mother's experience of fad dieting (1990: 201–8), *The Beauty Myth* arguably pursues the laudable goal of grounding socio-political analysis in personal experience. Yet in the cover copy for the Vintage paperback edition, evidence for the argument has become the argument itself. The confessional replaces the political as the book's dominant mode: *The Beauty Myth* 'has the power to change lives' (1991a).

From this cross-genre drift two central issues emerge: firstly, given that self-help literature occupies one of the lowest prestige niches of a publishing house's list, it is reasonable to expect that the marketing of political feminist tracts as home therapy will reduce feminist non-fiction's cultural capital and result in the commissioning of fewer rigorously analytical feminist texts. Secondly, how can twenty-first-century feminism recast issues of women's self-esteem as worthy of inclusion on the public political agenda without falling into the intellectually simplistic trap of classifying all questions of social experience as inherently personal? The question is complicated by women's historical entrapment within the realm of the personal and domestic, firstly in the nineteenth-century, post-Industrial Revolution ideology of separate spheres, and more recently in the post-war glorification of domesticity, the suburban platitudes of which Friedan so successfully demolished in order to provide women with entrée to a public realm. Legislative parity now having been substantially achieved for Western women, the question becomes how to fashion a sophisticated feminist analysis alive to issues of *cultural* coercion, one which does not become so dazzled by the possibilities of textual analysis that it loses sight of the cultural industries avidly constructing and distributing such media artefacts. In her attempt to 'define our self-esteem as political' (1991a: 281), Wolf gestures towards such a shift in analytic focus. Yet the deceptive ease with which the very book mounting such arguments is itself marketed as female self-help indicates how fraught with risks of containment such a manoeuvre may prove.

CONCLUSION

What are feminists to make of the mainstream publishing industry's most recent strategy to corner the market in feminist books – the feminist sequel? The announcement in February 1998 that Germaine Greer had accepted a £500,000 advance from Transworld/Doubleday to pen a sequel to *The Female Eunuch* (Viner, 1998) prompts the scurrilous query as to what a self-proclaimedly celibate 60-year-old might know about women's sexuality in the 1990s (the focus of *The Whole Woman*). It moreover prompts questions as to why Greer, and not a younger feminist writer, was contracted to address the issue. The obvious answer – the commercial reliability of Greer's name – triggers more searching enquiries into the current formulation of feminist bestsellerdom. Are older, already established feminist writers, with the willing collusion of multinational publishers, ossifying feminist thought by monopolising public debate? In the pre-publication comments of Doubleday's publishing director Marianne Velmans, it was the singular, essentially confining image of the feminist guru that predominated: 'It is the book we've all been waiting for, not only to revive the debate, but to reinvent the issues for a new generation' (Viner, 1998: 4). Greer, who herself in 1971 castigated publishers for falsely elevating 'hapless authoresses' to 'the roles of cult leaders' (Greer, 1971c: 355), has here come full circle; what has changed is that she is now perceived as a two-book, not merely a one-book, guru.

As a volume, *The Whole Woman* appears deeply marked by commercial publisher preferences – opening with a 'recantation' in which Greer explains that her volte-face on her promise never to pen a sequel to *The Female Eunuch* springs from awareness of how much worse women's position has become, further aggravated by the unsisterly backsliding of feminists of her own generation (2000: 1).

Yet the volume fails to dispel the creeping suspicion that it has been written to publisher prescription rather than out of the white-hot anger Greer alleges: its thematic structuring around clusters of abstract nouns – 'body', 'mind', 'love', 'power' – explicitly evokes that of *The Female Eunuch*, reinforcing the book's claims to sequel status; its unusually short 'chapterkins' do not develop an argument sequentially but essentially constitute parallel case-studies of the application of a central thesis, suggesting easily excisable sections tailor-made for broadsheet serialisation;[14] and breakout box quotes from a grab-bag of sources are scattered throughout the text with no contextualisa-tion within the main argument, suggesting their insertion during the post-writing production phase to give the appearance of readerly accessibility and to mimic use of the same device in *The Female Eunuch* (Cameron, 1999; Ward, 1999). Of all the texts discussed in this chapter, *The Whole Woman* exhibits most clearly the current lineaments of the feminist bestseller. Greer may be sufficiently perspicacious to diagnose feminism's gradual commodification by the marketing and cultural industries it originally sought to critique (2000: 11), yet she is conspicuously silent about the complicity of book publishers in this same process. Exuding the air of having been written to order, *The Whole Woman* represents not simply publisher commodification of feminist rage, as frequently alleged in the 1970s, but the *prescription* of rage itself. Doubleday's promotional posters for the title's March 1999 hardback launch, declaring boldly 'It's time to get angry again', were in this sense highly revealing: *The Whole Woman* was positioned by its multinational publisher not as capturing a wave of already brewing female revolt but as itself instigating that wave (Greer, 1999b).

The book industry apparatus within which contemporary feminist writing circulates determines that the majority of feminist bestsellers emanate from commercially driven mainstream houses and serve the financial interests of their parent conglomerates. To rephrase Beauvoir's famous maxim, the feminist book is not born, but rather becomes, a bestseller.[15] At each stage in the production of the mainstream feminist text, the institutional power of the multinational publishing apparatus is a determining presence: in its power to commission or reject a book proposal it crucially filters access to public discourse; in its editing of feminist texts it can subordinate a title's political analysis to the exigencies of profit and market whim; and in the design, packaging and promotion of feminist authors – as much as of their texts – the industry mediates public perceptions regarding the nature of feminism and its relevance to contemporary society.

Feminist critics would thus be insufficiently vigilant in assuming that mainstream publishers' influence over feminist thought begins and ends with the corporate colophon stamped on a book's spine. The publisher's logo is only the most explicit manifestation of a system of overarching institutional and cultural power.

Given that mainstream houses have published many of the most influential feminist critiques of the preceding 30 years, a resisting reader could yet be forgiven for asking why it is necessary, or even advisable, for feminist critics to remain circumspect in their treatment of corporate publishers. Inherently problematic is the tendency within the industry for feminism to be defined not by peer review but by publisher press release. Publishers increasingly hail a new release as a significant contribution to feminist thought even before its content has been surveyed and critiqued by the feminist community, much as Greer's publishers proclaimed *The Whole Woman* the 'most talked about, discussed and debated book of recent times' a full four months before its publication (Treneman, 1998: 1). Given the dissolution of anything approaching a unified political women's movement, the danger is that feminism will come to represent not a politico-cultural philosophy but a conveniently appropriable merchandising hook. A wary Sally Brampton, diagnosing this redefinition of feminism as a convenient niche market, suggests its concomitant risks of political containment and consumerist neutralisation: 'Comparisons have been made between *The Beauty Myth* and those seminal feminist tracts *The Second Sex* and *The Female Eunuch*. Unfortunately they have been made by the publishers themselves' (1990: 17).

Claims made by Chatto and Windus to the effect that Naomi Wolf represented 'the Beauvoir, the Friedan, the raving, ravishing Greer, of her generation' point, moreover, to the mainstream publishing industry's tendency towards recapitulation over innovation in its packaging of feminist thought (Turner, 1990: 29). Because they stand to profit from the continued prominence of established second-wave feminist authors whose titles appear on their backlists, publishers are frequently predisposed to support a new book from a familiar name rather than to search out newer, even previously unknown, talent. In Transworld/Doubleday's breathless pre-publication puffery for Greer's *The Whole Woman*, the potential constriction of the feminist canon can be felt at its keenest. While the elevation of certain feminist texts – *The Female Eunuch* among them – delineates a body of influential feminist writing and important political development, the process of canonisation is itself predicated upon a complementary process of denial and exclusion. For every title that is elevated to the feminist pantheon, multiple others are consigned to oblivion or declared to be unutterably beyond the political pale. The sales jargon of the bestseller relies, implicitly, upon singularity – a book represents the number one bestseller, *the* definitive analysis, the crucial text that alone 'changes lives'. As a result of this relentless selectivity, the vital diversity of feminist theorising is evermore concentrated into a handful of promotable titles. Just as the early second-wave women's movement was justifiably uneasy with the feminist 'star system', contemporary critics are right to be chary of the celebrity media feminist, tame product of what one radical critic recently dubbed 'the celebrity blockbuster industry (women's issues subdivision)' (Cameron, 1999: 4). Promotion of an elect of feminist mandarins has potential to stifle on-going debate and to frustrate revisionist accounts from movement mavericks.

Finally, the mainstream publishing industry's decisive role in setting the parameters of feminist debate is rendered doubly problematic by the current disinclination of feminism rigorously to explore its own media construction. This is not to claim that feminist critics have remained oblivious to developments in media studies. Indeed, the eagerness of feminists to explore the influence of popular culture and the political implications of its depictions has comprised one of the major energising strands within both women's studies and media studies over the preceding three decades. But feminist media critics have been predisposed to analyse disempowering representations of women or to deconstruct negative stereotypes of feminists, rather than to interrogate the media construction of supposed feminist success stories. Thus the landmark texts of the second-wave women's movement continue to be regarded as in some sense *beyond* media processes rather than as products themselves crucially mediated by the mainstream communications industries. Perhaps this skittishness is understandable – no radical movement is exactly heartened to discover that its rhetorical landmarks are tempered by the dominant paradigm. But until feminism reconceptualises itself as in part product – as are all political movements – of media mediation, it will remain in its current state of angry disbelief that its ground should be so co-opted by an opportunistic mainstream publishing industry.

The concluding chapters of this volume aim to destabilise standard divisions of feminist print activity into opposing categories of radical independents and the corporate mainstream. The weaknesses of both approaches – the financial instability and low output of the radical imprints, and the political opportunism and profit slavishness of the multinational firms – demand reconceptualisation of feminist publishing practice if the sector is to survive in recognisable form in the twenty-first century. This survey maintains that the dichotomised core/mainstream conceptualisation of feminist publishing has been proven redundant, and should be jettisoned in favour of a less rigidified, more interpenetrative, schema. By putting pressure on the boundary between a 'core' feminism and a hostile mainstream 'exterior' from alternate argumentative directions, this discussion works to highlight its ultimate arbitrariness. The experience of feminist houses over the preceding 30 years is in essence a narrative of interaction with and accommodation to larger media environments, just as the rise of the feminist bestseller marks the corporate publishing world's growing awareness of feminism's mainstream infiltration. To attempt to analyse one factor in the publishing equation without paying heed to developments in the other is fundamentally to misconstrue the complex interdependence of the modern media sector.

The challenge facing feminist publishing early in the new century is how the benefits of both production systems might be fused into a new working relationship – one sufficiently cognisant of media industry dynamics and profit generation to harness these skills for a feminist agenda. It is, admittedly, no simple undertaking. The politics/profit dialectic is one incapable of ultimate resolution. But by overcoming the self-defeating conceptualisation of ideological commitment and profit generation as necessarily in antithesis, feminist publishing optimises its chances of forging a new, dynamically hybrid model – that of commercial media savvy deployed to effect political change.

Afterword
Feminist Publishing Beyond the Millennium: Inscribing Women's Print Heritage in a Digital Future

Perhaps more than any other development in publishing in our century, women's publishing has attempted to bring about radical and wide-ranging change. Not only new writers, but new subjects have been introduced. Old, existing disciplines have been critiqued; the making of canons has been questioned, the definitions of what constitutes appropriate or acceptable subject matter for books have been expanded and stretched, as have given boundaries. And, most important, the whole process of the creation and production of knowledge has been looked at afresh, turned upside down, often rethought and remade. And all this in barely a quarter century.

Urvashi Butalia and Ritu Menon,
Making a Difference: Feminist Publishing in the South (1995: 1)

In the early 1980s I decided we'd got everything we ever set out to do, and then worked out that one of the reasons we had was because print wasn't the primary information medium any more and wasn't being defended by men in the way that it had been ... I don't have any difficulty saying – [feminist publishing] flowered, it was wonderful, they were heady days, I loved it. But almost everything has a timeframe. I'm just delighted I was there, and in it, and right at the centre of it. Now, I do not spend my days thinking – 'oh my God, it's over'.

Dale Spender, interview with the author (2003)

One characteristic of feminist publishing and the debates which surround it is that identical circumstances are frequently used to support wildly differing conclusions. Thus, as in the paired quotations with which this volume begins, feminist publishing simultaneously represents both manifest triumph and lamentable absurdity. As a movement, feminist publishing is held both to valorise a tradition of women's fiction, and simultaneously to ghettoise such writing with gendered prescriptions. That feminist-informed writing now occupies a significant place on the lists of mainstream and academic publishers is both testament to the force of the feminist publishing revolution and, ostensibly, the cause of its demise. Notable feminist houses have resonant imprint identity and are, allegedly, captive to second-wave nostalgia – so preoccupied with marketing their legacy they fail to discern their contemporary irrelevance. To read the mainstream press and the relatively sparse academic discussion of the fortunes of feminist publishing is to be continually disoriented; feminist publishing appears both everywhere and nowhere, unexplored by feminist critique yet also tediously passé.

The foregoing chapters explicate this contradictory situation by exploring feminist publishing's siting at the interstices of multiple industry, political, cultural, commercial and scholarly debates. But the present discussion's priority of excavating and critiquing three decades of feminist book publishing practice focuses on the recent past and primarily upon the print format. This afterword represents an acknowledgement of the necessarily incomplete ambit of such an enterprise. It attempts to cast its glance forward into the twenty-first century – specifically into the realm of digital communication – and to cast the auguries for feminist publishing in a communications realm in which both the terms 'feminist' and 'publishing' confront new challenges.

PRINT AS A SUPERSEDED MEDIUM

Dale Spender has been among the most vociferous critics of feminism's continuing investment in print culture, arguing that women gained influence in the sphere of book publishing from the 1970s onwards precisely because print was then being superseded by computer technology. In symbiotic manner, Spender argues that the feminisation of print culture further devalued the medium in the eyes of the technological and financial elite, thus allowing more female control over the written word. As women seep in, power, it seems, seeps out of cultural institutions and professions alike (Spender, 2003). Spender's long involvement in women's studies print culture, including co-establishing feminist presses and academic journals, makes her critique one which feminist publishing can ill afford to disregard, highly discomforting though it may be. Nevertheless, Spender and like-minded technophoric critics have arguably been unduly rash in rejecting the feminist publishing project in their eagerness to encourage women's embrace of emergent digital technologies. The implicit positing of digital and print communication as mutually exclusive media has worked to dichotomise a debate which, on closer inspection, suggests positions between the two extremes that may prove politically more productive.

A first concern with the technophoric project is that feminism's historical memory, particularly in the West, inheres in print culture. Second-wave feminist presses were themselves prime advocates of conceptualising feminism as a textually inscribed movement: in their recuperation and restoration of a tradition of women's writing, they aimed to put paid to charges that feminism lacked a history, that it amounted to merely a passing fad. Such presses were, in direct ways, also the beneficiaries of this approach: houses such as Virago and The Feminist Press were in their early phases underpinned financially by feminist reprint lists. The rescuing from oblivion of this work indirectly generated new, secondary manuscripts from academics analysing the tradition's importance, as well as from fiction writers responding to its precedents. Decrying the fact that writing of such quality should ever have fallen into obscurity, countless feminist theorists have railed against the academic and publishing orthodoxies that hid such works from eager would-be readers. Their conclusion was frequently that the process of publication is by its very nature political, and that women's traditional exclusion from loci of publishing power has worked to perpetuate women's historical silencing, forcing each subsequent generation of feminists to reinvent the wheel (Spender, D., 1983a: 4–7; 1983b: 369; Price and Owen, 1998).

The imbuing of publishing with specifically political power by critics such as Spender makes the wholesale rejection of print in favour of digital technology all the more puzzling. The legacy and contribution of feminist publishing has been a significant force in the contemporary knowledge industries and one in which feminist knowledge is now richly stored. To jettison this rich tradition before academia has come to terms with its significance appears rash and – in the political terms Spender herself outlines – tactically counter-productive. This is all the more so in that feminist theorists themselves have to date largely failed to factor feminist publishing into their analyses as an active agent in determining feminism's public profile, rather than relegating it to the status of a mere barometer of the women's movement's prominence in any given period. If feminist publishing is reconceptualised as not merely a *reflection* of wider women's activism, but as an *instigator* of political and cultural change, the traditional classification of feminist history into the peak-and-trough model of first, second and third waves is immediately problematised. Arguably, it is gatekeepers' periodic exclusion of feminist analyses from the privileged realm of public discourse that is in part *causative* of women's disaffiliation from feminism. Conversely, such research as exists on women's historical involvement in the publishing industries has frequently been published by feminist presses, journals and periodicals. By implication, the extent of knowledge about a movement's history depends crucially upon that movement's contemporary vibrancy. Introduction of a feminist publishing perspective into the disciplines of women's studies, book history and cultural studies thus prompts invigorating re-examination of received analytical paradigms. Reconceptualised as *cause* and not *symptom* of women's vacillating political consciousness, feminist publishing emerges as a vital tool for understanding twentieth-century social and cultural history – one with potentially revisionary effects.

Further – and more concretely material – grounds on which to query feminist rejection of print in favour of digital initiatives are developments within the information technology (IT) sector since the time of Spender's key publication in this area, *Nattering on the Net* (1995). The mid-1990s apogee of 'death of the book' rhetoric, of which Spender's work is representative, has been broadly disproved by the continued resilience of the book as a cultural and commercial artefact. 'Death of the book' arguments have been moreover discredited by the spectacular losses and subsequent retreat of companies that invested too early in speculative, often incompatible, electronic book formats. A recalcitrantly bibliocentric reading public demonstrates a marked lack of enthusiasm for e.book technology, whether because of the inadequacy of the reader experience offered, or because legal uncertainty prevented electronic formatting of sufficiently enticing content. Early entrants into markets for embryonic technologies commonly bear such heavy research and development costs. Even later entrants, such as the multinational houses that established e.book divisions with much fanfare in the mid- to late 1990s, have generally downsized or abolished these divisions in the face of huge losses. Feminist publishers constitute one of the least well-capitalised sectors of the book trade, making overly enthusiastic embrace of minimally tested and rapidly obsolescing technology an act of commercial self-annihilation. To argue for the abandonment of a media format in which feminism has demonstrated its greatest success, in favour of a format that even multinationals cannot yet profitably exploit, risks once again liquidating feminism's hard-won store of knowledge.

BOOK-ENDS: CO-OPTING DIGITAL TECHNOLOGY FOR THE BOOK

How then should feminist publishers remain open to the opportunities presented by digital technologies without becoming so enslaved by the technical capabilities of specific digital formats that they squander their corporate knowledge and operating capital? Successful contemporary feminist publishing initiatives suggest that engaging in the digital sphere while retaining a bibliocentric outlook yields optimal results. Where the Internet has been utilised to expand publicity and sales opportunities for traditional format books, feminist publishers have been able to strike a happy medium. Virtually all women's publishers now boast homepages highlighting their company profile and frontlist titles, but several have pioneered more innovative applications: brand-name feminist presses Virago and The Feminist Press have designed their websites as community centres and guides to the presses' history; numerous houses – among them The Women's Press, Spinifex and Naiad – offer online purchasing through third-party distributors; and, in a sign that e.book boosterism may be terminally on the wane, Virago has pioneered online print-on-demand ordering for 15 out-of-print Virago Modern Classics titles in traditional book format.

Such recalibration of digital technology for bibliocentric ends represents a cannily circumspect approach to a rapidly changing and still evolving medium. Yet it can at best pose only an interim solution to the question of feminist publishing's future. The longer-term sustainability of feminist publishing can only be assured if the sector comes to terms with the nature of the modern media industries as content-warehousing operations. The globalised media conglomerates that dominate the contemporary mediascape aim to own a broad array of intellectual property brands, which can be reformatted and repurposed in a wide variety of media forms, be they textual, visual, audio or any combination of these. Reconceptualising books not as stand-alone entities, but as component products in the life of a larger content property, may offer feminist publishing its best chance of survival in a greatly expanded and increasingly converged media landscape. Specific presses must respond to such shifts in industry structures by crafting individually tailored strategies. For feminist lists within larger corporations, maximum benefit may lie in promoting book properties to affiliate film, television or magazine divisions, and in reaping the cross-promotional benefits of tie-in editions, much as Virago engineered with screen-adapted bestsellers such as Vera Brittain's *Testament of Youth* (1933, republished 1978), Virginia Woolf's *Orlando* (1928, republished 1993) or, more recently, Sarah Waters' *Tipping the Velvet* (1998). In the case of independent feminist houses lacking such a conglomerate niche, press interests may best be served by contracting with authors to acquire the maximum range of rights, and actively brokering these rights for sale to outside parties, again benefiting from resultant cross-promotion. To embrace such cross-media traffic in content is not to admit the obsolescence of the book, but rather to acknowledge public enthusiasm for re-engaging with content already encountered in other media, and to harness this enthusiasm for the book sector.

Transforming publishing's key product from 'books' to 'rights' in such manner does, however, present feminist publishing with an especially destabilising challenge. The women's classics with which many feminist presses cut their teeth become vulnerable in a twenty-first-century media landscape for precisely the reasons they formerly represented a solid business proposition. 'Classic' titles, generally being already typeset, out of copyright and without living authors requiring royalty payments, formerly represented a low-cost, high-profit publishing opportunity. But in a publishing environment characterised by rights brokerage, such titles' out of copyright status renders them commercially disadvantageous, in that their content is already in the public domain. Contemporary feminist publishers may therefore be best advised to redirect their frontlists towards newly acquired titles by living authors, and to retain 'classics' backlists as commercial ballast, albeit continually depreciating ballast. The snag lies, of course, in the industry reality that notable living authors are almost certain to engage literary agents who will scrutinise overly generous rights clauses in publishers' contracts with the vigilant eye of self-interest. The trend would thus seem to lead back to feminist publishers' traditional ground: emerging writers who stand to benefit by association with a strong imprint identity, but who are not yet sufficiently successful to market themselves as their own authorial brand. Once again, feminist publishing finds its identity in pushing cultural margins, adroitly trafficking ideas between the periphery and the mainstream.

REFRAMING THE 'FEMINIST PUBLISHING' DEBATE

Throughout the preceding three decades of second-wave feminist publishing, debate has continuously swirled around the properly 'feminist' nature of such an activity, resulting in often arid debates over political 'purity' as opposed to commercial 'co-optation'. Yet, as the foregoing two chapters demonstrate, traffic between the margins and the mainstream of cultural production is now so plentiful and complex that any such attempts at watertight classifications obscure more than they illuminate. The as yet underexamined second term in the 'feminist publishing' tag – the nature of book publishing itself – now emerges as the front on which feminist publishing must regroup. The sector faces the challenge of keeping feminist issues prominent in a media environment in which the book represents only one of a plethora of competing communications platforms, and not the most pervasive or profitable platform at that. The skill lies in tactically engaging with ancillary media to promote book properties. To retain maximum manoeuvrability, and to be able to ride out battles between developing delivery mechanisms, book publishers need to prioritise control of rights in book properties. This involves the possibly chastening experience for publishers of accepting that the most profitable application of a book property may not necessarily be in book form, but that interest in content generated by a screen medium may be captured and redirected by publishers towards a textual form.

Such a strategic approach holds particular benefits for feminists interested in the interface of gender and communication. For if feminist ideas have historically been suppressed through denying women access to the most socially powerful media forms, there is always the possibility that feminists investing heavily in one specific communications platform will miscalculate the odds, and be relegated to a less pervasive or obsolescing medium. Directing movement energies into retaining ownership of feminist intellectual property by contrast insulates feminism from the unpredictable fates and rivalries of communications media, and ensures that premium women's content can be formatted in whichever media seem most appropriate at any given time. The strategy constitutes a quintessentially twenty-first-century reformulation of Virginia Woolf's assertion in *Three Guineas* (1938) that owning a printing press is *the* non-negotiable prerequisite for guaranteeing 'intellectual liberty'. Thirty years of feminist publishing activism have amply manifested the overriding importance of women controlling the medium. Yet in the emerging media environment, control of the medium is proving secondary to control of the message itself.

Notes

INTRODUCTION

1. The term 'womanist' is preferred by some women of colour as a means to avoid the white, middle-class connotations of the word 'feminist'. It was coined by African-American novelist and critic Alice Walker in the title essay of her volume of collected essays, *In Search of Our Mothers' Gardens: Womanist Prose* (1983 [1982]). For a fuller discussion of the interface between feminist thought and issues of racial identity refer to Chapter 2.

2. Perhaps anticipating further feminist fall-outs, newspaper literary editors solicited reviews of Weldon's *Big Women* from prominent feminist publishing figures internationally. Former Virago director Ursula Owen wrote a surprisingly benign review for the *Observer*, remarking that the naked frolicking with which the fictional Medusa was established was 'dear reader ... sadly not the ambience of the Virago office' (1998a: 17). Stephanie Dowrick, founder of The Women's Press, was more acerbic in her review for the *Sydney Morning Herald*, pronouncing: 'There is still a great book to be written about the writing that the women's movement inspired, and the feminist presses which published it. But Fay Weldon's most recent novel, *Big Women*, is not it' (1998: 11). Feminist non-fiction author Joan Smith, reviewing the novel for the *Financial Times* (UK), found it 'sardonic and sarcastic' in tone and stocked with two-dimensional characters acting out 'a kind of feminist soap opera' – a common complaint among reviewers (1998: 5). Though perhaps the vociferousness of Weldon's satire had built up steam during decades of pressure in the book world to maintain feminist solidarity; an anonymous publisher's reader for this book observed: 'Weldon's fictional attack was most unfair, but probably (in grotesque form) reflected much of what other feminists felt about feminist publishing and editors'.

3. Similarly glancing references to feminist publishing's emergence and achievements occur in one-sentence summaries in Anna Coote and Beatrix Campbell's *Sweet Freedom: The Struggle for Women's Liberation* (1987: 44, 226) and in Vicky Randall's *Women and Politics: An International Perspective* (1987: 246). Echoing Minogue's brief mention, Randall's terse discussion also misspells the names of both The Women's Press and Onlywomen Press, and in addition misdates the foundation of Virago to 1976 – rather betraying the peripherality of feminist publishing to her critical concerns. Angela Neustatter, writing three years after Randall, devotes one paragraph of *Hyenas in Petticoats: A Look at Twenty Years of Feminism* (1990 [1989]: 213–14) to the feminist press movement and its mainstream imitators, though her breezily celebratory assertion that 'the wealth of women's literature ... cannot now be erased and is an enduring and exhilarating record' simplifies the complexities

of the sector (1990: 214). For a more recent example of the passing mention, refer to Joannou, 2000: 9.

4. 'Cultural studies' and 'media studies' are used throughout this Introduction as largely interchangeable terms. Whether, in fact, they denote distinct fields of academic research or, more specifically, variant trends within a single area, has proven fodder for much critical debate over the foregoing three decades (Marris and Thornham, 1996). The task of definition is made particularly difficult by the fact that cultural studies, almost as its founding gesture, rejected the concept of disciplinary boundaries and their associated critical and methodological baggage (Turner, 1996: 4–5). For the purposes of this study, however, I perceive a distinction between cultural studies – a broad field encompassing virtually any form of social practice that can be analysed for meaning – and media studies – which has tended to concentrate its critiques around the print and broadcast media and, in recent years, the Internet. The distinction may be as much one of critical intent as it is of subject matter. Graeme Turner remarks that the purpose of cultural studies is 'to examine the power relations that constitute ... everyday life and thus to reveal the configuration of interests [their] construction serves' (1996: 6). Media studies, by contrast, in some of its streams presents descriptive rather than critical or politically engaged accounts of media industries – describing the state of contemporary British journalism, for example, without necessarily adopting an oppositional stance (see Bromley, 1995).

5. The sidelining of feminist analyses within the history of the book is manifest also in David Finkelstein and Alistair McCleery's *The Book History Reader* (2002), a publication that clearly positions itself as the textbook of choice for burgeoning courses in the discipline at undergraduate and postgraduate level. Feminist-informed extracts are almost exclusively confined to the *Reader*'s fourth section entitled 'Books and Readers', bypassing consideration of women's role as book producers, or of gender as an important variable in conceptualising book history. Publishing educator Paul Richardson observes in his review of the volume that 'women's perspectives are somewhat underrepresented in the book as a whole' (2002: 31).

6. Recently there have been signs that feminist academics are becoming increasingly restive with book history's gender-blind theoretical under-pinnings. A special issue of the *Leipziger Jahrbuch zur Buchgeschichte 6* contained three articles on women's historical involvement in the book trades, notably Leslie Howsam's attempt to 'address ... the question of the book trade from the perspective of gender' (1996: 68). Reprising her contribution to the *Jahrbuch*, Howsam in the autumn 1998 newsletter of the Society for the History of Authorship, Reading and Publishing (book history's international scholarly network) argues forcefully for book history practitioners 'to make use of the powerful theory and flexible methodology of feminist analysis when we think about and investigate the history of books' (*SHARP News*, 1998: 2). In the same issue of the newsletter, Maureen Bell and Gail Chester announce their joint-editorship of the proposed *Women and the Book: Female Participation in Print Culture from the Sixteenth Century to Today*, potentially a major

the Kali book?

contribution to understanding women's role in bibliographic history (1998: 4). Although Chester states in a more recent article that the volume has to date not been accepted by 'any publisher we have so far approached', stymieing the editors' desire 'to insert feminist scholarship into a nascent academic area, Book History, which has so far been only lightly touched by feminist analysis' (2002: 202).

7. By 1982, the feminist presses Virago, Onlywomen, The Women's Press and Sheba Feminist Publishers were all in operation in Britain.

8. To cite only one example of how acrimonious author–publisher relationships can become, in feminist houses as much as any other, see Gail Morgan's vituperative satire *The Day my Publisher Turned into a Dog* (1990 [1989]), a surreal fantasy of down-trodden authorial revenge upon celebrity feminist publishers seemingly inspired by Morgan's dissatisfaction with Virago over publication of her earlier novel, *Promise of Rain* (1985) (Miller, 1988: 78).

9. The Feminist Press founder Florence Howe notes how Olsen's recommendation of *Life in the Iron Mills* was instigatory in establishing The Feminist Press Reprint series, the earliest of the second-wave feminist reprint libraries: 'My reaction to that story spelled the mission of The Feminist Press to this day: If that amazingly brilliant story had been "lost" for more than a hundred years, what else had been lost? Was it not our business to find that "lost" literary output by women?' (2000b: 9–10).

10. Adapted from Emily Dickinson's poem 'Tell All the Truth But Tell It Slant' (c. 1868), *The Complete Poems of Emily Dickinson* (1960 [1945]: 506–7).

11. In an article published the same year, 'Who's Who and Where's Where: Constructing Feminist Literary Studies', Eagleton makes a similar point in arguing for greater academic attention to the economic, educational and institutional contexts within which feminist literary criticism is produced. She productively highlights the paucity of 'analysis of the development of feminist publishing' (1996b: 6). Jackie Jones, similarly writing about the interface of feminism and academic book publishing, states: 'a more detailed historically and culturally situated account of contemporary academic publishing – and of feminist publishing specifically – in Britain, is still to be written' (1992: 174).

12. A more recent publication co-authored by two members of the Indian feminist press Kali for Women, Urvashi Butalia and Ritu Menon's *Making a Difference: Feminist Publishing in the South* (1995), is centrally concerned with women's presses in the developing world (the 'South' of their somewhat confusingly worded subtitle) although the book also includes a (factually unreliable) five-page summary of 'Feminist Publishers Across the Atlantic' (1995: 10). At the time of writing Gerrard (1989), Duncker (1992), and Joan and Chesman (1978) are out of print.

13. See, for example, June Arnold's 'Feminist Presses & Feminist Politics' (1976), and Harriet Desmoines and Catherine Nicholson's 'Dear Beth' (1976), cf. Elizabeth Linder's 'An Editor's View' (1986).

CHAPTER 1 'BOOKS WITH BITE':
VIRAGO PRESS AND THE POLITICS OF FEMINIST CONVERSION

1. Time Warner became AOL Time Warner after its merger with Internet service provider America Online in January 2000. Little, Brown & Co. UK changed its name to Time Warner Books UK from 1 January 2002, and is a part of the AOL Time Warner Book Group. See http://www.time-warnerbooks.co.uk/company/company.htm.

2. An equally textbook example of how to reduce complex political and commercial differences to female catfights in order to dismiss feminism appeared in London's *Evening Standard*, complete with pat political homily: 'What happened to Virago is a cautionary tale. It shows that the sisterhood is too fragile for strong individuals. Feminism is fine in principle, but women can still fall out ... Virago is dead. Long live the Viragos' (Shakespeare, 1995: 12).

3. The exact meaning of the term 'radical' within feminist political discourse is a troubled one, as the word has altered in meaning and has, in addition, frequently sustained multiple meanings simultaneously (see Chapter 4 for an extended discussion of this issue). In the twentieth century, the term has contained three distinct meanings: firstly, it describes a non-conformist position to the left of progressive politics; secondly, it has been used to denote the separatist wing of the women's liberation movement, which prioritorised gender over other social categories; thirdly, and simultaneous with these other meanings, the term has continued to be used to denote the subversively non-conformist in a general sense (see Williams, 1983: 251–2). Clearly, when using the term in relation to the capitalist ethos of Virago Press, I intend this third sense of the term, as Virago was never an adherent of collectivist or avowedly separatist politics. In most cases, this terminological distinction will be apparent from the context in which the term is used. Though a slight potential for confusion exists, it seems essential to destabilise the word's received meaning in terms of the standard tripartite classification of feminism into liberal, socialist/Marxist and radical wings. For radicalism in the general sense is by no means confined to self-proclaimedly 'radical' feminist enterprises.

4. The 'Virago's History' page of the imprint's current website gives the date of the press's establishment as 1973, making 2003 the press's thirtieth anniversary. See http://www.virago.co.uk/virago/virago/history.asp.

5. The conflict in 1991 between The Women's Press's then managing director, Ros de Lanerolle, and the owner of Quartet Books, Naim Attallah, is explored in detail in Chapter 2. At the time of Virago's departure from the Quartet fold in 1976, however, John Booth and William Miller were in charge of the firm; Attallah did not become owner of Quartet until the following year. Yet speaking of Virago's time under Quartet's previous ownership, Ursula Owen recalls that 'a year of that was enough and we realised we had to go off and do our own thing' (1998b).

6. In March 1998 Random House was itself bought by German media conglomerate Bertelsmann for an undisclosed sum. It has since been merged with Bantam Doubleday Dell (also a Bertelsmann subsidiary) and restructured as Random House Inc. (Traynor and Foden, 1998). Virago's architecturally designed signature bookshop had generated positive industry attention upon its opening in January 1985 (*Bookseller*, 1985c: 15).

7. See Dale Spender, *Man Made Language* (1980) and *The Writing or the Sex? Or Why You Don't Have to Read Women's Writing to Know It's No Good* (1989).

8. Carol Ehrlich's early second-wave review article 'The Woman Book Industry' similarly decries mainstream publishers' release of books 'hastily and opportunistically thrown together to cash in on the lucrative new topic' (1973: 268).

9. Charlotte Bunch was involved in the women's liberation movement in Washington, D.C. from the late 1960s, as well as being a member of the *Furies* editorial collective (1971–72) and a founding editor of *Quest: A Feminist Quarterly*. She was, in addition, affiliated with the feminist press Daughters, Inc., owned by June Arnold and Parke Bowman (Bunch, 1977; Hartman and Messer-Davidow, 1982, II; Echols, 1989).

10. *Spare Rib* magazine was founded in 1972 by Rosie Boycott and Marsha Rowe and operated as a collective until its demise in March 1993 (Toynbee, 1982; Fairweather, 1993).

11. The specific marketing strategy behind this slogan, the broader relationship between Virago and The Women's Press, and the complex issues surrounding race and feminist publishing are examined further in Chapter 2.

12. Extracted from a speech by Carmen Callil to Women in Publishing: 'The biggest battle still to be fought by all feminist publishers is, I believe, the battle for the school and university curricula' (1986: 852).

13. A more sustained account of the complex politics of academic feminist publishing is contained in Chapter 3.

14. Harriet Spicer's response when asked in interview about the 'boy's own' atmosphere of the British publishing industry in the early 1970s (Spicer, 1996).

15. For details of pre-second-wave feminist book publishing endeavours, see Howsam, 1996; Murray, 2000b; Poland, 2003.

16. Fourth Estate was, however, subsequently sold to HarperCollins, part of the News Corporation conglomerate, in July 2000 (O'Connor, 2000: 31; Franklin, 2002: 54).

17. The contemporary reflection of such arguments might be Carol Anne Douglas' assertion that feminists who patronise Amazon.com or chain book retailers out of convenience directly jeopardise the existence of feminist bookstores (2000: 1).

18. See Chapter 3 for further discussion of such debates.

19. Virago's 2003 thirtieth-birthday slogan, featured on the Virago website, launched in 2000. See http://www.virago.co.uk.

20. The self-mythologising tendency to conflate Virago with women's writing per se is particularly manifest in Kasia Boddy, Ali Smith and Sarah Wood's

anthology *Brilliant Careers*, in which extracts from 100 Virago titles – predominantly the Modern Classics series – 'represent, chronologically, each year of the twentieth century' (2000: xiii).

21. See http://www.virago.co.uk/virago/virago/history.asp. By May 2003 Virago's annual turnover had doubled to nearly £4 million (Bostridge, 2003: 16).

22. *The Women's Room*'s new cover design not only sported the dark green livery of the Modern Classics, but also featured a bitten apple graphic, and a blurb from Fay Weldon attesting to the book's power to 'chang[e] lives' (French, 1997 [1977]). See Abbey, 1998 and http://www. virago.co.uk/virago/virago/history.asp.

23. In October 2002 Philippa Harrison announced her resignation as CEO of Time Warner Books UK to take up the position of editorial director at the Ed Victor Agency in London (Doran, 2002: 16).

CHAPTER 2 'BOOKS OF INTEGRITY': DILEMMAS OF RACE AND AUTHENTICITY IN FEMINIST PUBLISHING

1. This chapter, and the volume as a whole, utilises various terms to discuss race-based activism within the women's movement: black (or Black) feminism; third-world feminism; women of colour activism; multicultural feminism; Chicana/Latina feminism; and womanism. Because this chapter maps over 20 years of developments in women's movement thinking, and because it uses international examples to counterpoint British publishing experience, no one term can hope to capture the nuances of debates around gender and race across the period as a whole. Rather than select a single term, and thus preserve in aspic the parameters of the debate at any one point in time, this discussion utilises the terminology preferred by the writer or publishing house under discussion. Many writers and critics, for example Barbara Smith, moreover employ terms such as 'Black' and 'women of colo(u)r' contemporaneously, thus further militating against use of a misleadingly universalist terminology in framing this discussion (Smith and Smith, 1983 [1981]).

Briefly, the diverse origins and political associations of the various terms might be summarised as follows. 'Black' has become the most popularised term in racially focused feminist thought, continuing as it does the tactic of validating a formerly derogatory adjective originally championed by the Black Consciousness and Black Power movements of the late 1960s and early 1970s (see Smith, 1986 [1977]; Davis, 1981; hooks, 1981; Collins, 1991). The merits of capitalisation constitute a further sub-debate in this area, with some critics regarding the use of upper-case as a logical extension of the valorisation strategy. Others regard capitalisation as tactically inappropriate 'until the label white is also capitalized; otherwise the effect is, once again, the special and prejudicial setting aside of blacks as Other' (Kramarae and Treichler, 1992: 73).

The term 'women of colo(u)r' arose in protest against the dichotomising tendencies of the black/white binary, and attempts to destabilise such thought patterns by highlighting both the diversity of non-

Caucasian women (for example Puerto Rican-American women, Latinas, First Nation Canadians, Maori women and Aboriginal Australian women), as well as their commonalities and allied concerns (Moraga and Anzaldúa, 1983 [1981]). The denomination 'third-world women' achieved prominence in the early to mid-1980s in response to demands that first-world feminists (including feminists of colour) look beyond the borders of developed nations to acknowledge the international economic relationships that serve to perpetuate women's oppression in the developing world (Davies, 1983; Brydon and Chant, 1989).

'Multiculturalism', a term recurrent in policy statements of centre-left political parties during the 1980s (Cashmore, 1996), indicates a desired ethnic and cultural pluralism, which is not only multiracial (in the sense of advocating the peaceful interrelationship of black and white populations) but which also embraces the variety of ethnic identifications among Caucasians (for example Jews, Serbians, Greek-Australians, Italo-Canadians and Polish Americans). Finally, the term 'womanism', associated specifically with African-American writer Alice Walker, proposes a means for black feminists to distance their socio-intellectual programmes from the white, middle-class, WASP priorities traditionally associated with the term 'feminism'. Walker derives her neologism from the adjective 'womanish', used in black vernaculars to describe young girls displaying 'outrageous, audacious, courageous or *willful* behaviour (Walker, 1984 [1983]: xi).

2. The firm's website in mid-2003 stated: 'this year The Women's Press celebrates 25 spirited years of independent publishing'. See http://www.the-womens-press.com.

3. Dowrick sold her shareholding to Attallah around 1985; Attallah thus owned 100 per cent of The Women's Press by the time of the 1991 crisis (Hennegan, 1992: 6; Dowrick, 2003b).

4. Attallah announced his planned retirement from business in November 2000, offering for sale all of the Namara group's interests, including The Women's Press (Attallah, 2000: 64; Morrish, 2000: 5; Weale, 2000: 8). Namara was reported in December 2000 to be in negotiations with The Women's Press staff over a management buyout of the company (*Independent*, 2000: 10) although Namara was subsequently reported to be neogiating with the Barclay brothers for sale of the press in May 2002 (Waller, 2002: n.p.). Negotiations have similarly been reported for the sale of other Namara assets, specifically magazines the *Literary Review*, *The Oldie* and *The Wire* (Weale, 2000: 8). In November 1995, the Soho-based *Literary Review*, edited by the late Auberon Waugh, had been threatened with the withdrawal of Attallah's financial backing on account of its continued losses. Fortunately for the magazine's editorial board, powerful financiers John Paul Getty and Lord Hanson 'admire[d] the magazine and Bron Waugh's contribution to British life' sufficiently to cover its debts (*Bookseller*, 1995c: 8). *The Oldie* survived a similar 'near-death experience' and was bailed out with an injection of funds by Attallah in 1994 (Morrish, 2000: 5; Attallah, 2000: 64). The Women's Press, facing a similar cash-flow crisis some years earlier, was conspicuously denied a commensurate financial bailout. Attallah retired after 21

years as senior executive for the Asprey, Garrard, Mappin & Webb group in 1995 (Kay, 2000: 38).

5. Gale and Hemming continued as joint managing directors until the appointment of Elsbeth Lindner in 1999. Lindner, formerly head of Lime Tree press, announced plans for reinvigorating The Women's Press by 'developing strategies to increase our visibility' (Evans, 2001).

6. The 1991 crisis has subsequently been discussed in a number of academic and media articles: Hennegan, 1992: 6; Woddis, 1992: 26; Bonner, 1996: 104; Murray, 1998; Sullivan, 1998: 20.

7. Virago's 1998 *Spring/Summer Catalogue* revealed that Angelou long remained a crucial literary asset for the press. The fifth volume of Angelou's autobiography, *Even the Stars Look Lonesome* (1998), was Virago's leading frontlist title for the season, flanked by Dolly A. McPherson's critical analysis, *Order Out of Chaos: The Autobiographical Works of Maya Angelou* (1998), and the 'stunning new-look' reissue of the preceding four volumes of Angelou's memoirs. Given that Angelou is one of only four women of colour frontlisted in the catalogue, Virago's promotional tactics raise disconcerting questions about black women's subsidisation of white presses.

8. This is not to suggest that collectivist and consciousness-raising group models are in any way unproblematic or optimal production environments. Chapter 4 explores in detail the complexity of feminist organisational models and their interaction with the commercial publishing process. It is important to note also that models of publisher–author symbiosis like that proposed by Dowrick could, when put into practice, be experienced by writers as oppressively prescriptive and artistically inhibiting (see Maitland, 1979).

9. Perhaps more surprisingly, Dowrick also invokes such romantic discourse in her narration of The Women's Press's foundation: 'when I met Naim he and I fell instantly in love – not romantically – but entrepreunerially [sic]!! He backed me and The Women's Press came into being' (Dowrick, 2003a).

10. New York publisher Harcourt Brace Jovanovich originally published Walker's *The Color Purple: A Novel* for the US market in 1982. In 1992 Harcourt released a special tenth anniversary edition of the title.

11. At the time of its establishment in 1980, the Sheba collective consisted entirely of white women but, after lengthy internal debates over the imprint's racial make-up in 1983–84, it became increasingly multicultural and established a distinctive public profile as a publisher of books by British women of colour (Sheba Feminist Publishers Archive, 1980–94; Loach, 1986: 18–21). The complex and involved politics of this collective are considered in Chapter 4 as part of an analysis of group publishing models.

12. See Chapter 5 for a discussion of the power of mainstream book marketing to dilute or misrepresent the oppositional force of feminist texts.

13. This Canadian press, founded as a 'non-profit socialist feminist collective' in 1972, bears no official relationship to the British press of a similar name (Gabriel and Scott, 1993: 27). In a now familiar turn of events, it

suffered financial difficulties and was sold to Toronto-based Canadian Scholars Press in October 2000, where it remains as an imprint (Eichler, 2000: 22).

14. Margaret Busby was co-founder of the British publishing house Allison and Busby. She also edited the important multicultural anthology of black women's writing *Daughters of Africa* (1992).

15. Refer, for example, to the cover of X Press's controversial 1995 bestseller, Sheri Campbell's *Wicked in Bed*.

16. The cover of The Women's Press's 1998 title *Anything We Love Can Be Saved: A Writer's Activism* by Alice Walker is such an example of author-photo prominence (see also Kanneh, 1998 for a rare analysis of the racial dynamics at work in book design and marketing). The cover of The Women's Press's anthology of black British women's writing, *Bittersweet* (1998) features a close-up photograph of braided hair, unmistakably demarcating its target audience – Britain's African and Afro-Caribbean communities. The cross-racial cover appeal of The Women's Press's young adult Livewire! title, *Sorrelle* (1998) by Millie Murray, may illustrate how the very diversity of Britain's ethnic populations could itself become a marketing strength.

CHAPTER 3 OPENING PANDORA'S BOX: THE RISE OF ACADEMIC FEMINIST PUBLISHING

1. Philippa Brewster on the failure of Pandora's 1991 management buyout bid (quoted in *Bookseller*, 1991b: 829).

2. Spender's narrative of Pandora's emergence in reaction to a conservative sales force bears out Martha M. Kinney's observation that the mainstreaming of feminist knowledge owes much to 'women editors in publishing houses [who] encouraged and supported women writers and argued with predominantly male sales managers and publishing boards for the right to publish feminist books' (1982: 49).

3. Pandora Press's February 1985 Spring books announcement in UK trade periodical the *Bookseller* contains a one-paragraph blurb about the novel, promoting it as: 'A funny, eccentric jewel of a novel about growing up bewildered in a North Country Fundamentalist household' (*Bookseller*, 1985a: 595).

4. Jeanette Winterson (1986) introduced Amelia Opie's *Adeline Mowbray, or The Mother and Daughter* [1804], Fay Weldon (1986) wrote a new introduction to Mary Brunton's *Discipline* [1814], while Margaret Drabble (1988) introduced Fanny Burney's *The Wanderer, or Female Difficulties* [1814].

5. Ros de Lanerolle, (then) managing director of The Women's Press (quoted in Neustatter, 1988: 20).

6. See Howe's similar comments on the occasion of The Feminist Press's tenth anniversary: 'We have two kinds of success stories. One is numbers. The other is when we can drop a book from our list because another publisher has picked it up' (Dunning, 1980: 69). In the same vein, shortly after the press's twentieth anniversary in 1990 Howe stated, 'I thought

we would last a year or two', having 'assumed that other publishers would see the need for our kind of books and that we would soon be out of business' (Barbato, 1991: 46).

7. Ellen Messer-Davidow, 2002: 138.

8. The dismantling of author-editor hierarchies was not always in the best interests of book projects. Authors Susan Griffin and J.J. Wilson describe blurring of the boundaries of authorial identity, which feminist press structures can unwittingly instigate, whereby 'the women's press people [are] almost writing for the author the book they would like to be writing ... and then later, when the editor has to reemerge as publisher ..., there can be a sense of betrayal or of muddle at least' (1982: 82).

9. Routledge, Women's and Gender Studies catalogue, 2001: 2.

10. See Routledge UK's pioneering of this concept in its respective gender, publishing studies and media and cultural studies arenas, *inter alia* (http://www.routledge.co.uk/rcenters/rcen.html).

11. Routledge UK has demonstrated the most commitment to the field, in 1995 acquiring the Blueprint Professional Media list from Chapman and Hall, including titles such as Hugh Jones' *Publishing Law* (1996), and Patrick Forsyth and Robin Birn's *Marketing in Publishing* (1997), in addition to Blueprint Career Builder Guides such as Giles Clark's industry vade mecum *Inside Book Publishing* (3rd edn, 2000). Routledge UK has also originated important book history textbook anthologies such as David Finkelstein and Alistair McCleery's *The Book History Reader* (2002).

12. Sage Publications, a dominant force in contemporary English-language humanities publishing, currently adopts the terms 'gender studies' (UK) and 'gender and sexuality studies' (US). Rival multinational Routledge (since November 1998 an imprint of Taylor & Francis) formerly hedged its bets with the combined option 'women's and gender studies', although it has more recently preferred 'gender studies'. Princeton University Press denominates its list as 'gender studies', while Stanford University Press and Yale University Press both opt for 'women's studies and gender studies'. Columbia University Press, a leading US publisher in the field, meanwhile covers all bases with 'women's studies', 'gender studies' and 'gay and lesbian studies' lists. Neither Oxford University Press nor Cambridge University Press produces a specifically gender-themed catalogue.

CHAPTER 4 COLLECTIVE UNCONSCIOUS: THE DEMISE OF RADICAL FEMINIST PUBLISHING

1. Further evidence of radical feminism's posthumous influence can be found in the UK book retail chain Books etc.'s sampler of women's fiction, *Women etc.*, published to coincide with the announcement of the shortlist for the 1997 all-women Orange Prize for Fiction.

2. Onlywomen Press operated under the name the Women's Press from its 1974 foundation until Naim Attallah and Stephanie Dowrick registered the name for their new Namara-backed feminist publishing house (Onlywomen Press, c. 1977; Mohin, 1998; Dowrick, 2003b). The original

Women's Press had, 'in the thrill of political purity', decided against registering the name, and thus could only mount an ineffectual protest at Attallah's actions (Jackson, C., 1993: 48). Lilian Mohin has since remarked: 'We came up with "Onlywomen Press" with unseemly haste – and lived to regret it. People didn't get what we meant by "only women" and it overlapped too much with The Women's Press' (Jackson, C., 1993: 48). To avoid confusing Mohin's press with London-based The Women's Press, with the Toronto-based Women's Press, or with the early 1970s Californian operation of the same name, this discussion refers to the house as Onlywomen throughout.

3. The cross-subsidisation of book publishing with jobbing printing was a common organisational rationale among 1970s women's print collectives before the mass uptake of personal computers and desktop publishing software rendered such operations technologically and commercially obsolete (see Frank, 1982; *Co-operator*, 1985; Lynch, 1998).

4. The Women's Library operated as the Fawcett Library, a reference library of London Guildhall University, until a £7 million National Lottery grant enabled it to relocate to purpose-built premises in east London in February 2002 (Muir, 2001; Viner, 2002). It is now open to the public.

5. Titles originated by Naiad and purchased by Silver Moon Books (SMB) for the UK and Commonwealth markets include Katherine V. Forrest's strong backlist sellers *Curious Wine* (1983 Naiad/1990 SMB) and *An Emergence of Green* (1986/1990), and the erotic lesbian short fiction collections *Diving Deep* (1992/1993), *Diving Deeper* (1993/1994), *Deeply Mysterious* (1994/1995) and *The First Time Ever* (1995/1996), all co-edited by Barbara Grier.

6. Radical feminists' suspicion that mainstream publishers would misrepresent feminist ideas through their institutional control of the editorial, marketing and promotional processes was to some extent justified (see Chapter 5).

7. Somewhat ironically, Piercy's publications in the UK appeared under the colophons of the feminist press movement's most corporate-aligned houses – The Women's Press and Pandora Press (Piercy, 1979, 1983).

8. Radical feminist Ti-Grace Atkinson had in 1968 led a breakaway group of the New York NOW chapter, claiming that the overly hierarchical nature of the organisation founded by Betty Friedan served to inhibit revolutionary feminist action (see Atkinson, 1974: 68).

9. Jane Cholmeley adumbrates the tensions within Silver Moon women's bookshop, which led to the abandonment of collectivist practices and the forging of a 'modus vivendi' between capitalist management and collectivist consensus (1991: 224–9). More general discussions of collectivism's failures as a feminist organising practice (though not referring specifically to its implications for the feminist print sector) are found in Evans, 1980: 222–4; Bouchier, 1983: 217–23; and Randall, 1987: 254–7. Alice Echols in *Daring to Be Bad: Radical Feminism in America 1967–1975* (1989: 269–81) outlines US radical feminists' 1973–74 debate over the political implications of feminist entrepreneurialism (see also the article 'Taking Care of Business' (1974) by Coletta Reid, founder of Diana Press).

10. The festering issue of racism within feminist publishing did, in fact, re-emerge at the Women's Press (Canada) the following year, with a 'widely publicised split' precipitated by 'divisions over the content of and approval process for a fiction anthology [*Dykeversions*]' (Gabriel and Scott, 1993: 43). Press historians Chris Gabriel and Katherine Scott in their article 'Women's Press at Twenty: The Politics of Feminist Publishing' note that 'unable to reach an accommodation, eight members left the Press [in 1987], intending to found a new feminist press in Toronto' (1993: 45). This breakaway group subsequently established Second Story Press (Godard, 2002: 216).

11. Conservative opposition was already discernible at local government level by autumn 1981, when Tory opposition councillors in the Greater London Council responded to Sheba's request for a £20,000 loan by declaring certain of the press's publications both pornographic and blasphemous. After a barrage of adverse publicity in the right-wing press, Sheba reduced their loan application to £12,000 (Sheba Feminist Publishers Archive, 1981: box 2.3).

12. See Naiad Press's homepage: http://www.naiadpress.com/index.htm.

CHAPTER 5 'THIS BOOK COULD CHANGE YOUR LIFE': FEMINIST BESTSELLERS AND THE POWER OF MAINSTREAM PUBLISHING

1. The sales statistics cited throughout this chapter are, unless otherwise indicated, the US sales figures for individual titles as derived from *Publishers Weekly*'s non-fiction 'Best Sellers' listing, one compiled with commendable professionalism 'on a percentage basis from reports from 48 booksellers in 35 communities in the U.S.A.' (*Publishers Weekly* – hereafter *PW* – 17 June, 1963: 118). Because British bestseller listings in the *Bookseller* and the *Sunday Times* did not appear until the mid-1970s, the actual British sales figures for the majority of the books analysed here are unreliable. Sales statistics acquired from British publishers have been included where this information was forthcoming. As Sutherland accurately observes in *Bestsellers*, 'anyone attempting [a] comprehensive and numerically informative account of British bestsellers would face a Herculean task' (1981: 13).

2. Sample titles of two of these 1963 extracts include: 'G.I. Bill for Women? Excerpts from *The Feminine Mystique*'. *Ladies' Home Journal*, January: 24–9; and 'Fraud of Femininity: Excerpts from *The Feminine Mystique*'. *McCall's*, March: 81–7.

3. Friedan's estimate of the book's sales appears reasonably accurate, if erring somewhat on the side of generosity. Alice Payne Hackett and James Henry Burke in *80 Years of Best Sellers: 1895–1975* calculate that by 1975 *The Feminine Mystique* had sold approximately 2 million copies (1977: 20). Margaret Bluman, editor of Penguin UK's women's studies list, states that although Penguin does not now directly promote Friedan's book, it continues to sell 500–600 copies annually as a backlist title (Bluman, 1999).

4. Self-consciously echoing such publishers' cover blurbs, Kate Millett recalls of reading Simone de Beauvoir's *The Second Sex* in 1950s America: 'This book could change your life, it could make you dissatisfied. It could make you not just want to be one of the good girls that went to college, but you wanted to kick the windows in too' (quoted in Forster and Sutton 1989: 22).

5. The publicist's dream debate between Norman Mailer, Germaine Greer and other speakers took place in New York Town Hall in April 1971 (see *Uncensored*, 1998b).

6. Recently, there have been tentative signs that this crucial interface of literature and marketing is beginning to receive belated attention. Elaine Jordan explores the paperback packaging of Angela Carter's work in 'Her Brilliant Career: The Marketing of Angela Carter', one of the papers collected in Judy Simons and Kate Fullbrook's *Writing: A Woman's Business: Women, Writing and the Marketplace* (1998) – a pioneering text in its fusion of literary and commercial approaches. Robin Roberts's spirited analysis of the gender dynamics at work in 1950s sci-fi pulp magazine covers explores related ideas in a tangential wing of the publishing industry (1993).

7. The other side of author–publisher conflicts over cover design can be glimpsed in Germaine Greer's debate with design representatives of Doubleday, publisher of Greer's *The Female Eunuch* 'sequel', *The Whole Woman* (1999). Wanting a cover 'that's shocking, like the original cover was shocking', Greer insists upon using her photograph of a Filipino female fertility symbol pressed into raw steak, overriding the designers' fear that the cover will alienate potential book-buying vegans (*Close-Up*, 1999). Interestingly, in the mass-market Anchor paperback edition (2000), the image background has been reticulated, so as to be scarcely recognisable as meat.

8. Millett, 1976 [1974]: 214.

9. Notably, the UK paperback and the US hardback editions of *The New Feminism* (1999) were released under the Virago imprint. Either Walter's reasoning underwent a radical revision in the period between making this statement and early 1999, or the incident represents an interesting example of list traffic within publishing conglomerates owning feminist imprints.

10. Millett, 1976 [1974]: 83.

11. *Observer*, 1995: 24.

12. Wolf, 1991a: 275.

13. The Fawcett Columbine US paperback edition of *Fire With Fire* (1994) is particularly revealing in its modulation of Wolf's image and public positioning for maximum sales impact. The cover of this edition is dominated by a colour photograph of the author herself, and the book's subtitle has been changed to *The New Female Power and How to Use It*. The author's photographic prominence, the subtitle and the use of block typography all work to package *Fire With Fire* as an upmarket feminist self-help manual – one offering 'political' solutions for troubled individual psyches.

14. *The Whole Woman* was serialised in Britain's Conrad Black-owned broadsheet, the *Daily Telegraph*, during March 1999. Greer also granted the *Daily Telegraph* an exclusive pre-publication interview (Coward, 1999: 2). Greer's lecture at the London Festival of Literature on 23 March 1999, ostensibly discussing critical reception of her book, was further sponsored by the same newspaper (*Marketing Week*, 1999: 35).

15. For an exploration of this argument in relation to Beauvoir's own bestseller, *The Second Sex*, see Murray, 2000c.

Bibliography

Abbey, Sally. (1998) Interview with the author. London. 9 Sep.

Abbey, Sally, with Lydia Millet and Alice Thompson. (1997) 'Virago Voices'. Platforms series. London: Lyttelton Theatre, National Theatre. 15 Apr.

Abbott, Charlotte. (2001) 'Battening Down the Niche: Amid Turmoil: Gay and Lesbian Publishers, Retailers and Book Clubs Struggle for Security'. *Publishers Weekly* 23 Apr.: 32–5.

Adaba, A. Tom, Olalekan Ajia and Ikechukwu Nwosu, eds. (1988) *The Crisis of Publications: Communication Industry in Nigeria* [sic]. Africa Media Monograph Series. Nairobi, Kenya: African Council on Communication Education.

Adams, Kate. (1992) 'Making the World Safe for the Missionary Position: Images of the Lesbian in Post-World War II America'. *Lesbian Texts and Contexts: Radical Revisions.* Eds Karla Jay and Joanne Glasgow. London: Onlywomen Press. 255–74.

—— (1998) 'Built Out of Books: Lesbian Energy and Feminist Ideology in Alternative Publishing'. *Journal of Homosexuality* 34.3–4: 113–41.

Aftab, Tahera. (2002) 'Lobbying for Transnational Feminism: Feminist Conversations Make Connections'. *National Women's Studies Association Journal* 14.2: 153–6.

Ahmad, Rukhsana. (1991) 'What's Happening to the Women's Presses?' *Spare Rib* May: 10–13.

Alberge, Dalya. (1995) 'Heavyweight Publishers Vie for Virago'. *The Times* [UK] 25 Oct.: 3.

Allen, Sandra, Lee Sanders and Jan Wallis, eds. (1974) *Conditions of Illusion: Papers from the Women's Movement.* Leeds: Feminist Books.

Altbach, Philip G. (1975) *Publishing in India: An Analysis.* Delhi: Oxford University Press.

Anderson, Patricia J. and Jonathan Rose, eds. (1991) *British Literary Publishing Houses, 1820–1880.* Dictionary of Literary Biography, vol. 106. Detroit, MI: Gale Research.

Ang, Ien. (1995) 'The Vicissitudes of "Progressive Television"'. *Cultural Remix: Theories of Politics and the Popular.* London: Lawrence & Wishart. 167–87.

Angelou, Maya. (1981) *The Heart of a Woman.* New York: Bantam/Random House.

—— (1984) *I Know Why the Caged Bird Sings.* [1969] London: Virago Press.

Ardill, Susan. (1984) 'At the Fair'. *Spare Rib* Jun.: 21.

Arnold, June. (1976) 'Feminist Presses & Feminist Politics'. *Quest: A Feminist Quarterly* 3.1: 18–26.

Atkinson, Ti-Grace. (1974) 'The Equality Issue'. *Amazon Odyssey.* New York: Link Books. 65–75.

Attallah, Naim, ed. (1987) *Women.* London: Quartet.

—— (2000) 'I'm Too Old for *The Oldie*'. *Evening Standard* [UK] 15 Nov.: 64.

Atwood, Margaret. (1978) 'Obstacle Course'. Review of Tillie Olsen, *Silences*. *New York Times Book Review* 30 Jul.: 1, 27.

234

Austen, Jane. (1978) *Love and Freindship [sic], and Other Early Works*. London: The Women's Press.

Australian Financial Review. (1998) 'Greer Plans *Female Eunuch* Sequel'. 26 Feb.: 55.

Badawi, Leila. (1987) 'Naim of the Game'. *Guardian* [UK] 29 Apr.: 10.

Baehr, Helen, ed. (1980) *Women and Media*. *Women's Studies International Quarterly*. 3.1: 1–133.

Baehr, Helen and Gillian Dyer, eds. (1987) *Boxed In: Women and Television*. London: Pandora Press.

Baehr, Helen and Ann Gray, eds. (1996) *Turning It On: A Reader in Women and Media*. London: Arnold.

Barbato, Joseph. (1990) 'Irish Women on the Move'. *Publishers Weekly* 13 Jul.: 34.

—— (1991) 'Lighting Fires at The Feminist Press'. *Publishers Weekly* 12 Jul.: 46.

Bardsley, Barney. (1982) 'Sweet Words and Sour Cream'. *Undercurrents* 55/56 Sep.: 36.

Barker, Nicolas. (1990) 'Reflections on the History of the Book'. *The Book Collector* 39.1: 9–26.

Barrett, Michèle. (1980) *Women's Oppression Today: Problems in Marxist Feminist Analysis*. London: Verso.

—— (1988) *Women's Oppression Today: The Marxist/Feminist Encounter*. London: Verso.

Barrett Browning, Elizabeth. (1978) *Aurora Leigh and Other Poems*. London: The Women's Press.

Battles, Jan. (1998) 'Irish Feminists Rage as Publisher Loses the Plot'. *Sunday Times* [UK] 8 Feb.: n.p.

Baxter, Sarah. (1990) 'The Carmen Touch'. *New Statesman & Society* 21 Sep.: 10–11.

—— (1995) 'Why Did the Apple Crumble?' *Observer* [UK] 29 Oct.: Review, 9.

Beauvoir, Simone de. (1949) *Le Deuxième Sexe*. Paris: Gallimard.

—— (1953a) *The Second Sex*. [1949] Trans. H. M. Parshley. New York: Alfred A. Knopf and London: Cape.

Beddoe, Deirdre. (1983) *Discovering Women's History: A Practical Manual*. Pandora Handbook series. London: Pandora Press.

Belle, Jennifer. (1997) *Going Down*. Virago Vs. London: Virago Press.

Bennett, C. (1993) 'The House that Carmen Built'. *Guardian* [UK] 14 Jun.: G2, 10–11.

Bereano, Nancy. (2001) 'The Bottom Line'. *Women's Review of Books* [US] Jul.: 19–20.

Betterton, Rosemary, ed. (1987) *Looking On: Images of Femininity in the Visual Arts and Media*. London: Pandora Press.

Big Women. (1998) BBC TV. Channel 4, London. 2 Jul., 9 Jul., 16 Jul., 23 Jul.

Birch, Helen. (1991) 'Bold Types in a Buyer's Market'. *New Statesman & Society* 31 May: 39.

Black Woman Talk Collective. (1984a) 'Black Woman Talk'. *Feminist Review* 17: 100.

—— (1984b) 'Black Woman Talk'. *Spare Rib* Jun.: 28.

Blain, Virginia, Patricia Clements and Isobel Grundy, eds. (1990) *The Feminist Companion to Literature in English: Women Writers from the Middle Ages to the Present*. New Haven, CT: Yale University Press.

Bluman, Margaret. (1999) Telephone conversation with the author. London. 22 Jan.

Boddy, Kasia, Ali Smith and Sarah Wood, eds. (2000) *Brilliant Careers: The Virago Book of Twentieth-Century Fiction*. London: Virago Press/Little, Brown UK.

Bonfante, Jordan. (1971) 'Germaine Greer'. *Life* 7 May: 30–3.

Bonner, Frances. (1996) 'From *The Female Man* to the *Virtual Girl*: Whatever Happened to Feminist SF?' *Hecate* 22.1: 104-19.

Bonner, Frances, Lizbeth Goodman, Richard Allen, Linda Jones and Catherine King, eds. (1992) *Imagining Women: Cultural Representations and Gender*. Cambridge: Polity Press and the Open University.

Book Marketing Council. (1982) *Impulse Buying of Books*. London: Book Marketing Council.

Bookseller. (1984) 'A Fantastic First Feminist Book Fair'. 16 Jun.: 2420.

Bookseller. (1985a) 'Pandora Press'. Spring books advertisement. 9 Feb.: 595.

Bookseller. (1985b) 'Routledge Rift After ABP Bid'. 23 Mar.: 1255–6.

Bookseller. (1985c) 'Virago Bookshop: "Stylish and Fun"'. 5 Jan.: 15.

Bookseller. (1987) 'International Thomson Buys ABP'. 19 Jun.: 2301.

Bookseller. (1988) 'Pandora's New Home?' 22 Jan.: 242.

Bookseller. (1990a) 'Unwin Hyman to be Dismembered'. 13 Jul.: 73–4.

Bookseller. (1990b) 'Collins Close to Deal to Buy Unwin Hyman'. 6 Jul.: 5.

Bookseller. (1991a) 'Hundreds Lose Jobs as Publishers Retrench'. 22 Mar.: 851–3.

Bookseller. (1991b) 'Pandora Buyout Collapses'. 27 Sep.: 829.

Bookseller. (1995a) 'Is Virago's Independence Under the Hammer?' 27 Oct.: 5.

Bookseller. (1995b) 'Little, Brown Pips Bloomsbury in Battle for Virago'. 10 Nov.: 8.

Bookseller. (1995c) 'Review Saved'. 17 Nov.: 8.

Bookseller. (1995d) 'Virago Loses Another Virago'. 13 Oct.: 6.

Bookseller. (1996a) 'The Word is Virago'. Publicity insert. 12 Jul.: 1–4.

Bookseller. (1996b) 'Women's Fiction Prize Finally Launched'. 2 Feb.: 13.

Bookseller. (1996c) 'X Press Route to Success'. 1 Mar.: 55-6.

Bordwell, David, Janet Staiger and Kristin Thompson. (1985) *The Classical Hollywood Cinema: Film Style and Mode of Production to 1960*. London: Routledge.

Bostridge, Mark. (2003) 'The Apple Bites Back'. *Independent on Sunday* [UK] 18 May: 16.

Bouchier, David. (1983) *The Feminist Challenge: The Movement for Women's Liberation in Britain and the USA*. London: Macmillan.

Brampton, Sally. (1990) 'Hit and Myth'. *Guardian* [UK] 12 Sep.: 17.

Brewster, Philippa. (1999) 'An Erudite and Original Challenge: Publishing *The Politics of Reproduction*'. *Canadian Women's Studies* 18.4: 111.

—— (2003) Telephone interview with the author. Brisbane. 6 Jun.

Bright, Susie, ed. (2002) *The Best American Erotica 2002*. New York: Simon & Schuster.

Briscoe, Joanna. (1990a) 'Feminists Fatales'. *Guardian* [UK] 1 Feb.: 17.

—— (1990b) 'Feminist Presses: Who Needs Them?' *Guardian* [UK] 6 Jun.: 43.

—— (1992) 'Publish or Be Damned'. *Guardian* [UK] 10 Jun.: 17.

—— (1993) 'The Penguin Book of Lesbian Short Stories edited by Margaret Reynolds'. Review. *Guardian* [UK] 7 Sep.: 9.

Brittain, Vera. (1978) *Testament of Youth: An Autobiographical Study of the Years 1900–1925*. [1933] Virago Modern Classics. London: Virago Press.

Bromley, Michael. (1995) *Media Studies: An Introduction to Journalism*. London: Hodder & Stoughton.

Broughton, Trev. (1993) 'Cross Purposes: Literature, (In)discipline and Women's Studies'. *Women's Studies in the 1990s: Doing Things Differently*. Eds Joanna de Groot and Mary Maynard. London: Macmillan. 62–85.

Brown, Di[ane]. (1997) 'Feminist Publishing in Australia – Sisters Publishing 1979–1983'. *Publishing Studies* 4: 7–11.

—— (1998) 'Feminist Publishing in Australia: Commercial and Cultural Practices'. *Overland* 153: 8–13.

Brydon, Lynne and Sylvia Chant. (1989) *Women in the Third World: Gender Issues in Rural and Urban Areas*. New Brunswick, NJ: Rutgers University Press.

Buckingham, Lisa. (1995) 'Women's Imprint Virago Sold'. *Guardian* [UK] 3 Nov.: 4.

Bunch, Charlotte. (1977) 'Feminist Publishing: An Antiquated Form? – Notes for a Talk at the Old Wives Tales Bookstore'. *Heresies* 3: 24–6.

Burford, Barbara. (1987) 'The Landscapes Painted on the Inside of My Skin'. *Spare Rib* Jun.: 36–9.

Burford, Barbara, et al. (1984) *A Dangerous Knowing: Four Black Women Poets*. London: Sheba Feminist Publishers.

Burnham, Jonathan. (1998) 'Gay Fiction R.I.P.?' *W: The Waterstone's Magazine* 12 Winter/Spring: 30–5.

Busby, Margaret. (1984) 'Black Books'. *New Statesman* 6 Apr.: 12.   — (9/)

——, ed. (1992) *Daughters of Africa: An International Anthology of Words and Writings by Women of African Descent from the Ancient Egyptian to the Present*. London: Cape.

Butalia, Urvashi. (1995) 'Kali for Women: Publishing for Development'. *Genderly Speaking*. Ottawa, Ontario: MATCH International. 9–11.

—— (2000) 'Feminist Publishing in the Third World'. *Routledge International Encyclopedia of Women*. Eds Cheris Kramarae and Dale Spender. New York: Routledge. 1708–11.

Butalia, Urvashi and Ritu Menon, eds. (1993) *In Other Words: New Writing by Indian Women*. London: The Women's Press.

—— (1995) *Making a Difference: Feminist Publishing in the South*. Bellagio Studies in Publishing. Boston, MA: Bellagio Publishing Network.

Butterworth, Sue. (1998) Interview with the author. London. 23 Feb.

Cadman, Eileen, Gail Chester and Agnes Pivot. (1981) *Rolling Our Own: Women as Printers, Publishers and Distributors*. Minority Press Group series. London: Minority Press Group.

Callil, Carmen. (1980) 'Virago Reprints: Redressing the Balance'. *Times Literary Supplement* 12 Sep.: 1001.

—— (1986) 'The Future of Feminist Publishing'. *Bookseller* 1 Mar.: 850–2.

—— (1995) 'The Book, the Chief, the Hype and the Other Cover'. *The Female Eunuch* 25th anniversary supplement. *Weekend Australian* 7 Oct.: 8.

—— (1996) Telephone interview with the author. London. 31 Aug.

—— (1998) 'Women, Publishing and Power – Judy Simons Interviews Carmen Callil'. *Writing: A Woman's Business: Women, Writing and the Marketplace*.

Eds Judy Simons and Kate Fullbrook. Manchester: Manchester University Press. 183–92.

Callil, Carmen and Rayner Unwin. (1980) 'My Ideal Author'. *Author* 91: 67–70.

Cambridge Women's Peace Collective. (1984) *My Country is the Whole World: An Anthology of Women's Work on Peace and War*. London: Pandora Press.

Cameron, Debbie. (1999) 'The Price of Fame – I'. *Trouble & Strife* Summer 39: 4–8.

Cameron, Marsaili. (1987) 'What the Hell Is Feminist Editing?' *In Other Words: Writing as a Feminist*. Eds Gail Chester and Sigrid Nielsen. London: Hutchinson Education. 119–25.

Caplette, Michele. (1982) 'Women in Book Publishing: A Qualified Success Story'. *Books: The Culture and Commerce of Publishing*. Eds Lewis A. Coser, Charles Kadushin and Walter W. Powell. New York: Basic Books. 148–74.

Carter, Angela, ed. (1986) *Wayward Girls & Wicked Women*. London: Virago Press.

Case, John and Rosemary C.R. Taylor, eds. (1979) *Co-ops, Communes and Collectives: Experiments in Social Change in the 1960s and 1970s*. New York: Pantheon.

Cashmore, Ellis, ed. (1996) *Dictionary of Race and Ethnic Relations*. 4th edn. London: Routledge.

Catapano, Joan and Marlie P. Wasserman. (1998) 'Is Publishing Perishing?' *Women's Review of Books* Feb.: 22.

Chapple, Steve and Reebee Garofalo. (1977) *Rock 'n' Roll Is Here to Pay*. Chicago: Nelson-Hall.

Chartier, Roger. (1989) 'Texts, Printing, Readings'. *The New Cultural History*. Ed. Lynn Hunt. Berkeley, CA: University of California Press. 154–75.

Chester, Gail. (1996) 'Book Publishing – the Gentleperson's Profession?' *Writing on the Line: Twentieth Century Working-Class Women Writers*. Eds Sarah Richardson, Sammy Palfrey, Merylyn Cherry and Gail Chester. London: Working Press. 141–8.

—— (2002) 'The Anthology as a Medium for Feminist Debate in the UK'. *Women's Studies International Forum* 25.2: 193–207.

Chester, Gail and Sigrid Nielsen, eds. (1987) *In Other Words: Writing as a Feminist*. London: Hutchinson Education.

Cholmeley, Jane. (1986) 'Feminist Book Fair Success in Oslo'. *Bookseller* 16 Aug.: 630.

—— (1991) 'A Feminist Business in a Capitalist World: Silver Moon Women's Bookshop'. *Working Women: International Perspectives on Labour and Gender Ideology*. Eds Nanneke Redclift and M. Thea Sinclair. London: Routledge. 213–32.

Chopin, Kate. (1978) *The Awakening*. London: The Women's Press.

Chronicle of Higher Education. (1999) 'Founder and Director of Feminist Press Will Step Down'. 29 Oct.: A26.

Clardy, Andrea Fleck. (1983) 'Creating the Space: Feminist Publications Outside the Mainstream'. *Women's Studies International Forum* 6.5: 545–6.

—— (1986) 'Somebody Else's Crisis: Feminist Publishers and Midlist Books'. *Book Research Quarterly* 2.1: 5–8.

Clark, Giles. (2000) *Inside Book Publishing*. 3rd edn. Career Builders Guides. London: Routledge.

Close-Up. (1999) 'Germaine Greer: Close to the Bone'. ABC TV, Brisbane. 21 Mar.

Cobham, Rhonda and Merle Collins, eds. (1987) *Watchers and Seekers: Creative Writing by Black Women in Britain*. London: The Women's Press.

Coleman, Sarah. (1998) 'Sex Please, We're Brits!' *Salon.com*. 6 Jan. <http://www.salon.com/media/1998/01/06media.html> (19 Jun. 2003).

Collins, Jean. (1975) 'The Feminist Press'. *Women on Campus: The Unfinished Liberation*. Eds *Change* Magazine editors. New Rochelle, NY: *Change* Magazine. 102–9.

Collins, Patricia Hill. (1991) *Black Feminist Thought: Knowledge, Consciousness, and the Politics of Empowerment*. New York: Routledge.

Co-operator. (1985) 'Sybylla Co-operative Press'. 5: 9–12.

Coote, Anna and Beatrix Campbell. (1987) *Sweet Freedom: The Struggle for Women's Liberation*. 2nd edn. Oxford: Blackwell.

Cornwell, Jane. (2001) 'London Letter'. *Weekend Australian* 24 Nov.: Books Extra, 12.

Cosic, Miriam. (1997) 'Life, Death and the Whole Damn Thing'. *Australian Magazine* 28–9 Jun.: 26–31.

Coultrap-McQuin, Susan. (1990) *Doing Literary Business: American Women Writers in the Nineteenth Century*. Chapel Hill, NC: University of North Carolina Press.

Coward, Ros[alind]. (1980) '"This Novel Changes Lives": Are Women's Novels Feminist Novels?' *Feminist Review* 5: 53–64.

—— (1999) 'Germaine Bites Back'. *Guardian* [UK] 24 Feb.: 2.

Croom, David. (1993) 'Academic and Textbook Publishing'. *Publishing Now*. Ed. Peter Owen. London: Peter Owen. 134–41.

Dale, Martin. (1997) *The Movie Game: The Film Business in Britain, Europe and America*. London: Cassell.

Dalley, Jan. (1995) 'Was Virago Too Successful?' *Independent on Sunday* [UK] 29 Oct.: 21.

Dangarembga, Tsitsi. (1988) *Nervous Conditions*. London: The Women's Press.

Darnton, Robert. (1987) 'Histoire du Livre. Geschichte des Buchwesens. An Agenda for Comparative History'. *Publishing History* 22: 33–41.

—— (1990) 'What Is the History of Books?' [1982] *The Kiss of Lamourette: Reflections in Cultural History*. London: Faber. 107–35.

Davenport-Hines, Richard. (1990) 'Torments of the Flesh'. Review of Naomi Wolf, *The Beauty Myth*. *Times Literary Supplement* 12 Oct.: 1097.

Davies, Margaret Llewelyn, ed. (1977) *Life as We Have Known it*. [1931] Virago Reprint Library. London: Virago Press.

Davies, Miranda, ed. (1983) *Third World – Second Sex: Women's Struggles and National Liberation*. London: Zed Books.

Davis, Angela Y. (1981) *Women, Race & Class*. New York: Random House.

Davis, Rebecca Harding. (1972) *Life in the Iron Mills; or, The Korl Woman*. [1861] The Feminist Press Reprint series. Old Westbury, NY: The Feminist Press.

de Lanerolle, Ros. (1990) 'Publishing Against the "Other Censorship"'. *Index on Censorship* Oct.: 8–9.

—— (1991) 'The Women's Press'. *Spare Rib* Jul.: 4.

De La Vars, Lauren Pringle. (1991) 'Victoria Press'. *British Literary Publishing Houses, 1820–1880. Dictionary of Literary Biography*, vol. 106. Eds Patricia J. Anderson and Jonathan Rose. Detroit, MI: Gale Research. 311–14.

dell'Olio, Anselma. (1970) 'Divisiveness and Self-Destruction in the Women's Movement'. *Chicago Women's Liberation Newsletter* Aug.: n.p.

Desmoines, Harriet and Catherine Nicholson. (1976) 'Dear Beth'. *Sinister Wisdom* 1: 126–9.

Dickinson, Emily. (1960) 'Tell All the Truth But Tell It Slant'. [1945] *The Complete Poems of Emily Dickinson*. Ed. Thomas H. Johnson. Boston: Little, Brown. 506–7.

Dijkstra, Sandra. (1980) 'Simone de Beauvoir and Betty Friedan: The Politics of Omission'. *Feminist Studies* 6.2: 290–303.

Doran, Amanda-Jane. (2002) 'Harrison Joins Victor Agency'. *Publishers Weekly* 7 Oct.: 16.

Dougary, Ginny. (1992) 'Balancing the Books'. *The Times* [UK] 31 Oct.: Review, 10–12.

Doughty, Frances. (1980) 'Printers and Publishers: Frances Doughty Talks to Charlotte Bunch About Women's Publishing'. *Sinister Wisdom* 13: 71–7.

Douglas, Carol Anne. (1997) 'Plenary – The Future of Feminist Education'. *off our backs* Aug.: 16–18.

—— (2000) 'Support Feminist Bookstores!' *off our backs* Dec.: 1.

Dowrick, Stephanie. (1981) 'Women, Men and the Power of Words'. *Bookseller* 7 Nov.: 1599–600.

—— (1997) Interview with Margaret Throsby. Sydney: ABC Radio National, 30 Jun.

—— (1998) 'Big, But Not Big Enough'. Review of Fay Weldon, *Big Women*. *Sydney Morning Herald* 28 Feb.: Spectrum, 11.

—— (2003a) 'Who Are You Anyway & What Do You Have to Say?' Interview with Orchard Somerville-Collie. *StephanieDowrick.com*. <http:// www. stephaniedowrick.com/FAQ.html> (20 May 2003).

—— (2003b) Interview with the author. Sydney. 2 Jul.

Dreifus, Claudia. (1971) 'The Selling of a Feminist'. Review of Germaine Greer, *The Female Eunuch*. *Nation* 7 Jun.: 728–9.

Duncker, Patricia. (1992) *Sisters and Strangers: An Introduction to Contemporary Feminist Fiction*. Oxford: Blackwell.

Dunning, Jennifer. (1980) 'Feminist Press to Mark 10th Birthday Tuesday'. *New York Times* 16 Nov.: 69.

Durrant, Sabine. (1993) 'How We Met: Carmen Callil and Harriet Spicer'. *Independent* [UK] 23 May: Review, 93.

Dworkin, Andrea. (1997) *Life and Death*. London: Virago Press.

Eagleton, Mary, ed. (1991) *Feminist Literary Criticism*. Harlow, Essex: Longman.

——, ed. (1996a) *Feminist Literary Theory: A Reader*. 2nd edn. Oxford: Blackwell.

—— (1996b) 'Who's Who and Where's Where: Constructing Feminist Literary Studies'. *Feminist Review* 53: 1–23.

—— (1996c) *Working With Feminist Criticism*. Oxford: Blackwell.

Eaves, Morris. (1977) 'What Is the "History of Publishing"?' *Publishing History* 2: 57–77.

Echols, Alice. (1989) *Daring to Be Bad: Radical Feminism in America 1967–1975*. Minneapolis, MN: University of Minnesota Press.

Edgeworth, Maria. (1986a) *Belinda*. [1811] Mothers of the Novel series. London: Pandora Press.

—— (1986b) *Patronage*. [1814] Mothers of the Novel series. London: Pandora Press.

Ehrlich, Carol. (1973) 'The Woman Book Industry'. *Changing Women in a Changing Society*. Ed. Joan Huber. Chicago: University of Chicago Press. 268–82.

Eichler, Leah. (2000) 'CS Acquires Women's Press'. *Publishers Weekly* 13 Nov.: 22.

Eisenbach, Helen. (1997) *Lesbianism Made Easy*. Virago Vs. London: Virago Press.

Eliot, Simon. (1994) *Some Patterns and Trends in British Publishing 1800–1919*. London: Bibliographical Society.

Ellmann, Mary. (1971) 'Women'. Review of Kate Millett, *Sexual Politics*. *Yale Review* 60.4: 590–3.

—— (1979) *Thinking About Women*. [1968] London: Virago Press.

Engel, Mary. (1963) 'Chercher l'Homme'. Review of Betty Friedan, *The Feminine Mystique*. *Contemporary Psychology* 8.11: 423–4.

Epstein, Jason. (2002) *Book Business: Publishing Past Present and Future*. New York: Norton.

Evans, Grace. (1986) 'Feminist Book Fortnight'. *Spare Rib* Jun.: 22–3.

—— (1991) 'Pushing the Boat Out'. *Everywoman* Jun.: 12–14.

Evans, Kate. (2001) 'Should the Women's Press Stow its Irons? [sic]' Homestead.com. Jul. <http://as0701.homestead.com/feminist.html> (20 May 2003).

Evans, Sara. (1980) *Personal Politics: The Roots of Women's Liberation in the Civil Rights Movement and the New Left*. New York: Vintage.

Evening Standard. [UK] (1995) 'Official: The Feminist Dream is Dead'. 13 Sep.: 8.

Everywoman. (1987) 'Upheavals in Women's Publishing'. Sep.: 11.

Ezard, John. (1995) 'Virago Facing Sale after Rows and Recession'. *Guardian* [UK] 25 Oct.: 3.

Fairbairns, Zoë. (1994) 'Still Backing Feminist Basics'. *Bookseller* 24 Jun.: 34.

Fairweather, Eileen. (1993) 'Death By Suicide'. *Guardian* [UK] 15 Mar.: II, 12.

Faludi, Susan. (1992) *Backlash: The Undeclared War Against Women*. London: Chatto and Windus.

Fava, Sylvia Fleis. (1963) 'Book Reviews'. Review of Betty Friedan, *The Feminine Mystique*. *American Sociological Review* 28: 1053–4.

Feather, John. (1988) *A History of British Publishing*. London: Routledge.

Febvre, Lucien and Henri-Jean Martin. (1976) *The Coming of the Book: The Impact of Printing 1450–1800*. Trans. David Gerard from *L'Apparition du Livre* [1958]. London: NLB.

Feinberg, Renee and Susan Vaughn. (1976) 'Feminist Publishing: An Exploration'. *Library Journal* 1 Jun.: 1263–5.

Feminist Anthology Collective, ed. (1981) *No Turning Back: Writings from the Women's Liberation Movement 1975–80*. London: The Women's Press.

Feminist Collections. (1998) 'Feminist Publishing'. 19.3: 16–17.

Field, Michelle. (1995) 'Jeanette Winterson: "I Fear Insincerity"'. *Publishers Weekly* 20 Mar.: 38–9.

Finkelstein, David and Alistair McCleery, eds. (2002) *The Book History Reader*. London and New York: Routledge.

Forrest, Katherine V. and Barbara Grier, eds. (1993) *Diving Deeper: More Erotic Lesbian Love Stories*. Tallahassee, FL: Naiad Press.

Forster, Clare. (1993) 'Shrewish Maybe, But Shrewd as Well'. Review of *A Virago Keepsake* and Angela Carter, ed., *The Second Virago Book of Fairy Tales*. *Brisbane Weekend Times* 16 Oct.: 5.

Forster, Penny and Imogen Sutton, eds. (1989) *Daughters of de Beauvoir*. London: The Women's Press.

Forsyth, Patrick, Robin Birn and Dag Smith. (1997) *Marketing in Publishing*. London: Routledge/Blueprint.

Frank, Shirley. (1982) 'Feminist Presses'. *Women in Print: Opportunities for Women's Studies Publication in Language and Literature*. Eds Joan E. Hartman and Ellen Messer-Davidow. New York: Modern Language Association of America. II, 89–116.

Franklin, Andrew. (2002) 'The End of a Great Tradition'. *New Statesman* 27 May: 54–5.

Frawley, Maria. (1998) 'The Editor as Advocate: Emily Faithfull and "The Victoria Magazine"'. *Victorian Periodicals Review* 31.1: 87–104.

Fredeman, William E. (1974) 'Emily Faithfull and the Victoria Press: An Experiment in Sociological Bibliography'. *Library* 29: 139–64.

Freely, Maureen. (1994) 'US and Them: When the Circus Has Left Town'. *Guardian* [UK] 2 Feb.: II, 9.

Freeman, Alexa and Valle Jones. (1976) 'Creating Feminist Communications'. *Quest: A Feminist Quarterly* 3.2: 3–10.

Freeman, Jo[reen]. (1970) 'The Tyranny of Structurelessness'. *The Second Wave* 2.1: 20–5, 42.

—— (1973) 'The Origins of the Women's Liberation Movement'. *Changing Women in a Changing Society*. Ed. Joan Huber. Chicago: University of Chicago Press. 30–49.

—— (1982) *The Tyranny of Structurelessness*. [1970] London: Dark Star Press.

French, Marilyn. (1997) *The Women's Room*. [1977] Virago Modern Classics. London: Virago Press.

Friedan, Betty. (1963) *The Feminine Mystique*. New York: W.W. Norton.

—— (1965) *The Feminine Mystique*. [1963] London: Penguin.

—— (1976) *It Changed My Life: Writings on the Women's Movement*. New York: Random House.

—— (1985) *'It Changed My Life' [sic]: Writings on the Women's Movement*. Revised edn. New York: Norton.

Fritz, Leah. (1986a) 'Publishing and Flourishing'. *Women's Review of Books* Feb.: 16–17.

—— (1986b) 'Publishing and Flourishing (II)'. *Women's Review of Books* Sep.: 14–15.

Furman, Laura. (1970) ' "A House is Not a Home": Women in Publishing'. *Sisterhood Is Powerful: An Anthology of Writings from the Women's Liberation Movement*. Ed. Robin Morgan. New York: Random House. 66–70.

Gabriel, Chris and Katherine Scott. (1993) 'Women's Press at Twenty: The Politics of Feminist Publishing'. *And Still We Rise: Feminist Political Mobilizing in Canada*. Ed. Linda Carty. Toronto: Women's Press. 25–52.

Gale, Kathy. (1997) 'Reading Between the Lies'. *Women Making a Difference: A Directory for Change, 1997/1998*. London: Feminist Publishing Limited co-op. 74.

Gallagher, Catherine. (1994) *Nobody's Story: The Vanishing Acts of Women Writers in the Marketplace, 1670–1820*. Oxford: Clarendon Press.

Garner, Helen. (1995) *The First Stone, Some Questions About Sex and Power*. Sydney: Picador.

Gaskell, Elizabeth. (1983) *Four Short Stories*. Introduced by Anna Walters. London: Pandora Press.

Geare, M. (1986) 'Carmen Callil'. *Author* 97 Spring: 15–16.

Geraghty, Christine and David Lusted, eds. (1998) *The Television Studies Book*. London: Arnold.

Gerrard, Nicci. (1989) *Into the Mainstream: How Feminism Has Changed Women's Writing*. London: Pandora Press.

—— (1993) 'Sisters on the Shelves'. *Observer* [UK] 13 Jun.: 61.

—— (1994) 'The Ultimate Self-Produced Woman'. *Observer* [UK] 5 Jun.: Review, 7.

—— (1995a) 'Middle-aged Feminist Rage Shocks and Amuses'. *Observer* [UK] 21 May: 12.

—— (1995b) 'Young, Sozzled, Certain and Sunk Before we'd Really Begun'. *Observer* [UK] 27 Aug.: 10.

Gilbert, Harriet. (1981) 'Speaking Volumes: Feminist Bookshops'. *Guardian* [UK] 27 Aug.: 9.

Ginsberg, Elaine and Sara Lennox. (1996) 'Antifeminism in Scholarship and Publishing'. *Antifeminism in the Academy*. Eds VèVè Clark, Shirley Nelson Garner, Margaret Higonnet and Ketu H. Katrak. New York: Routledge. 169–99.

Gledhill, Christine. (1997) 'Genre and Gender: The Case of Soap Opera'. *Representation: Cultural Representations and Signifying Practices*. Ed. Stuart Hall. London and Milton Keynes: Sage in association with the Open University. 337–84.

Glendinning, Matthew and Victoria Glendinning, eds. (1996) *Sons & Mothers*. London: Virago Press.

Godard, Barbara. (2002) 'Feminist Periodicals and the Production of Cultural Value: The Canadian Context'. *Women's Studies International Forum* 25.2: 209–23.

Gold, Karen. (1993) 'Women Published and Were Damned'. *Times Higher Education Supplement* 3 Dec.: 16.

Goode, Jennie. (1998) 'Adiós, Assumptions – "Young" Feminists Publish'. *Feminist Bookstore News* Sep./Oct.: 25–7.

Goodings, Lennie. (1993) 'Cleaning the Office, Changing the World'. *Bookseller* 4 Jun.: 26–7.

Goodkin, Judy. (1992) 'Pressing for Change'. *Guardian* [UK] 3 Jun.: 17.

Grant, Jaime M. (1996) 'Building Community-Based Coalitions from Academe: The Union Institute and the Kitchen Table: Women of Color Press Transition Coalition'. *Signs* 21.4: 1024–33.

Greer, Germaine. (1970) *The Female Eunuch*. London: MacGibbon & Kee.

—— (1971a) *The Female Eunuch*. [1970] St Albans, Herts.: Granada.

—— (1971b) 'Germaine Greer … Answers Questions Telephoned to the Studio by Listeners to Radio 4'. *Listener* 21 Jan.: 79–80, 82.

—— (1971c) 'Lib and Lit'. Review of Kate Millett, *Sexual Politics*, and Shulamith Firestone, *The Dialectic of Sex*. *Listener* 25 Mar.: 355–6.

—— (1975) 'When the Courting Has to Stop: Germaine Greer Faces Her Image'. Interview with David Dimbleby. *Listener* 13 Mar.: 331–2.

—— (1981) 'Interview'. With Nat Lehrman. *The Playboy Interview*. Ed. G. Barry Golson. n.p.: Wideview Books. 326–51.

—— (1987) 'The Sultan of Soho and His Harem'. *Observer* [UK] 11 Oct.: Magazine 54–5, 57.

—— (1991) *The Female Eunuch*. [1970] Revised foreword edn. London: Paladin.

—— (1993) *The Female Eunuch*. [1970] Flamingo Modern Classics. London: HarperCollins.

—— (1995) 'Jeremy Isaacs Talks to Germaine Greer'. *Face to Face*. BBC2, London. 6 Nov.

—— (1999a) 'Site Seeing'. *Guardian* [UK] 13 Jan.: 13.

—— (1999b) Lecture and reading from *The Whole Woman*. Dillons/Doubleday book promotion. Friends House, London. 10 Mar.

—— (2000) *The Whole Woman*. [1999] London: Anchor.

Grier, Barbara and Christine Cassidy, eds. (1995) *The First Time Ever: Love Stories by Naiad Press Authors*. Tallahassee, FL: Naiad Press.

Griffey, Harriet. (1998a) 'The Women's Boom'. *Guardian* [UK] 17 Feb.: G2, 5.

—— (1998b) 'More Than the Sum of Her Parts'. *Herald* [Glasgow] 2 Jul.: 8.

Griffin, Susan and J.J. Wilson. (1982) 'Making Choices: Can Two Small-Town Feminists Publish With a Big-City Trade House and Remain Pure?' *Women in Print: Opportunities for Women's Studies Publication in Language and Literature*. Eds Joan E. Hartman and Ellen Messer-Davidow. New York: Modern Language Association of America. II, 79–86.

Guardian. [UK] (1997) 'Wayward Girls & Wicked Women'. Virago advertising insert. 7 Jun. 1–16.

Guardian. [UK] (2001) 'The Loafer'. 13 Oct.: 8.

Hackett, Alice Payne and James Henry Burke. (1977) *80 Years of Best Sellers: 1895–1975*. New York: Bowker.

Hall, Radclyffe. (1982) *The Well of Loneliness*. [1928] Virago Modern Classics. London: Virago Press.

Hancock, Julia. (1994) 'Putting the Heart and Soul into Feminist Publishing'. *Australian Women's Book Review* Dec.: 20–2.

Harris, Bertha. (1993) *Lover*. [1976] New York: New York University Press.

Hartman, Joan E. and Ellen Messer-Davidow, eds. (1982) *Women in Print: Opportunities for Women's Studies Publication in Language and Literature* Vols I and II. New York: Modern Language Association of America.

Hattenstone, Simon. (2001) 'Ursula Owen: Voices from the Margins'. *Guardian* [UK] 21 Jul.: Review, 6–12.

Hawthorne, Susan. (2001) 'Spinifex: Feminists Publishing in Australia'. Interview by Carol Anne Douglas. *off our backs* Jun.: 10–11.

Heller, Zoë. (1990) 'Live and Let Diet'. Review of Naomi Wolf, *The Beauty Myth*. *Independent* [UK] 6 Oct.: 33.

Hennegan, Alison. (1992) 'Weathering the Storm'. *Women's Review of Books* Apr.: 5–7.

—— (1998) Interview with the author. Cambridge. 17 Nov.

Henry, Scott. (1995) 'Taming of the Shrew'. *Australian* 27 Oct.: 13.

Hermes, Joke. (1992) 'Sexuality in Lesbian Romance Fiction'. *Feminist Review* 42: 49–66.

Hernton, Calvin. (1984) 'The Sexual Mountain and Black Women Writers'. *Black American Literature Forum* 18: 139–45.

Higgins, A.C. (1964) 'Briefer Comment'. Review of Betty Friedan, *The Feminine Mystique*. *Social Forces* 42.3: 396.

Hodges, Beth, ed. (1975) 'Lesbian Feminist Writing and Publishing'. Special issue. *Margins* 23: 1–72.

hooks, bell. (1981) *Ain't I a Woman: Black Women and Feminism*. Boston, MA: South End Press.

Howe, Florence. (1974) 'Literacy and Literature'. *PMLA* 89.3: 433–41.

——, ed. (1975) *Women and the Power to Change*. New York: McGraw-Hill.

—— (1976) 'Feminism and the Study of Literature'. *The Radical Teacher* Nov.: 3–11.

—— (1989) 'A Symbiotic Relationship'. *Women's Review of Books* 6.5: 15–16.

—— (1995) 'Feminist Publishing'. *International Book Publishing: An Encyclopedia*. Eds Philip G. Altbach and Edith S. Hoshino. New York: Garland. 130–8.

——, ed. (2000a) *The Politics of Women's Studies: Testimony from Thirty Founding Mothers*. Women's Studies History series. New York: Feminist Press at CUNY.

—— (2000b) 'Learning from Teaching'. *The Politics of Women's Studies: Testimony from Thirty Founding Mothers*. Ed. Florence Howe. Women's Studies History series. New York: Feminist Press at CUNY. 3–15.

Howell, Kevin. (2000) 'Changes Hit Gay/Lesbian Businesses'. *Publishers Weekly* 24 Jul.: 12.

Howsam, Leslie. (1996) 'Women in Publishing and the Book Trades in Britain, 1830–1914'. *Leipziger Jahrbuch zur Buchgeschichte* 6: 67–79.

Humm, Maggie. (1986) *Feminist Criticism: Women as Contemporary Critics*. Brighton: Harvester Press.

Independent. [UK] (1993) 'Virago Was the Only Name to Pick'. 5 Jun.: 14.

Independent [UK] (2000) 'Cover Stories'. 9 Dec.: 10.

Independent [UK]. (2001) 'The Literator'. 24 Nov.: 12.

Independent on Sunday [UK] (1990) 'Last Word'. 9 Sep.: 21.

Jackson, Cath. (1993) 'A Press of One's Own'. *Trouble & Strife* 26: 45–52.

Jackson, Stevi, et al., eds. (1993) *Women's Studies: A Reader*. Hemel Hempstead, Herts.: Harvester Wheatsheaf.

Jakubowski, Maxim, ed. (2002) *Mammoth Book of Best New Erotica: 2002*. London: Constable & Robinson.

James, Clive. (1970) 'Getting Married Later'. Review of Germaine Greer, *The Female Eunuch*. *Listener* 22 Oct.: 552.

Jay, Karla. (1993) 'Is Lesbian Literature Going Mainstream?' *Ms.* Jul.–Aug.: 70–3.

Jay, Karla and Joanne Glasgow, eds. (1992) *Lesbian Texts and Contexts: Radical Revisions*. London: Onlywomen Press.

Joan, Polly and Andrea Chesman. (1978) *Guide to Women's Publishing*. Paradise, CA: Dustbooks.

Joannou, Maroula. (2000) *Contemporary Women's Writing: From* The Golden Notebook *to* The Color Purple. Manchester: Manchester University Press.

Jones, Hugh. (1996) *Publishing Law*. London: Routledge.

Jones, Jackie. (1992) 'Publishing Feminist Criticism: Academic Book Publishing and the Construction and Circulation of Feminist Knowledges'. *Critical Survey* 4.2: 174–82.

Jones, Nicolette. (1991a) 'A Way With Words'. *Guardian* [UK] 30 May: 32.

—— (1991b) 'The Need to Publish and Be Feminist'. *Independent* [UK] 11 Sep.: 16.

—— (1992) 'Harriet Spicer – The Punctilious Professional'. *Bookseller* 3 Jan.: 20–3.

Jones, Richard Glyn and A. Susan Williams, eds. (1996) *The Penguin Book of Erotic Stories by Women*. London: Penguin.

Jopson, Debra. (1986) 'Feminist Writing Now Has Joined the Mainstream' *National Times* [Aus.] 28 Feb.: 34.

Jordan, Elaine. (1998) 'Her Brilliant Career: The Marketing of Angela Carter'. *Writing: A Woman's Business: Women, Writing and the Marketplace*. Eds Judy Simons and Kate Fullbrook. Manchester: Manchester University Press. 81–94.

Jordan, John O. and Robert L. Patten, eds. (1995) *Literature in the Marketplace: Nineteenth-century British Publishing and Reading Practices*. Cambridge Studies in Nineteenth-Century Literature and Culture. Cambridge: Cambridge University Press.

Kanneh, Kadiatu. (1998) 'Marketing Black Women's Texts: The Case of Alice Walker'. *Writing: A Woman's Business: Women, Writing and the Marketplace*. Eds Judy Simons and Kate Fullbrook. Manchester: Manchester University Press. 145–60.

Kaplan, Cora. (1986) 'Radical Feminism and Literature: Rethinking Millett's *Sexual Politics*'. *Sea Changes: Essays on Culture and Feminism*. Questions for Feminism. London: Verso. 15–30.

Kappeler, Suzanne. (1988) 'What Is a Feminist Publishing Policy?' *Feminism and Censorship: The Current Debate*. Eds Gail Chester and Julienne Dickey. Bridport, Dorset: Prism Press. 233–7.

Kay, William. (2000) 'My Nightmare at the Queen's Jewellers, by Angry Attallah'. *Evening Standard* [UK] 11 Jul.: 38.

Keller, Nicole. (1995) 'Feminist Bookstores Celebrate First "Week"'. *Publishers Weekly* 15 May: 19.

Kinney, Martha M. (1982) 'Boards and Paper: Feminist Writing and Trade Publishing'. *Women in Print II: Opportunities for Women's Studies Publication in Language and Literature*. Eds Joan E. Hartman and Ellen Messer-Davidow. New York: Modern Language Association of America. 41–55.

Klein, Naomi. (2001) *No Space, No Choice, No Jobs, No Logo*. [2000] London: Flamingo/HarperCollins.

Koski, Fran and Maida Tilchen. (1975) 'Some Pulp Sappho'. *Margins* 23: 41–5.

Kramarae, Cheris and Dale Spender, eds. (1992) *The Knowledge Explosion: Generations of Feminist Scholarship*. Athene series. New York: Teachers College Press.

Kramarae, Cheris and Paula A. Treichler. (1992) *Amazons, Bluestockings and Crones: A Feminist Dictionary*. 2nd edn. London: Pandora Press.

Kuzwayo, Ellen. (1985) *Call Me Woman*. London: The Women's Press.

Lauber, Peg. (1998) 'A Celebration of Feminist Publishing'. *Feminist Collections* 19.3: 9–10.

Lauter, Paul. (1984) 'Reconstructing American Literature: A Synopsis of an Educational Project of The Feminist Press'. *MELUS: Journal of the Society for the Study of Multi-Ethnic Literature of the US*. 11.1: 33–43.

Lawson, Mark. (1990) 'The Secret Success'. *Independent* [UK] 3 Nov.: Magazine, 56–8.

Lehmann-Haupt, Christopher. (1971) 'The Best Feminist Book So Far'. Review of Germaine Greer, *The Female Eunuch*. *New York Times* 20 Apr.: 45.

Lesbian Writing and Publishing Collective, ed. (1986) *Dykeversions: Lesbian Short Fiction*. Toronto: Women's Press.

Leser, David. (1993) 'In Search of Stephanie'. *HQ* Nov./Dec.: 80–5.

Linder, Elizabeth. (1986) 'An Editor's View'. *Women's Review* 8: 11.

Lister, David. (1997) 'Fay Weldon Turns from Feminism to Boy Power'. *Independent* [UK] 26 Apr.: 2.

Lloyd, Betty-Ann. (1987) 'Hearing Women into Speech: The Feminist Press and the Women's Community'. *Canadian Woman Studies / Les Cahiers de la Femme* 8.1: 29–32.

Loach, Loretta. (1986) 'Can Black and White Women Work Together?' *Spare Rib* Jul.: 18–21.

Lorde, Audre. (1984) 'The Master's Tools Will Never Dismantle the Master's House'. *Sister Outsider: Essays and Speeches*. Crossing Press Feminist series. Freedom, CA: The Crossing Press. 110–13.

—— (1987) *Our Dead Behind Us*. London: Sheba Feminist Publishers.

Lowry, Suzanne. (1977) 'Three's Company'. *Guardian* [UK] 19 Aug.: 9.

Lumby, Catharine. (1997) *Bad Girls: The Media, Sex and Feminism in the 90s*. Sydney: Allen & Unwin.

Lynch, Maryanne. (1998) 'A Collective History of One: Sybylla Feminist Press 1989–92'. *Arena Magazine* [Aus.] 37 Oct.–Nov.: 41–3.

Macaskill, H. (1989) 'Publishing: A Woman's Place?' *British Book News* Apr.: 256–7.

—— (1990) 'Virago Press: From Nowhere to Everywhere'. *British Book News* Jul.: 432–5.

—— (1991) 'The Women's Press: Live Authors, Live Issues'. *British Book News* Feb.: 82–5.

—— (1993) 'Virago at 20'. *British Book News* Jun.: 362–4.

Mahl, Mary R., and Helene Koon, eds. (1977) *The Female Spectator: English Women Writers Before 1800*. Bloomington, IA and Old Westbury, NY: Indiana University Press and The Feminist Press.

Mailer, Norman. (1971) *The Prisoner of Sex*. London: Weidenfeld and Nicholson.

Maitland, Sara. (1979) 'Novels Are Toys Not Bibles, But the Child Is Mother to the Woman'. *Women's Studies International Quarterly* 2.2: 203–7.

Mallis, Ronald. (1982) 'Textbook Publishing: Some Notes on Responsibility'. *Women in Print: Opportunities for Women's Studies Publication in Language and Literature*. Eds Joan E. Hartman and Ellen Messer-Davidow. New York: Modern Language Association of America. II, 35–40.

Mann, Peter H. (1979) *Book Publishing, Book Selling and Book Reading*. London: Book Marketing Council.

Mansbridge, Jane J. (1979) 'The Agony of Inequality'. *Co-ops, Communes & Collectives: Experiments in Social Change in the 1960s and 1970s*. Eds John Case and Rosemary C.R. Taylor. New York: Pantheon. 194–214.

Marchant, Anyda and Muriel Crawford. (1976) 'The Naiad Press'. Interview with Barbara Grier (aka Gene Damon). *Sinister Wisdom* 1: 116–19.

Marcuse, Herbert. (1986) *One-Dimensional Man: Studies in the Ideology of Advanced Industrial Society*. [1964] London: Ark.

Marek, Jayne E. (1995) *Women Editing Modernism: 'Little' Magazines and Literary History*. Lexington, KT: University Press of Kentucky.

Marketing Week. (1999) 'Is Feminist Icon Losing Her Ethics?' 1 Apr.: 35.

Marris, Paul and Sue Thornham, eds. (1996) *Media Studies: A Reader*. Edinburgh: Edinburgh University Press.

McAleer, Joseph. (1992) *Popular Reading and Publishing in Britain 1914–1950*. Oxford Historical Monographs. Oxford: Clarendon Press.

McCann, Paul. (1997) 'Daniella Finds Feminist Life in Channel 4 Drama'. *Independent* [UK] 4 Nov.: 2.

McDermott, Patrice. (1994) *Politics and Scholarship: Feminist Academic Journals and the Production of Knowledge*. Urbana, IL: University of Illinois Press.

McDowell, Paula. (1998) *The Women of Grub Street: Press, Politics, and Gender in the London Literary Marketplace 1678–1730*. Oxford: Oxford University Press.

McGuire, Scarlett. (1992) *Best Companies for Women: Britain's Top Employers*. London: Pandora Press.

McLuhan, Marshall. (2001) *Understanding Media: The Extensions of Man*. [1964] London and New York: Routledge.

McPhee, Hilary. (2001) *Other People's Words*. Sydney: Picador.

Melville, Pauline. (1990) *Shape-shifter*. London: The Women's Press.

Menkes, Vivienne. (1988) 'Thomson Sells Pandora Books to Unwin Hyman'. *Publishers Weekly* 19 Feb.: 16.

Menon, Ritu. (2001) 'Dismantling the Master's House ...: The Predicament of Feminist Publishing and Writing Today'. *Australian Feminist Studies* 16.35: 175–84.

Messer-Davidow, Ellen. (2002) *Disciplining Feminism: From Social Activism to Academic Discourse*. Durham, NC: Duke University Press.

Miller, Jane. (1990) *Seductions: Studies in Reading and Culture*. London: Virago Press.

Miller, Jill. (1983) *Happy as a Dead Cat*. London: The Women's Press.

Miller, Julie. (1988) 'Return of the Strong Character'. *Sydney Morning Herald* 8 Oct.: 78.

Millet, Lydia. (1997) *Omnivores*. Virago Vs. London: Virago Press.

Millett, Kate. (1972) *Sexual Politics*. [1970] London: Abacus.

—— (1976) *Flying*. [1974] Frogmore, Herts.: Paladin.

—— (1977) *Sexual Politics*. [1970] London: Virago Press.

—— (1990) *Flying*. [1974] New York: Touchstone.

Minogue, Sally, ed. (1990) *Problems for Feminist Criticism*. London: Routledge.

Mitchell, Susan. (1995) 'Legacy of a Daring Liberation'. *The Female Eunuch* 25th anniversary supplement. *Weekend Australian* 7 Oct.: 1, 8.

—— (1997) *Icons, Saints & Divas: Intimate Conversations With Women Who Changed the World*. London: Pandora Press.

Mizzell, Ellen. (1992a) 'Margins and Mainstreams'. *New Statesman & Society* 21 Feb.: 36.

—— (1992b) 'More Iron in the Spine'. *New Statesman & Society* 10 Jul.: 36.

Moberg, Verne. (1974) 'The New World of Feminist Publishing'. *Booklegger* 1 Jul.–Aug.: 14–18.

Mohin, Lilian, ed. (1979) *One Foot on the Mountain: An Anthology of British Feminist Poetry, 1969–1979*. London: Onlywomen Press.

—— (1998) Interview with the author. London. 11 Feb.

Moi, Toril. (1985) *Sexual/Textual Politics: Feminist Literary Theory*. New Accents series. London: Routledge.

Moncur, Andrew. (1992) 'Diary'. *Guardian* [UK] 9 Oct.: 23.

Montag, Tom. (1973) 'Notes on Women's Publications and Other Things'. *Margins* 7: 37, 21–5 [sic].

Moore, Suzanne. (1991) *Looking for Trouble: On Shopping, Gender and the Cinema*. London: Serpent's Tail.

—— (1992) 'Overhyped, Overrated and Over Here'. *Independent* 26 Mar.: 16.

—— (1993) 'Power Cut'. *Guardian* [UK] 8 Nov.: II, 10.

Moraga, Cherríe and Gloria Anzaldúa, eds. (1983) *This Bridge Called My Back: Writings by Radical Women of Color*. [1981] 2nd edn. New York: Kitchen Table: Women of Color Press.

Morgan, Gail. (1985) *Promise of Rain*. London: Virago Press.

—— (1990) *The Day My Publisher Turned into a Dog*. [1989] Sydney: Frances Allen.

Morgan, Robin. (1977) 'Rights of Passage.' *Going Too Far: The Personal Chronicle of a Feminist*. New York: Random House. 3-17.

——, ed. (1985) *Sisterhood Is Global: The International Women's Movement Anthology*. Harmondsworth, Middlesex: Penguin.

Morrish, John. (2000) '"Oldie" Magazine in Need of Life Support'. *Independent* [UK] 12 Nov.: 5.

Muir, Kate. (2001) 'Fraught & Social'. *The Times* [UK] 24 Nov.: n.p.

Mulford, Wendy. (1983) 'Notes on Writing: A Marxist/Feminist Viewpoint'. *On Gender and Writing*. Ed. Michelene Wandor. London: Pandora Press. 31–41.

Mumby, Frank Arthur and Ian Norrie. (1974) *Publishing and Bookselling*. 5th edn. London: Jonathan Cape.

Murray, Sharon. (2002) 'Silver Moon Finds New Home at Foyles on the Charing Cross Road'. *Silver Moon Quarterly* Mar.: 2.

Murray, Simone. (1998) '"Books of Integrity": The Women's Press, Kitchen Table Press and Dilemmas of Feminist Publishing'. *European Journal of Women's Studies* 5.2: 171–93.

—— (2000a) '"Live Authors. Live Issues": Dilemmas of Race and Authenticity in Feminist Publishing'. *Alternative Library Literature, 1998/1999: A Biennial Anthology*. 9th edn. Eds Sanford Berman and James P. Danky. Jefferson, NC: McFarland & Co. 42–56.

—— (2000b) '"Deeds *and* Words": The Woman's Press and the Politics of Print'. *Women: A Cultural Review* 11.3: 197–222.

—— (2000c) 'One Is Not Born, But Becomes, a Bestseller: The Publishing Politics of Simone de Beauvoir's *The Second Sex*'. *Hecate* 26.1: 144–60.

Myers, Robin and Michael Harris, eds. (1983) *Author/Publisher Relations During the Eighteenth and Nineteenth Centuries*. Oxford: Oxford Polytechnic Press.

—— (1985) *Economics of the British Booktrade 1605–1939*. Cambridge: Chadwyck-Healey.

Myron, Nancy and Charlotte Bunch, eds. (1975) *Lesbianism and the Women's Movement* Baltimore, MD: Diana Press.

Naher, Gaby. (1994) 'Spreading the Word'. *Everywoman* Jun.: n.p.

Nasta, Susheila, ed. (1991) *Motherlands: Black Women's Writing from Africa, the Caribbean and South Asia*. London: The Women's Press.

Negus, Keith. (1992) *Producing Pop: Culture and Conflict in the Popular Music Industry*. London: Arnold.

Neil, Andrew. (1998) 'Murdoch Diminished by Bowing to China'. *Guardian* [UK] 8 Mar.: Weekly 12.

Neustatter, Angela. (1988) 'A Cause for Celebration'. *Guardian* [UK] 13 Apr.: 20.

—— (1990) *Hyenas in Petticoats: A Look at Twenty Years of Feminism.* [1989] London: Penguin.

News from Neasden. (1979) 'An Exceptional Few Weeks in the Life of a Bookselling Collective'. 11: 34–6.

Nichols, John. (1995) 'A Home Girl Who Rewrote the Rules of Publishing'. *Capital Times* [Madison, WI] 3 Mar.: 11.

Nicholson, Joyce. (1982) 'Sisters Publishing: Problems of a Feminist Publishing House'. *Refractory Girl [Writes]* Oct.: 77–8.

Norden, Barbara. (1993) 'Coat of Many Colours'. *Everywoman* Jun.: 15–16.

Norrie, Ian. (1982) *Mumby's Publishing and Bookselling in the Twentieth Century.* 6th edn. London: Bell & Hyman.

Nwapa, Flora. (1993) 'Confessions of a Business Woman'. *Everywoman* Jun.: 17.

Oakley, Ann. (1976) *Housewife.* [1974] London: Penguin.

Observer. [UK] (1995) 'Germaine Greer: Feminist Guru, or Tarnished Old Icon'. 26 Mar.: 24.

O'Connor, Ashling. (2000) 'Fourth Estate Founder Sells Up But Stays On'. *Financial Times* [UK] 12 Jul.: 31.

Olsen, Tillie. (1980) *Silences.* [1978] London: Virago Press.

Onlywomen Press. (c. 1977) Information sheet. Publishing archive. Glasgow Women's Library.

Orbach, Susie. (1978) *Fat Is a Feminist Issue: The Anti-Diet Guide to Permanent Weight Loss.* London: Paddington Press.

—— (1979) *Fat Is a Feminist Issue…: How to Lose Weight Permanently – Without Dieting.* Middlesex: Hamlyn.

O'Sullivan, Sue. (2003) 'Obituary: Araba Yacoba Mercer – Feminist Publisher and Activist Committed to Black and Lesbian Writers'. *Guardian* [UK] 17 Apr.: 29.

Owen, Peter, ed. (1988) *Publishing – The Future.* London: Peter Owen.

——, ed. (1993) *Publishing Now.* London: Peter Owen.

Owen, Ursula. (1983) *Fathers: Reflections by Daughters.* Introduction. London: Virago Press. 9–14.

—— (1988) 'Feminist Publishing'. *Publishing – The Future.* Ed. Peter Owen. London: Peter Owen. 86–100.

—— (1998a) 'Wimmin Against the Tide'. Review of Fay Weldon, *Big Women. Observer* [UK] 25 Jan.: Review, 17.

—— (1998b) Interview with the author. London. 21 Dec.

Pallister, David. (1991) 'Under Pressure'. *Guardian* [UK] 27 Mar.: 38.

Palmer, Gabrielle. (1988) *The Politics of Breastfeeding.* London: Pandora Press.

Paton, Maureen. (2001) 'Eclipse of Silver Moon'. *Guardian* [UK] 23 Oct.: 9.

Patten, Christopher. (1998) *East and West.* London: Macmillan.

Phillips, Angela. (1993) *The Trouble with Boys.* London: Pandora Press/HarperCollins.

Picardie, Justine. (1990) 'The Suffering Sex'. Review of Naomi Wolf, *The Beauty Myth. New Statesman & Society* 21 Sep.: 39–40.

Piercy, Marge. (1979) *Woman on the Edge of Time.* London: The Women's Press.

—— (1982) 'Councils'. [1973] *Circles on the Water: Selected Poems.* New York: Alfred Knopf. 116–17.

—— (1983) *Stone, Paper, Knife.* London: Pandora Press.

Pitman, Joanna. (1995) 'Mother of All Rows'. *The Times* 18 Nov.: Magazine, 27–8, 30, 32.

Pitman, Joy. (1987) 'Why There's a Light-Box Where My Typewriter Should Be – Being a Feminist Publisher'. *In Other Words: Writing as a Feminist*. Eds Gail Chester and Sigrid Nielsen. London: Hutchinson Education. 104–8.

Plant, Marjorie. (1974) *The English Book Trade: An Economic History of the Making and Sale of Books*. 3rd edn. London: Allen & Unwin.

Poland, Louise. (2001) 'Printing Presses and Protest Banners: Feminist Presses in Australia'. *Lilith: A Feminist History Journal* 10: 121–36.

—— (2003) 'Out of Type: Bessie Mitchell (Guthrie) and Viking Press (1939–44)'. *Hecate: An Interdisciplinary Journal of Women's Liberation* 29.1: 19–33. (224)

Porter, Henry. (1995) 'The Feminist Fallout that Split Virago'. *Daily Telegraph* [UK] 3 Nov.: 1, 25.

Price, Marion and Mairead Owen. (1998) 'Who Studies Women's Studies?' *Gender and Education* 10.2: 185–98.

Pringle, Alexandra. (1996) Interview with the author. London. 8 Aug.

Randall, Vicky. (1987) *Women and Politics: An International Perspective*. 2nd edn. London: Macmillan Educational.

Ratcliffe, Eric. (1993) *The Caxton of Her Age: The Career and Family Background of Emily Faithfull, 1835–95*. Upton-upon-Severn: Images.

Ravenscroft, Alison, for Sybylla Press. (1989) 'Sybylla Press – A Radical Change'. *Womanspeak* Sep.–Oct.: 6–7.

Rawsthorn, Alice. (1995) 'Virago Sold to Time Warner'. *Financial Times* [UK] 3 Nov.: 7.

Reeves, Maud Pember. (1979) *Round About a Pound a Week*. [1913] Virago Reprint Library. London: Virago Press.

Reid, Coletta. (1974) 'Taking Care of Business'. *Quest: A Feminist Quarterly* 1.2: 6–23.

Reynolds, Margaret, ed. (1993) *The Penguin Book of Lesbian Short Stories*. London: Viking.

Richardson, Jean. (1998) 'Murdoch Critical of HC London in China Book Controversy'. *Publishers Weekly* 9 Mar.: 11, 15.

Richardson, Paul. (2002) 'New Page in Old Story'. Review of David Finkelstein and Alistair McCleery, eds, *The Book History Reader*. *Times Higher Education Supplement* 1 Nov.: 31.

Riley, Joan. (1985) *The Unbelonging*. London: The Women's Press.

Roberts, Helen, ed. (1981) *Doing Feminist Research*. London and New York: Routledge.

Roberts, Robin. (1993) *A New Species: Gender and Science in Science Fiction*. Urbana, IL: University of Illinois Press.

Robinson, Lillian S. (1978) *Sex, Class, and Culture*. Bloomington, IA: Indiana University Press.

Robinson, Victoria and Diane Richardson. (1994) 'Publishing Feminism: Redefining the Women's Studies Discourse'. *Journal of Gender Studies* 3.1: 87–94.

——, eds. (1997) *Introducing Women's Studies: Feminist Theory and Practice*. 2nd edn. London: Macmillan.

Rolfe, Patricia. (1993) 'Profits of Feminist Publishing'. *Bulletin*. 19 Oct.: 96.

Root, Jane. (1985) 'Distributing *A Question of Silence*: A Cautionary Tale'. *Screen* 26.6: 58–64.

Rosenwasser, Marie J. (1972) 'Rhetoric and the Progress of the Women's Liberation Movement'. *Today's Speech* 20: 45–56.

Rothschild-Whitt, Joyce. (1979) 'Conditions for Democracy: Making Participatory Organizations Work'. *Co-ops, Communes & Collectives: Experiments in Social Change in the 1960s and 1970s.* Eds John Case and Rosemary C.R. Taylor. New York: Pantheon. 215–44.

Russ, Joanna. (1984) *How to Suppress Women's Writing.* London: The Women's Press.

Sanborn, Margaret. (1995a) 'The Feminist Press at 25'. *Publishers Weekly* 27 Feb.: 39.

—— (1995b) 'Pride of Presence'. *Publishers Weekly* 19 Jun.: 28–30, 32–5, 38–9.

Sawyer, Miranda. (1998) 'The Fickle Hand of Fay'. *Good Weekend* [Aus.] 14 Mar.: 26–7, 29–30.

Scanlon, Joan and Julia Swindells. (1994) 'Bad Apple'. *Trouble & Strife* 28: 41–6.

Schiffrin, André. (2001) *The Business of Books: How International Conglomerates Took Over Publishing and Changed the Way We Read.* New York and London: Verso.

Schmoller, Hans. (1974) 'The Paperback Revolution'. *Essays in the History of Publishing.* Ed. Asa Briggs. London: Longman. 283–318.

Scott, Hilda. (1984) *Working Your Way to the Bottom: The Feminization of Poverty.* London: Pandora Press.

Sen, Mandira and Moushumi Bhowmik. (2002) 'Publishing Women's Studies in India: Stree's Experience'. *Women's Studies International Forum* 25.2: 185–92.

Shacklady, Helen. (2002) *The Stolen Crate.* London: Onlywomen Press.

Shah, Shaila. (1987) 'Producing a Feminist Magazine'. *In Other Words: Writing as a Feminist.* Eds Gail Chester and Sigrid Nielsen. London: Hutchinson Education. 93–9.

Shakespeare, Sebastian. (1995) 'When Viragos Fall Out'. *Evening Standard* [UK]14 Sep.: 12.

SHARP News. (1998) Newsletter of the Society for the History of Authorship, Reading and Publishing. Autumn 7.4: 1–16.

Sheba Collective, ed. (1989) *Serious Pleasure: Lesbian Erotic Stories and Poetry.* London: Sheba Feminist Publishers.

Sheba Feminist Publishers Archive. (1980–94) London: The Women's Library/Fawcett Library collection, London Guildhall University.

Shelley, Martha. (1976) 'Women's Press Collective: Interview with Harriet Desmoines'. *Sinister Wisdom* 1: 120–2.

Showalter, Elaine. (1978) *A Literature of Their Own: British Women Novelists from Brontë to Lessing.* [1977] London: Virago Press.

Simons, Judy and Kate Fullbrook, eds. (1998) *Writing: A Woman's Business: Women, Writing and the Marketplace.* Manchester: Manchester University Press.

Simons, Margaret A. (1979) 'Racism and Feminism: A Schism in the Sisterhood'. *Feminist Studies* 5.2: 384–401.

Smith, Barbara. (1984) 'Women of Colour: Our Stories'. *New Statesman* 8 Jun.: 23–4.

—— (1986) 'Toward a Black Feminist Criticism'. [1977] *The New Feminist Criticism: Essays on Women, Literature, and Theory.* Ed. Elaine Showalter. London: Virago Press. 168–85.

—— (1989) 'A Press of Our Own – Kitchen Table: Women of Color Press'. *Frontiers: A Journal of Women Studies* [sic] 10.3: 11–13.

—— (1998) *The Truth That Never Hurts: Writings on Race, Gender, and Freedom*. New Brunswick, NJ: Rutgers University Press.

Smith, Barbara and Beverly Smith. (1983) 'Across the Kitchen Table: A Sister-to-Sister Dialogue'. *This Bridge Called My Back: Writings by Radical Women of Color*. [1981] Eds Cherríe Moraga and Gloria Anzaldúa. 2nd edn. New York: Kitchen Table: Women of Color Press. 113–27.

Smith, Barbara and Cherríe Moraga. (1996) 'Lesbian Literature: A Third World Feminist Perspective'. *The New Lesbian Studies: Into the Twenty-First Century*. Eds Bonnie Zimmerman and Toni A.H. McNaron. New York: The Feminist Press at The City University of New York. 23–33.

Smith, Joan. (1990) 'Thin Reasoning, Slender Resources'. Review of Naomi Wolf, *The Beauty Myth*. *Independent on Sunday* [UK] 9 Sep.: Review, 22.

—— (1998) 'Women Behaving Badly'. Review of Fay Weldon, *Big Women*. *Financial Times* [UK] 24 Jan.: 5.

Sojourner: The Women's Forum. (1993) 'Packing Boxes and Editing Manuscripts: Women of Color in Feminist Publishing'. Aug.: 10–11.

Solotaroff, Ted. (1995) 'The Post-Cold-War Scene and the Literary Market'. *Tri-Quarterly* Fall: 145–50.

Sorensen, Rosemary. (1998) 'The Million-Dollar Woman'. *Courier-Mail* [Aus.] 14 Mar.: Weekend, 5.

Souter, Fenella. (1995) 'The Point of Purple (and Other Mysteries of the Book Cover Business)'. *HQ* Sep.–Oct.: 46–50.

Spare Rib. (1982) 'Community Publishing'. Feb.: 31–3.

Spare Rib. (1987) 'Liberation, the Lady Said ...' Jul.: 38–40.

Spare Rib Collective. (1979) 'Balancing'. *News from Neasden* 11: 38–9.

Spender, Dale. (1980) *Man Made Language*. London: Routledge & Kegan Paul.

—— (1981) 'The Gatekeepers: A Feminist Critique of Academic Publishing'. *Doing Feminist Research*. Ed. Helen Roberts. London: Routledge. 186–202.

—— (1983a) *There's Always Been a Women's Movement This Century*. London: Pandora Press.

——, ed. (1983b) *Feminist Theorists: Three Centuries of Women's Intellectual Traditions*. London: The Women's Press.

—— (1985) *For the Record: The Making and Meaning of Feminist Knowledge*. London: The Women's Press.

—— (1986) *Mothers of the Novel: 100 Good Women Writers Before Jane Austen*. London: Pandora Press.

—— (1989) *The Writing or the Sex? Or Why You Don't Have to Read Women's Writing to Know It's No Good*. Athene series. New York: Pergamon Press.

—— (1995) *Nattering on the Net: Women, Power and Cyberspace*. Melbourne, Vic.: Spinifex Press.

—— (2003) Interview with the author. Brisbane. 28 May.

Spender, Lynne. (1983a) *Intruders on the Rights of Men: Women's Unpublished Heritage*. London: Pandora Press.

—— (1983b) 'The Politics of Publishing: Selection and Rejection of Women's Words in Print'. *Women's Studies International Forum* 6.5: 469–73.

Spicer, Harriet. (1996) Interview with the author. London. 16 Jul.

Spongberg, Mary. (1993) 'If She's So Great, How Come So Many Pigs Dig Her?: Germaine Greer and the Malestream Press'. *Women's History Review* 2.3: 407–19.

Stanley, Liz, ed. (1997) *Knowing Feminisms: On Academic Borders, Territories and Tribes*. London: Sage.

Steel, Mel. (1998) 'Left on the Shelf'. *Independent on Sunday* [UK] 19 Apr.: 28–9.

Steinem, Gloria. (1992) *Revolution from Within: A Book of Self-Esteem*. London: Bloomsbury.

Stimpson, Catharine R. (1975) 'The New Feminism and Women's Studies'. *Women on Campus: The Unfinished Liberation*. Eds *Change* Magazine editors. New Rochelle, NY: *Change* Magazine. 69–84.

Sullivan, Jane. (1998) 'Woman's Own'. *Sydney Morning Herald* 8 Aug.: Good Weekend, 16–18, 20, 23.

Sulter, Maud. (1989) *As a Blackwomen [sic], Poems 1982–1985*. 2nd edn. Hebden Bridge, West Yorks.: Urban Fox Press.

Sunday Times. [UK] (1981) 'Germaine Greer Keeping Faith'. 15 Nov.: Magazine 33, 35–7.

Sutherland, John. (1978) *Fiction and the Fiction Industry*. London: Athlone Press.

—— (1981) *Bestsellers: Popular Fiction of the 1970s*. London: Routledge & Kegan Paul.

—— (1988) 'Publishing History: A Hole at the Centre of Literary Sociology'. *Critical Inquiry* 14.3: 574–89.

Tally, Justine. (1987) 'The Making of the Feminist Press: An Interview with Florence Howe'. *Revista Canaria de Estudios Ingleses* 13–14: 281–8.

Taverner, Jay. (2002) *Something Wicked*. London: Onlywomen Press.

The Second Wave. (1974) 'From Us: Thoughts on the Feminist Media'. 3: 2–4.

Thompson, Jane. (1994) *Still Crazy*. London: Silver Moon Books.

—— (1996) *Diamonds and Rust*. London: Silver Moon Books.

Time. (1970a) 'Who's Come a Long Way, Baby?' 31 Aug.: 14–19.

Time. (1970b) 'Women's Lib: A Second Look'. 14 Dec.: 41.

Times Literary Supplement. (1970) 'Feminising Our Folklore'. Review of Germaine Greer, *The Female Eunuch*. 25 Dec.: 1508.

Times Literary Supplement. (1971) 'A New Vindication of the Rights of Women'. Review of Kate Millett, *Sexual Politics*. 9 Apr.: 410.

Tindall, Gillian. (1979) 'Sisterly Sensibilities, or, Heroines Revived'. *New Society* 19 Jul.: 144–5.

Todd, Richard. (1996) *Consuming Fictions: The Booker Prize and Fiction in Britain Today*. London: Bloomsbury.

Tomalin, Claire. (1970) 'What Does a Woman Want?' Review of Eva Figes, *Patriarchal Attitudes, inter alia. New Statesman* 26 Jun: 917–18.

Tomlinson, F., S.A. Fischer and C. Baker. (1987) 'Twice as Many, Half as Powerful'. *Bookseller* 11 Dec.: 2302–3.

Toynbee, Polly. (1981) 'We Tend to Publish What Feels Right and Then See What It All Adds Up to Afterwards'. *Guardian* [UK] 26 Jan.: 8.

—— (1982) 'Lesbianism Is a Central Issue'. *Guardian* [UK] 23 Jul.: 8.

Traynor, Ian and Giles Foden. (1998) 'German Giant Buys Random House'. *Guardian* [UK] 24 Mar.: 1.

Treneman, Ann. (1998) 'Dr Greer, I Presume'. *Independent* [UK] 4 Nov.: 1.

Tuchman, Gaye, with Nina E. Fortin. (1989) *Edging Women Out: Victorian Novelists, Publishers, and Social Change*. London: Routledge.

Turner, Graeme. (1996) *British Cultural Studies: An Introduction*. 2nd edn. London: Routledge.

Turner, Jenny. (1990) 'Knife Attacks'. Review of Naomi Wolf, *The Beauty Myth*. *Listener* 13 Sep.: 29.

Uncensored. (1998a) 'Germaine Greer'. ABC TV, Brisbane. 22 Jul.

Uncensored. (1998b) 'Norman Mailer'. ABC TV, Brisbane. 29 Jul.

Viner, Katharine. (1997) 'How Was it for You?' *Guardian* [UK] 22 Apr.: II, 4.

—— (1998) 'Look Forward in Anger'. *Guardian* [UK] 26 Feb.: II, 4–5.

—— (2002) 'Look Back in Awe'. *Guardian* [UK] 26 Jan.: 16.

A Virago Keepsake to Celebrate Twenty Years of Publishing. (1993) London: Virago Press.

Virago publicity pamphlet. (1977) 'Virago Press'. London: Virago Press.

Virago publicity pamphlet. (1996) 'A Short History of Virago, 1973–1995'. London: Virago Press.

Virago 'V's. (1997) Promotional fiction sampler. London: Virago Press.

Walker, Alice. (1983) *The Color Purple*. [1982] London: The Women's Press.

—— (1984) *In Search of Our Mothers' Gardens: Womanist Prose*. [1983] London: The Women's Press.

Wallace, Christine. (1998) *Greer: Untamed Shrew*. [1997] Sydney: Picador.

Waller, Martin. (2002) 'A Fresh Chapter for Neil'. *The Times* [UK] 11 May: n.p.

Wallsgrove, Ruth. (1979) 'From Work "in Publishing" to *Spare Rib*'. *News from Neasden* 11: 36–8.

Walter, Natasha. (1998) *The New Feminism*. London: Little, Brown.

—— (1999) *The New Feminism*. [1998] London: Virago Press.

Wandor, Michelene, ed. (1983) *On Gender and Writing*. London: Pandora Press.

——, ed. (1990) *Once a Feminist: Stories of a Generation*. London: Virago Press.

Ward, Elizabeth. (1999) 'The Trouble With Women'. Review of Germaine Greer, *The Whole Woman* and Christine Wallace, *Germaine Greer: Untamed Shrew*. *Washington Post* 23 May: X8.

Waters, Sarah. (1998) *Tipping the Velvet*. London: Virago Press.

Watts, Janet. (1988) 'Feminist Publishing: Reading Between the Lines'. *Observer* [UK] 8 May: 36.

Weale, Sally. (2000) 'Farewell, My Lovelies'. *Guardian* [UK] 27 Nov.: 8.

Webby, Elizabeth. (1998) 'Publishing'. *Australian Feminism: A Companion*. Eds Barbara Caine et al. Melbourne: Oxford University Press. 477–80.

Weldon, Fay. (1997) *Big Women*. London: Flamingo.

West, Celeste and Valerie Wheat. (1978) *The Passionate Perils of Publishing*. San Francisco: Booklegger Press.

White, Antonia. (1978) *Frost in May*. [1933] Virago Modern Classics. London: Virago Press.

Wigutoff, Sharon. (1979–1980) 'The Feminist Press: Ten Years of Nonsexist Children's Books'. *The Lion and the Unicorn: A Critical Journal of Children's Literature* 3.2: 57–63.

Williams, Raymond. (1983) *Keywords: A Vocabulary of Culture and Society*. 2nd edn. London: Flamingo.

Williams, Rhys. (1995) 'Feminist Publisher at Centre of Tangled Plot'. *Independent* [UK] 26 Oct.: 6.

Willis, Pauline. (1988) 'Tuesday Women'. *Guardian* [UK] 16 Feb.: n.p.

Winant, Fran. (1975) 'Lesbian Publish Lesbians: My Life and Times With Violet Press'. *Margins* 23: 62, 64, 66.

for Mootoo/Macdonald article

Winterson, Jeanette. (1991) *Oranges Are Not the Only Fruit*. [1985] London: Vintage.

Woddis, Carole. (1992) 'Press for Change'. *Times Educational Supplement* 10 Jul.: 26.

Wolf, Naomi. (1990) *The Beauty Myth*. London: Chatto and Windus.

—— (1991a) *The Beauty Myth: How Images of Beauty Are Used Against Women*. [1990] London: Vintage.

—— (1991b) 'Last But by No Means Least'. *Guardian* [UK] 21 Feb.: 19.

—— (1993) *Fire With Fire: The New Female Power and How It Will Change the 21st Century*. London: Chatto and Windus.

—— (1994) *Fire With Fire: The New Female Power and How to Use It*. [1993] New York: Fawcett Columbine.

—— (1997a) *Promiscuities: A Secret History of Female Desire*. London: Chatto and Windus.

—— (1997b) Reading from *Promiscuities: A Secret History of Female Desire*. Platform series. National Theatre, London. 24 April.

—— (1998) *Promiscuities: A Secret History of Female Desire*. [1997] London: Vintage.

Wolfe, Margie. (1980) 'Feminist Publishing in Canada'. *Canadian Women's Studies* 2.2: 11–14.

Women etc. (1997) Promotional booklet. London: Books etc.

The Women's Press. (1979) 'Feminism and Publishing'. *News from Neasden* 11: 32–4.

The Women's Press. (2003) 'The Women's Press: Great Writing by Great Women'. <http://www.the-women's-press.com> (25 May 2003).

The Women's Press Twentieth Anniversary New Books Catalogue. (1998) Feb.–Jul. London: The Women's Press.

—— (1998–99) Aug.–Jan. London: The Women's Press.

Women's Report . (1974) 'Feminism: Getting into Print'. Jul.–Aug.: 10–11.

Woolf, Virginia. (1992) *A Room of One's Own/Three Guineas*. [1929/1938] World's Classics. Oxford: Oxford University Press.

—— (1993) *Orlando: A Biography*. [1928] London: Virago Press.

Workforce. (1975) 'Ma Revolution: Women's Press'. 47: 7–8.

Worpole, Ken. (1984) *Reading by Numbers: Contemporary Publishing & Popular Fiction*. London: Comedia.

Worrell, Kris. (2000) 'Fighting Words: Writer Barbara Smith Takes Her Work as an Activist Seriously'. *Times Union* [Albany, NY] 2 Jul.: G1.

Wrenn, Marie-Claude. (1970) 'The Furious Young Philosopher Who Got It Down On Paper'. *Life* 14 Sep.: 16–17.

Young, Elizabeth. (1989) 'The Business of Feminism: Issues in London Feminist Publishing'. *Frontiers: A Journal of Women [sic] Studies*. 10.3: 1–5.

Young, Stacey. (1997) *Changing the Wor(l)d: Discourse, Politics and the Feminist Movement*. New York: Routledge.

'Zest & Artery'. (1997) Promotional leaflet. London: Onlywomen Press.

Zoonen, Liesbet van. (1991) 'Feminist Perspectives on the Media'. *Mass Media and Society*. Eds James Curran and Michael Gurevitch. London: Arnold. 33–54.

—— (1994) *Feminist Media Studies*. Media, Culture & Society series. London: Sage.

Index

FBNews - 24
FBs - 107, 110